PRELUDE TO PEARL HARBOR

The United States Navy and the Far East, 1921-1931

PRELUDE TO PEARL HARBOR

The United States Navy and the Far East, 1921-1931

Gerald E. Wheeler

―――――――――

UNIVERSITY OF MISSOURI PRESS

COLUMBIA, MISSOURI

TO
J. F. W.

Preface

IN THE years following the announcement of the Truman Doctrine and Marshall Plan the American nation has been forced to live with the ever-present possibility that war, with all of its atomic-thermonuclear potentialities, may again beset it. In facing up to this situation Americans and their armed forces have become more candid. The State Department speaks of "containing" Soviet Russia; generals and admirals describe the striking power of the eight-jet intercontinental Stratofortress, the intercontinental ballistic missile, and the "atomic capability" of the Mediterranean-based Sixth Fleet; and those shouldering responsibilities for nuclear energy research and public health judge that danger to America at present overrides concern for the health of unborn generations. Most Americans, whether they read the editorial page or the comic page, have become aware that the Soviet Union is the national enemy.

For those defending the country, this national awareness has solved a major problem in defense planning. To keep their country secure, Americans now willingly spend enormous sums and bear the taxation necessary to prevent equally enormous budget deficits. When multibillion-dollar spending programs have been presented to Congress, budget trimmers have preferred to cut foreign aid, agricultural supports, and on occasions a bit of fat from the traditional "pork barrel." But the over-all tendency has been to accept without question the military's needs, especially when presented by a popular President with a military background. A billion or two may be deleted from a current defense budget, but percentage cuts equivalent to those imposed on other budget items are seldom considered. The American taxpayer has now accepted a slight alteration of the homily: "The price of liberty is eternal vigilance—and taxation."

During the years 1921 to 1931 American naval leaders faced a problem in some ways similar to the situation after 1947. They were convinced that the United States had a national enemy in Japan. But the United States Congress, like the public that elected it during the 1920's, was less than impressed; in fact it was positively hostile to any suggestion that America might again go to war. The President

vii

and his executive departments—save perhaps the War Department—were also reluctant to accept the Navy's conclusions or its premises. How the United States Navy solved its problem of preparing for war in an unsympathetic climate of opinion is the story here presented.

In the preparation of this book I have built up obligations to friends and colleagues that I can hardly discharge by preface acknowledgment. To Dr. Lyle H. Kendall, Jr., of Texas Christian University and Dr. Rex Burbank of San Jose State College I owe a special debt for their invaluable editorial commentary on the total manuscript. For advice, counsel, and much eye-wearying labor I am grateful to Mr. William F. McCoy of the University of California (Davis) Library and to Dr. Daniel M. Smith of the University of Colorado. Dr. Paolo E. Coletta of the United States Naval Academy and Lieutenant Colonel George V. Fagan of the United States Air Force Academy were most helpful in their research and editing suggestions. Guidance, encouragement, thorough criticism, and almost unlimited time were made available to me by my University of California (Berkeley) mentor, Dr. Armin Rappaport. While I was preparing the manuscript for publication, Dr. John D. Hicks of the faculty at Berkeley and Dr. Benjamin F. Gilbert of San Jose State College offered much good advice and caution. Not only I, but almost all who have worked in the field of United States diplomatic history, cannot help but feel grateful to the late Dr. Carl Lokke and to Mrs. Julia B. Carroll of the National Archives. As a research assistant, editor, critic, and typist, my wife Jean French Wheeler was a constant source of help and encouragement. I am grateful to all for their help; they do not, of course, share the responsibility of any errors in this book.

GERALD E. WHEELER

San Jose State College
San Jose, California

Table of Contents

Introduction

PEARL HARBOR came as no great surprise to United States naval officers. Wardroom talk for years had centered on war possibilities in the Far East. Private correspondence among ranking officers betrayed concern over American naval weakness in the Pacific, and a significant number felt that the enemy would be Japan. To the War Plans Division and the Naval War College the primary maritime enemy of the United States was "Orange"—Japan; the principal Continental enemy was "Black"—Germany. And by the 1930's uneasiness over Japanese conduct in the Far East had begun to sift down to the grass roots. The United States Navy, however, did not wait for the Manchurian "Incident" of 1931 or the *Panay* bombing in 1937 to begin its preparations.

The Navy Department had never been blind to its role as the strong arm of American diplomacy, but at no time did the United States in the forty years before Pearl Harbor have at hand the requisite force necessary to sustain such commitments as the defense of its territorial possessions in the Pacific, safeguarding the Panama Canal, maintaining the Open Door and territorial integrity of China, and securing the continental limits of the American nation. The force available to meet these commitments consisted merely of the United States Fleet, its Fleet Marine Force, and small army garrisons in the Philippines and Hawaii. Additional strength in the form of dependable military alliances was lacking until 1941. In the 1920's the idea of alliances was diplomatic or political heresy.

From the viewpoint of the Navy Department two basic limitations hampered the effective implementation of American Far Eastern policy: the Washington treaties of 1921-22 and the unrealistic attitude toward military support of foreign policy manifested by the Republican administrations in the years 1921 to 1931. The Washington treaties represented an attempt to freeze the *status quo* in naval and political relationships in the Far East, but Japan was left free to use its navy as a potent agency of diplomacy where it counted most heavily—on the China coast. Furthermore, the policies of maintaining the territorial integrity of China and of defending the Open Door were not abandoned. The Nine-Power Treaty multilateralized to some extent these unilateral American policies, but through the 1920's the nation still clung to the position that it should be the treaty's conscience. With these traditional commitments still on the record, and with a new firm policy toward the Philippines that promised nothing to the independence movement in the foreseeable future, Congress proceeded to whittle away at the remains of American naval power. Slowly and most reluctantly the legislators considered the Navy's suggestions to balance and modernize the fleet. In turning out the Wilsonians the Republicans had accepted one cliché—the world *had* been made safe for democracy—so naval power was not needed. It was too costly in view of promised economies.

By 1922 the General Board of the Navy and the Office of Naval Intelligence had come to the conclusion that the foreign policies of Japan were antithetical to America's Far Eastern interests. They believed that Japan's policies included the eventual domination of the Far East both politically and economically, and that such domination would include American holdings in the Philippine Islands. The most elementary knowledge of economic geography showed that Japan needed low-cost, easily accessible raw materials and guaranteed markets close enough to hold down shipping costs. Labor was cheap and plentiful in the island empire, and the industrial plant was relatively new—a monument to rapid westernization. The only obstacles to Japan's further aggrandizement were policy statements by the United States, an Asiatic Fleet led by the rather aged cruiser *Pittsburgh,* and the American Battle Fleet tethered closely to its Pacific base in the Hawaiian Islands.

With the policy of defending the interests of the United States as a guide, and the probability of war with Japan as a premise, the Navy Department from 1922 to 1931 began to set its house in order. This study is an account of the manner in which the United States Navy was readied for action in the years between the Washington Conference and Japan's move into Manchuria during September, 1931.

1

The Commitments of American Far Eastern Policy: China and the Philippine Islands

FOREIGN policy making has never been simple for Americans, particularly when such activity has dealt with the Far East. Ideally it should not be troublesome. The Constitution is reasonably explicit in leaving foreign policy formulation in the hands of the President. The State Department and its secretary are executive creatures; therefore, no complications should arise from this quarter. However, the Constitution does make the conduct of foreign affairs a little less simple by giving the Senate a voice in treaty matters and in the business of consenting to appointments. The House of Representatives also has its say through the powers to appropriate and to investigate. And in this American democracy the man in the street feels he should share some of the legislative and executive burden. He does, as a voter; but this approach leaves the citizen many times removed from the formulation, implementation, and execution of policy.

In the absence of direct grass-roots stimulation or control, organized pressure groups and lobbyists have acquired a disproportionately important voice in the field of foreign affairs. Unfortunately for all concerned, this voice traditionally has been raucous and disparate in its advices. At times its stridency has bemused even the deafest secretary of state. In Far Eastern matters the loudest sounds, in the 1920's, emanated from those representing religious and business interests. As could be expected, these lobbyists did not speak from a single point of view; in fact, when there was unity of viewpoint the shrewdest observers were somewhat amazed. Admiral Mark L. Bristol, Com-

1

mander-in-Chief of the Asiatic Fleet in 1928, regretfully called attention to this situation when he wrote to an old friend:

> I find the Americans out here very much divided, as they were in Turkey when I first went there. It is the same old thing: missionaries divided against the businessmen, and due to the various missionary activities of different denominations, there is a great deal of discord amongst them; and in the same way businessmen do not pull together.[1]

Despite his amateur status as a diplomat, Bristol recognized one of the most potent sources of pressure on the State Department. How much the missionary community has influenced American Far Eastern policy has never been measured—it is doubtful that it can be. But many writers and observers have commented on the efficacy of missionary activity in the field.[2] During the nineteenth century missionaries provided the American public with its few histories and travel accounts of China and the Far East; and because of their facility in the use of Asiatic languages they were the only interpreters and translators available to the American legations and consulates in eastern Asia for many years. During the nineteenth and the early years of the twentieth century the missionary community grew in numbers and in the value of its physical assets.[3] While their freedom of travel and residence was covered by treaty, these religious workers found it necessary to move with the currents of Chinese politics, devious though they might be. It was not unusual, therefore, in the 1920's to find missionary bodies in the interior of China joining with the Young China nationalist movement and demanding an end of extraterritorial privileges. Yet it

---

[1]Bristol to Lewis Heck, Manila, March 22, 1928, Mark L. Bristol Papers, Box 83, MLB 42-28, Library of Congress Manuscripts Division. Hereafter, papers in the Library of Congress Manuscripts Division will be cited as LCMD.

[2]See particularly Tyler Dennett, *Americans in Eastern Asia* (New York: The Macmillan Company, 1922), pp. 555-77; A. Whitney Griswold, *The Far Eastern Policy of the United States* (New York: Harcourt, Brace & Company, Inc., 1938), pp. 468-71; T'ien-yi Li, *Woodrow Wilson's China Policy, 1913-1917* (New York: University of Kansas City Press, 1952), pp. 5, 203-4; John W. Masland, "Missionary Influence Upon American Far Eastern Policy," *Pacific Historical Review*, X (September, 1941), 279-96.

[3]C. F. Remer, *Foreign Investments in China* (New York: The Macmillan Company, 1933), pp. 302-8; Dorothy Borg, *American Policy and the Chinese Revolution 1925-1928* (New York: American Institute of Pacific Relations and The Macmillan Company, 1947), pp. 68-70.

was equally commonplace to find other evangelical groups in the International Settlement and treaty ports demanding a continuance of old treaty rights.[4] The voice of this missionary body was heard through the denominational magazines, papers, letters, and the never-ending resolutions of their governing bodies.

As Bristol suggested, the other major pressure group, the business community, similarly was not united in the methods it used or the goals it sought. This is easily demonstrated by examining the response of businessmen when Philippine independence or loans to Japan were discussed. The businessman who processed sugar in the Philippines felt retention of the islands was vital to his best interests; the Louisiana sugar miller and the Utah sugar beet farmer, on the other hand, felt Filipino freedom and its attendant tariff liability was good for the "little brown brothers," and even more so for themselves. Again, the American banker wanted to lend money to Japan for developments in Korea and Manchuria; the American manufacturer preferred to see those areas remain undeveloped and thus become markets for American steel products. To formulate and implement a policy in the Far East that would satisfy all these segments of American society was a Herculean task.

A final factor that has required special consideration by agencies devising policies for the Far East has been the level of political and economic development within the area. By the 1920's the government of Japan was highly centralized through its institutional developments and the nature of its constitution. Political parties had existed for many decades, and experimentation was going forward to make them politically responsible. China on the other hand was badly split, with a

---

[4]Westel W. Willoughby, *Foreign Rights and Interests in China,* 2 vols. (Baltimore: The Johns Hopkins Press, 1927), pp. 719-21; Henry Kittredge Norton, *China and the Powers* (New York: The John Day Company, Inc., 1927), pp. 127-30; Borg, *American Policy,* pp. 93-94. Assistant Secretary of State Nelson T. Johnson, later Minister to China, corresponded regularly with A. L. Warnshuis, representing the Foreign Missions Conference of North America. Warnshuis noted that several foreign mission groups in the United States favored protecting American missionaries in China diplomatically, but not by the use of force or by recourse to any of the unequal treaties with the Chinese. A. L. Warnshuis to Johnson, New York, December 21, 1927, Nelson T. Johnson Papers, Vol. IV, LCMD.

central government that represented not the whole country but a few northern provinces. Though Peking was the seat of the central government, it was unable to speak diplomatically for the Manchurian provinces or the area south of the Yangtze River. Foreign gunboats still ascended the Yangtze for a thousand miles to protect alien nationals, foreigners collected the country's customs and determined what rates should prevail, and foreign citizens were tried in foreign courts established in China. By 1900 Japan had thrown off these vestiges of humiliating subservience, and by 1905 had become firmly established as one of the Great Powers of the world. China had not.

There was a corresponding economic disparity. By the 1920's Japan was a modern industrial nation possessing fairly modern machinery and blessed with enough surplus population to make a cheap labor supply possible. Social and political institutions kept the workers docile and relatively unorganized. Possessing few natural resources for their industrial plant, the Japanese aggressively sought sources of cheap raw materials and outlets for their manufactured products. China—especially the area north of the Yangtze, including the Manchurian provinces—provided the solution. Compared with the Japanese, the Chinese were still in the handicraft stage. Their industrial concerns were largely foreign-owned and -managed, native capital being insufficient for major developments and state capital being unavailable because of political chaos. Money that might have gone into industrial developments was hoarded from grasping *tuchuns,* who warred constantly among themselves for political control.[5] Japan, therefore, was able to duplicate the role of the western nations in exploiting China, and by reason of propinquity to do so more efficiently.

Thus any policy of the United States in regard to China had necessarily to consider her more aggressive neighbor. Relations between Japan and the United States were conducted in terms of international equality—the same obviously could not be said for China. When America and Japan conferred on mutual problems, the chances for a satisfactory solution were good; however, when the two nations dis-

---

[5]The Legation in China to the Department of State, Peking, October 19, 1918, U. S., Department of State, *Papers Relating to the Foreign Relations of the United States, 1918* (Washington, 1930), pp. 112-13. Hereafter cited as *Foreign Relations.* See also Remer, *Foreign Investments in China,* pp. 229-36.

cussed general Far Eastern matters, particularly those in which China was concerned, the Japanese could never admit equality of interest —their future was too closely tied to the mainland.[6]

In summation, American Far Eastern policy in the decade of the 1920's was a program complicated by the many conflicting interests it was designed to serve, and further tangled by the nature of the area with which it dealt. The policy itself was basically the fabrication of three agencies: the executive branch of the Government, the Congress, and organized pressure groups. Simply stated, this policy was the traditional one vis-à-vis China; a program of vacillation toward Japan, but with strong efforts made to create mutual good feeling; and a policy toward the Philippines that promised good government, indefinite territorial status, and recognition that they were expendable in Far Eastern power politics.

The policy of the United States toward China in the 1920's had three characteristics: it was designed to serve the American business community, it was a policy of friendship, and it did not involve the use of military force to any great extent. These points were not distinct and separate parts of a total policy but were overlapping. At times they were conflicting, at times they fell into disuse, and always they were subject to broad interpretation.

President A. Whitney Griswold of Yale University in the early pages of his study of the Far Eastern policy of the United States wrote that: "Its fundamental aim was commercial not political. Equal commercial opportunity for Americans; no territorial concessions for the

---

[6]In a document presented to the League of Nations the Japanese stated their case simply:

> The only, and at the same time the best, means for Japan to solve the problem of over-population, is to develope [sic] new industries with Chinese raw materials, and to export the manufactured articles to China. Japan's fate hangs upon the realisation or non-realisation of this project. This indeed constitutes for her a question of life or death. Herein lies the reason why Japan attaches so much importance to the Chinese question, and especially the question of Manchuria and Mongolia.

Japan, Foreign Office, *The Present Condition of China: With Reference to Circumstances Affecting International Relations and the Good Understanding Between Nations Upon Which Peace Depends,* "Document A" (Printed July, 1932).

United States; a strong Eastern Asia to resist a designing Europe. . . ."[7] At the end of his remarkably prescient study, Griswold reaffirmed his basic description of America's policy in China and the Far East but admitted mystification. America in the years to 1935 had achieved very little in the way of financial gain from its preferential policy toward China and had probably lost considerably owing to its treatment of Japan. He wondered why America had chosen such a policy.[8] The answer to this question is not a rational one but deals to some extent with wishful thinking and the perpetuation of a myth.

The American attitude toward China in the 1920's was shaped by the magic statistic—400,000,000 Chinese—and by the belief that the American industrial plant was turning out more than could be absorbed in the home market. What was required then was to guarantee that American businessmen and their products would have access to China's markets. General Leonard Wood, President Warren G. Harding's appointee as governor-general of the Philippines, voiced this belief when writing to the widow of an old friend: "Our people are being rapidly industrialized. We must have foreign markets and plenty of them. The four hundred and odd millions of people of China present the great trading area in the world. . . ." Writing to President Harding, Wood spoke even more cogently: "Again, our country is becoming so rapidly industrialized that foreign markets for our surplus output will be an imperative necessity. The greatest future trade area in the world is China. . . ."[9] The Commander of

---

[7]Griswold, *Far Eastern Policy*, p. 8.

[8]*Ibid.*, pp. 466-71. Griswold's question has been re-examined many times since 1938 and several times before. See Charles Callan Tansill, *Back Door to War: The Roosevelt Foreign Policy 1933-1941* (Chicago: Henry Regnery Company, 1952), 690 pp. In this volume Tansill concluded that the United States backed the wrong horse in its Far Eastern planning. A more thoughtful and temperate analysis of this situation is found in William L. Neumann's chapter, "Ambiguity and Ambivalence in Ideas of National Interest in Asia," in *Isolation and Security*, Alexander De Conde, ed. (Durham: Duke University Press, 1957), pp. 133-58.

[9]Wood to Mrs. Whitelaw Reid, Baguio, August 29, 1922, Leonard Wood Papers, Box 162, LCMD; Leonard Wood to the President of the United States, Manila, November 29, 1922, U. S., Department of the Interior, File 364-504A, National Archives. See also Herbert Feis, *The Diplomacy of the Dollar, First Era 1919-1932* (Baltimore: The Johns Hopkins Press, 1950), pp. 4-5.

the South China Patrol, whose task was the protection of American interests in the South Seas, wrote to a friend, "If the Foreigner would forego a temporary selfish advantage, China with its four hundred and fifty million people would be the best market in the world for Foreign business interests. . . . There is lots of money to be made in China by Foreigners if they go about it properly. America is the favored nation."[10] The genesis of this idea, like so many basic concepts of American foreign policy, has historical roots.

The expansionist propaganda drive of the late nineteenth century was effective enough to leave the United States with certain fixed attitudes. One of these has been called "the bogey of the surplus."[11] It was widely advertised in business journals and magazines that the United States at the end of the nineteenth century was industrially mature. The nation was producing more than the home market could absorb, because of machine efficiency and a slowing down of the economy with the halt in westward expansion. To make the picture even more desperate, it was held that foreign markets in Europe and Latin America might be closed. Thus businessmen reasoned that the urgency of the situation called for "an all-out drive for overseas markets, because unless the country succeeded in adding substantially to its outlets abroad it would in time be swamped with an ever-growing surplus; the standard of living would decline; the social order would be disturbed; even revolution might break out. . . ."[12] The

---

[10]Captain E. T. Constein to Vice Admiral Welles, Canton, August 4, 1925, Roger Welles Papers, Box 201, LCMD. It is interesting to note that the president of the American Chamber of Commerce of Shanghai, when trying to encourage the State Department to pursue a firmer policy in China, wrote: "This Chamber has repeatedly emphasized the fact that America requires a future outlet for the rapidly increasing surplus products of her industries and that the welfare of the people of the United States demands that our Government do everything possible to retain and develop this great potential market in Asia. . . ." *Bulletin* of the American Chamber of Commerce of Shanghai, August, 1927, quoted in Borg, *American Policy*, p. 354.

[11]Charles S. Campbell, Jr., *Special Business Interests and the Open Door Policy* (New Haven: Yale University Press, 1951), pp. 1-9.

[12]*Ibid.*, p. 2. See also the contemporary works by Brooks Adams, *America's Economic Supremacy* (New York: The Macmillan Company, 1900), 222 pp., and *The New Empire* (New York: The Macmillan Company, 1902), 243 pp.

solution to this problem at the turn of the century was to be resolved by full exploitation of the China market.

The concept that China's markets were necessary for America's well-being continued to be accepted into the 1920's. The years between the administrations of Secretaries of State John Hay and Charles Evans Hughes saw no basic change in the strategy of the China policy. Such tactics as the abortive "Knox Neutralization Policy" of 1909, participation in financial consortia, nonrecognition of Japan's "Twenty-one Demands of China," participation in the Siberian expedition, and the attempted settlement of the Shantung question between China and Japan were undertaken to preserve the Open Door and China's territorial integrity, both of which would serve importantly to preserve the China market. A scholar has pointed out recently that one cannot overlook the aspect of American idealism in this pattern of action, but commercial considerations are quite evident.[13]

In pursuing a policy of friendship toward China the United States adhered to a program of encouraging unification and the erection of a strong central government; yet great pains were taken to insure that the Chinese accomplish these goals without American interference. In August, 1923, suggestions were made to Secretary of State Hughes toward strengthening the program of the new Four-Power Consortium, but they received scant consideration.[14] For the purpose of indicating what conditions really were, the President of the American Group of the Chinese consortium sent Hughes several letters received from the group's representative in China. One letter noted that "the Central Government has completely broken down. . . . It is my belief that there is not in China any power capable of bringing order out of this chaotic condition of affairs. . . . Unless one is prepared to see the country drift into anarchy rather than infringe its sovereignty one must sooner or later face the fact that a measure of

---

[13]Li, *Wilson's China Policy*, pp. 203, 211-12; Frederick V. Field, *American Participation in the China Consortiums* (Chicago: University of Chicago Press, 1931), pp. 34-36, 115-17, 192-242; Russell H. Fifield, *Woodrow Wilson and the Far East; The Diplomacy of the Shantung Question* (New York: Thomas Y. Crowell Company, 1952), pp. 61-62, 110; Griswold, *Far Eastern Policy*, pp. 153-57, 174-75.

[14]*Foreign Relations, 1923*, II, 503-9.

foreign intervention is necessary and wise. . . ."[15] To this plea Hughes merely gave his customary polite acknowledgment. The next day Hughes wrote to the secretary of the Republican National Committee, George B. Lockwood, answering an inquiry whether Hughes was ". . . reversing our traditional policy of being the defender of China rather than a mere disinterested looker-on while aggressions against China are undertaken by other powers." In his answer Hughes made a fairly clear and candid statement of the American position toward China at that time. He felt the Washington Conference had done much to free China of its foreign problems and had cleared the air between Japan and the United States.

> The direct and indirect results of the conference were, in fact, such as afforded ground for hope that China might proceed without foreign interference or incumbrance, with the political evolution necessitated by the transition . . . from the imperial to the republican form of government. . . . The difficulty of the situation in the Far East, as you will perceive, lies in the weakness of the Chinese Government. We have done what we could to strengthen it and to give it the opportunity for development. But that development must of necessity take place within.[16]

The policy of the Coolidge administration toward China during the period of the most intensive internecine strife from 1925 to 1928 was, consistently, "hands off." When the civil war began in earnest again in the spring of 1925, the British and the Japanese asked the State Department whether the United States wanted to participate in an international attempt to control the scope of the fighting around Shanghai. Jacob Gould Schurman, the United States minister to China, suggested that America steer clear of any joint activity with the British and Japanese. He believed such participation would merely enhance the Japanese position and could only help one side in China. Acting on Schurman's advice, the department informed the British of its attitude on April 2, 1925. "Aside from the question of the doubtful efficacy of the course proposed, this Government cannot escape the

---

[15]Thomas W. Lamont to Hughes, New York, August 1, 1923, Charles Evans Hughes Papers, Box 30, LCMD.

[16]Charles E. Hughes to George B. Lockwood, Washington, August 2, 1923, U. S., State Department, File 711.94/57, National Archives. Hereafter cited as D/S . . . Archives.

conviction that such an effort to influence by external pressure the course of Chinese domestic politics would almost certainly aggravate, and perhaps render critical, the present widespread anti-foreign sentiment among certain classes of the Chinese people. . . . This Government . . . regrets it cannot . . . adopt the course of action proposed in your note of March 27."[17]

This statement of April 2, 1925, became policy for the State Department under Secretary Frank B. Kellogg. While concerned about any endangerment of American lives or property in China, the United States would join no international expeditions to support the treaty system then extant. One writer has even concluded that Secretary Kellogg believed it was time that treaties relating to China be cast aside, and that a new liberalized treaty system be effected with that nation. In this attitude President Calvin Coolidge and his secretary of state were encouraged by missionary boards in the United States, the press, and the House of Representatives.[18]

By September, 1929, this policy of friendship for China had become doctrine for the Asiatic Fleet. Upon assuming command Admiral Charles V. McVay issued Asiatic Fleet General Order No. 3-20, which noted that the American policy in China was the Open Door policy, nonintervention in internal Chinese affairs, maintenance of the territorial integrity of China, and traditional friendship for China. Fleet policy was to be protection of American lives, protection of American property, the promotion of American interests, and "the cultivation of friendly relations with the Chinese."[19] The State Department undoubtedly concurred.

In contrast with the Far Eastern policy of the United States today, the China policy in the years 1900 to 1931 was a fairly simple affair. The heart of the policy was the protection of the China market

---

[17]Schurman to Kellogg, Peking, March 29, 1925, *Foreign Relations, 1925,* I, 603-5; Kellogg to British Ambassador (Howard), *ibid.,* 607-9.

[18]MacMurray to Kellogg, Peking, November 29, 1926, *Foreign Relations, 1926,* I, 651-54, 662-63. See also: Joseph G. Grew, *Turbulent Era: A Diplomatic Record of Forty Years,* 2 vols. (Boston: Houghton Mifflin Company, 1952), I, 689-90; Borg, *American Policy,* pp. 68-94, 242-66, 419-21; Wesley R. Fishel, *The End of Extraterritoriality in China* (Berkeley and Los Angeles: University of California Press, 1952), pp. 100-8.

[19]D/S, File 811.30 Asiatic Fleet/47, Shanghai, November 2, 1929, Archives.

for American businessmen, and to some extent of the "soul market" for American missionaries. To achieve this policy it was necessary to maintain the Open Door, or the right of American businessmen to trade in China on equal terms with other foreign nations. Protecting the territorial integrity of China was a similar guarantee that segments of China's geographical area would not pass under foreign control and thus become colonialized. The traditional friendship between China and the United States was a product of missionary zeal, but more importantly, it was a by-product of America's insistence that the Chinese melon not be carved. Yet no administration felt that the policy could be supported by armed force.[20] With the benefit of many years of hindsight, one of the chief architects of our China policy, Elihu Root, wrote, "It never entered the head of any President or Secretary of State or Chairman of the Committee on Foreign Relations of the Senate or Chairman of the Committee on Foreign Affairs of the House that we would ever send forces to China to maintain the Open Door."[21] In the eyes of a State Department historical adviser, sanctions for America's China policy were lacking because ". . . American interests in the Far East, while considerable, were not worth fighting for. If they could be conserved by agreement, well and good; if not, at least they were not worth the cost of preparedness to defend them."[22]

---

[20]In September, 1929, Admiral Mark L. Bristol, then commanding the Asiatic Fleet, issued the following instruction to his fleet concerning the use of force in China:

a. Don't use force unless you mean it. Don't bluff. A dignified evacuation is better than defeat.
b. If fired upon the ships are to return the fire just to silence it.
c. Protect American lives by evacuation.
d. Protect property but avoid killing on either side. It would be better to be indemnified later.
e. Avoid any possible creations of another Boxer situation.
f. U. S. forces have no concessions to protect except their part of the Shanghai concession, thus U. S. forces shall not be used to assist in holding foreign concessions. U. S. forces are not to operate under a unified command.

D/S File 811.30 Asiatic Fleet/39, Shanghai, September 6, 1929, Archives.

[21]Elihu Root to Philip Jessup, July 6, 1931, quoted in Philip C. Jessup, *Elihu Root*, 2 vols. (New York: Dodd, Mead & Company, 1938), II, 452.

11

The possession and defense of the Philippine Islands represented a second aspect of America's Far Eastern policy. At the time of their seizure, and through the years until the early 1930's, the islands were the embodiment of a commercial dream. As our policy toward China was built upon the magic statistic of 400,000,000 potential consumers and souls to be saved, so our policy toward the Philippines was built upon the premise that they would be an entrepôt in the Oriental trade, and that their inhabitants would likewise become consumers and Christian neophytes. Unforeseen by many, and eagerly accepted by others, was the hard fact that possession of those verdant isles meant a plunge into the morass of Far Eastern politics, and a part of this new responsibility would be the commitment to their defense.

With a few exceptions, it has been the studied conclusion of American diplomatic historians that the acquisition of the Philippine Islands was an accidental by-product of the Spanish-American War.[23] The islands were not unknown to American commercial interests or the Department of State, but a reading of the consular letters from Manila in the years before the war reveals a singularly apathetic attitude toward the Spanish Isles by both the American Government and business. It was by coincidence that the war with Spain occurred at the same time that the United States began to take an active interest in the possible partitioning of China, and as noted before, this interest in China was based upon commercial considerations; thus when Dewey's victory at Manila became known, the retention of the Philippines became a means of preserving our stake in the trade of the East. However, as clearly demonstrated by Professor J. W. Pratt, the missionary interests were also interested in keeping the Philippines for evangelization purposes. Though the islands were 90 per cent Roman Catholic, the various Protestant sects in the United States apparently

[22]Tyler Dennett, "The Open Door Policy as Intervention," *The Annals of The American Academy of Political and Social Science,* 168 (July, 1933), 81.

[23]Julius W. Pratt, *Expansionists of 1898: The Acquisition of Hawaii and the Spanish Islands* (Baltimore: The Johns Hopkins Press, 1936), pp. 252-78; Garel A. Grunder and William E. Livezey, *The Philippines and the United States* (Norman: University of Oklahoma Press, 1951), pp. 27-38. An opposite viewpoint can be obtained in the Communist-inspired interpretation of Victor Perlo in his *American Imperialism* (New York: International Publishers, 1952), chap. i, *passim.*

felt that an "American" Christianity had to be introduced to replace "Popish" influences. More important than introducing Protestantism into the Philippines was using the islands as a Christian outpost in spreading the gospel to China and Southeast Asia. Thus business and missionary interests had an eye to the future when advocating retention of the Philippines, and that future lay not in the archipelago but on the Asiatic mainland.[24]

Once acquired, the Philippines presented a defense problem of immense proportions, but all strategic difficulties were temporarily solved through a series of diplomatic settlements. Japanese aggressiveness in eastern Asia and irritation with the United States concerning the treatment of Japanese immigrants, coupled with the reluctance of Congress and the Navy Department to concentrate the American fleet in the Far East, resulted in the "Agreed Memorandum of 1905," the Root-Takahira Agreement of 1908, and the Lansing-Ishii Agreement of 1917.[25] All three of these agreements, among other things, protected the American position in the Philippines and in varying degrees freed Japan to pursue a policy of pressure on the Asiatic mainland. Through such agreements the United States continued its control over the Philippines without solving the problem of their defense. Furthermore, a justification was provided for continued rejection of Philippine independence demands—the islands were secure from Japanese aggression; therefore, delay was reasonable until their true value could be determined.

---

[24]Pratt, *Expansionists of 1898*, pp. 273, 279-315. See also John A. Garraty, *Henry Cabot Lodge: A Biography* (New York: Alfred A. Knopf, Inc., 1953), pp. 204-5; Grunder and Livezey, *Philippines*, p. 28.

[25]Tyler Dennett, *Roosevelt and the Russo-Japanese War* (Garden City, New York: Doubleday, Page & Company, 1925), pp. 112-15; Jessup, *Elihu Root*, II, 34-43; Griswold, *Far Eastern Policy*, pp. 129, 214-17. The best account of the "Japanese problem" and its many ramifications is to be found in Thomas A. Bailey, *Theodore Roosevelt and the Japanese-American Crises* (Stanford: Stanford University Press, 1934), 353 pp. See also Kikujiro Ishii, *Diplomatic Commentaries*, William R. Langdon, ed. (Baltimore: The Johns Hopkins Press, 1936), pp. 111-32; U. S., Department of State, *Papers Relating to the Foreign Relations of the United States: The Lansing Papers, 1914-1920*, 2 vols. (Washington: Government Printing Office, 1940), II, 432-53.

The twelve years of Republican administration, from 1921 to 1933, revealed a division of thought within the dominant party when Philippine problems were considered. Presidents Harding, Coolidge, Hoover, and their official families consistently adhered to the policy of retaining the Philippines and re-exerting American control over many governmental functions that had been "Filipinized" during the Francis B. Harrison regime (1913-21). In Congress, on the other hand, there was a tendency to follow presidential leadership until 1924, but in the years thereafter pressures steadily built toward cutting the Philippine dependency adrift. The final revolt of Congress was evidenced by the resounding repassage of the Hare-Hawes-Cutting Act over the President's veto in January, 1933. Throughout these years the Filipinos never ceased their drumfire demands for independence.[26] Yet the question was never put to the democratic test in the Philippines, and in the end it was the American laborer, farmer, dairyman, and sugar-grower who resolved that the politicos were right and the President wrong. Finally, from the strategic viewpoint, the Philippine problem was portentous. Early in 1922 Governor-General Leonard Wood described the measures necessary for holding the Philippines, maintaining the Open Door, and preserving free trade and fair competition throughout the Pacific. He felt the United States must build adequate bases on the Pacific Coast at San Francisco and Puget Sound; the defenses of Oahu must be completed to make the island impregnable; a strongly fortified establishment must be created around Manila Bay; submarine

---

[26]The principal challenge to the Administration position came in 1924 when H.R. 8856 was reported favorably from the House Committee on Insular Affairs. The bill provided for the immediate establishment of a commonwealth and for a 30-year period of continued control by the United States, with a plebiscite at the end of the period to determine whether the Filipinos desired independence. General Frank McIntyre wrote to Govennor-General Wood that "Dominant sentiment seems to be [the] desire to get rid of the Philippine Islands. Opposition to free admission of Philippine sugar, cigars and other products, has great weight in determining attitude of many. . . ." Frank E. McIntyre to Leonard Wood, March 11, 1924, quoted in Hermann Hagedorn, *Leonard Wood: A Biography*, 2 vols. (New York and London: Harper and Brothers, 1931), II, 447-48. See also Grayson L. Kirk, *Philippine Independence* (New York: Farrar, Rinehart, Inc., 1936), pp. 33-54; Gerald E. Wheeler, "Republican Philippine Policy, 1921-1933," *Pacific Historical Review*, XXVIII (November, 1959), 377-90.

and air defenses should be built up considerably in the Philippines; an adequate fleet should be maintained in the Pacific; and a large American army garrisoned in the Philippines.[27] Few of these measures were or could be undertaken after February, 1922, because of the Washington Conference treaty settlements; yet the Presidents continued to reject Filipino independence demands that would possibly have absolved them from responsibility for Philippine defense.

A search of the correspondence of General Leonard Wood helps to explain their position. Wood was a key figure in constructing the attitudes of the executive branch toward the Philippines. Among his many personal friends were the most important figures in the Republican party. That he was a leading candidate for the presidential nomination in 1920 suggests his basic political connections. As a Rough Rider, pacifier of the Philippines, and well-known general during World War I, he formed many friendships and built much grass-roots support. Likewise, he formed a reputation for stubbornness, high-handedness, single-mindedness, integrity, administrative ability, and inability to cooperate. Working independently he could be outstanding; but it is significant that General Pershing did not want him in France. Republican leaders preferred the more malleable Harding as a candidate, and President Harding preferred Wood in the Philippines rather than in his cabinet as Secretary of War.[28]

Once in office, President Harding selected General Wood and W. Cameron Forbes to visit the Philippines and determine whether the Philippine government was in a position to warrant its total separation from the United States. The selection of Wood for the task practically assured a strong report for retaining the islands and reversing Harrison policies. Two months before his appointment the General had written

---

[27]Wood to Captain J. M. Scammell, Manila, February 4, 1922, Leonard Wood Papers, Box 162, LCMD.

[28]Without doubt the best biography of General Leonard Wood is that by Hermann Hagedorn. He and Wood were close personal friends and the biography was written from the rather voluminous Wood papers. See also Grunder and Livezey, *Philippines,* pp. 162-83; Kirk, *Philippine Independence,* pp. 50-54. Cross references for material on General Wood can be found in the Elihu Root, Charles Evans Hughes, W. Cameron Forbes, Calvin Coolidge, John J. Pershing, and Frank R. McCoy Papers in the Library of Congress Manuscripts Division, and in the Henry L. Stimson Papers at Yale University.

a confidant, the editor of the *Boston American*: "I am not in accord
with the policy of scuttling in the Philippines until the people are ready
to govern themselves, and the people know my attitude."[29] Accordingly, the Wood-Forbes Commission reported the Filipinos were unready
for independence, and:

> It is the general opinion among Filipinos, Americans and foreigners
> that the public services are now in many particulars relatively ineffi-
> cient; that there has occurred a slowing down in the dispatch of
> business, and a distinct relapse toward the standards and administra-
> tive habits of former days. This is due in part to bad example, incom-
> petent direction, to political infection of the services, and above all
> to lack of competent supervision and inspection.[30]

At the completion of his survey of the Philippines, Wood was appointed governor-general. He proceeded to remedy the defects noted
in the Commission Report.

Through the years until Wood's death in 1927, the Malacañan
Palace in Manila was the seat of a vigorous propaganda campaign to
maintain American sovereignty over the Philippines. As governor-
general of the islands, Wood was responsible to the President through
the Secretary of War, whose Bureau of Insular Affairs was the home
office for the Manila government. Wood never hesitated to write the
various Presidents directly, and he was on the best of terms with
Secretary of War John W. Weeks and his successor, Dwight F. Davis.
With the long-time chief of the War Department's Bureau of Insular
Affairs, Brigadier General Frank E. McIntyre, Wood was usually
in agreement. Outside of the official cabinet Wood counted among
his personal friends such illustrious names as former President Taft,
Elihu Root, Henry Cabot Lodge, Henry L. Stimson, W. C. Forbes,
Franklin D. Roosevelt, Theodore Roosevelt, Jr., Mrs. Whitelaw Reid,

---

[29]Wood to James T. Williams, Jr., Fort Sheridan, Illinois, January 25, 1921,
Leonard Wood Papers, Box 158, LCMD. General Wood's attitude was shared
by W. Cameron Forbes. In answer to a letter from Forbes, a former governor-
general wrote: "The view you express that it is a piece of criminal folly to
grant independence now seems to me incontestable. . . ." Luke E. Wright to
Forbes, Memphis, February 9, 1921, Journal of W. C. Forbes (typescript), 2d
Series, Vol. II (1921-1929), 37-38, LCMD.

[30]*Report of the Special Mission to the Philippines* (Manila: Bureau of
Printing, 1921), 27 pp.

and Mrs. Theodore Roosevelt; such writers as Isaac F. Marcosson of the *Saturday Evening Post,* Nicholas Roosevelt of the *New York Times,* James T. Williams, Jr., of the *Boston American,* Henry Cabot Lodge, Jr., and Edward Price Bell; such a big-Navy publicist as William Howard Gardiner; and such military men as Generals Frank R. Mc-Coy, Douglas MacArthur, and James G. Harbord, who became president of R.C.A. upon retirement. Wood's vigorous correspondence was supplemented by the views of his subordinates and ex-subordinates upon their return to the United States. Folder after folder of the Wood papers tell of a loyal legion of turn-of-the-century imperialists still beating the drum and still fighting for empire during a period of relative isolationism in America. They pitched their arguments for Philippine retention in terms of Far Eastern markets, moral obligations, maintenance of Far Eastern stability, and strategic needs, and generally concluded their pleas by arguing *ad horrendum* that Japan would probably seize the islands were the United States to free them.

From the egocentric viewpoint of a Philippines governor-general it was probably reasonable to expect that the Philippines would become a great economic asset to the United States. Wood certainly preached a gospel of unlimited opportunity and never departed from the principle that early independence would rob both the islands and the United States of the benefits of economic interdependence. He worried that American businessmen were not interested in the Philippines and complained that "the people at home have little or no appreciation as a whole of the far-reaching importance of the Philippines in the development of United States commerce and progress."[31] To remedy this lack of appreciation Wood urged writers

---

[31]Wood to Isaac F. Marcosson, Manila, May 16, 1922, Leonard Wood Papers, Box 161, LCMD. Wood's views were faithfully reiterated by his chief, the Secretary of War, when he wrote: "We have, as a people, utterly failed to take advantage of the commercial and financial opportunities offered us by the Philippines. . . . This probably is the most profitable field for the cultivation of sugar in the world. Americans have been given every opportunity therein. It is observed that they neither cultivate the sugar, nor mill it, nor do they get the brokerage profits thereon. . . . The lack of American participation in the tobacco and cigar industry is even more marked. . . ." John W. Weeks to Charles G. Washburn, Washington, November 15, 1923, U. S., Interior Department, File 364-467, Archives.

to present the facts to the American people. Response came in books by Nicholas Roosevelt and Katherine Mayo and in plenty of newsprint in various magazines and newspapers.[32] Yet Wood could not guarantee the one thing that American investors wanted—assurance that the Philippines would be kept indefinitely.

President Coolidge did his part to assure American businessmen that the Government did not anticipate Philippine independence in the foreseeable future. He discouraged the annual Philippine independence missions, and in 1924 when the House Committee on Insular Affairs was considering an independence bill, the President made public his reply to Manuel Roxas, the tenor of which was that the Filipinos should be grateful for American protection and aid.[33] In 1926 Coolidge sent Colonel Carmi Thompson, an Ohio politician, as a personal representative to the Philippines to investigate economic conditions in the islands. Thompson's report to Coolidge, which was later given wide circulation, sustained the President's convictions:

> From the standpoint of American commercial interests in the Far East, it would be unwise to relinquish control of the Philippines at the present time. Our trade with the Orient has been expanding year by year and all indications point to an increased volume of business for the future. We need the Philippines as a commercial base, and the retention of the Philippines will otherwise be of great benefit to our Eastern situation.

Thompson had been provided with full news coverage during the trip, and his viewpoint was given further support by press predictions that the islands would be used to break the British and Dutch strangle hold on the world's rubber production.[34]

---

[32]Nicholas Roosevelt, *The Philippines: A Treasure and a Problem* (New York: Sears Publishing Company, 1927); *The Restless Pacific* (New York: Charles Scribner's Sons, 1928). A more recent work by Mr. Roosevelt gives some added highlights on the Philippines and General Wood: *A Front Row Seat* (Norman: University of Oklahoma Press, 1953); Katherine Mayo, *The Isles of Fear* (New York: Harcourt, Brace & Company, Inc., 1925).

[33]Coolidge to Manuel Roxas, Washington, February 21, 1924, Calvin Coolidge Papers, Box 400, Philippines: 1, LCMD.

[34]"Report of Conditions in the Philippine Islands, Cleveland, December 4, 1926," Calvin Coolidge Papers, Box 3467-88, Folder 3477, LCMD; Julius W. Pratt, *America's Colonial Experiment* (New York: Prentice-Hall, Inc., 1951), p.

An examination of the trade statistics for the decade 1921-31 reveals the hollowness of the Thompson report and suggests that Wood and his followers were overoptimistic. American world trade was healthy, with an average positive dollar balance of approximately 800 millions annually. European trade provided a positive balance of 1,200 millions annually; but Asiatic trade had an annual negative balance of 500 millions, of which 128 millions were a part of the East Asiatic trade and 34 millions due to Philippine trade:[35] American businessmen were selling heavily in Europe and buying heavily in the Far East. During the period that the United States had an average trade deficit with the Philippines of 34 millions annually, the islands were selling the United States 72.3 per cent of their exports, but buying just 58.7 per cent of their imports from the United States. There was no established upward trend in Philippine buying to cause the American exporter to become overenthusiastic. The Philippines never became the entrepôt for American Far Eastern trade as expected, because the islands were too far removed from the principal sea routes to Tokyo and Shanghai. Nothing was gained by transshipment from Manila, because the islands were American territory and imposts against Philippine products were the same as duties against American goods.[36] One can only conclude that General Wood, his associates, and the Administration were infected with the same myth of the great Asiatic trade that caused the Polo brothers to journey to Cambaluc and Magellan to die on the Philippine isle of Cebu; yet it was the same myth that was basic not only to Philippine policy but to China policy as well.

300; "The Next Step in the Philippines," *The Literary Digest,* October 23, 1926, pp. 12-13.

[35]U. S., Department of Commerce, *Foreign Commerce and Navigation of the United States, 1921-1931,* 11 vols. (Washington: Government Printing Office, 1922-1932), Table IV in all volumes.

[36]Philip G. Wright, *Trade and Trade Barriers in the Pacific* (Stanford: Stanford University Press, 1935), Table 221, p. 525; U. S., Department of State, "Foreign Economic Interests in the Far East," *Memoranda for the American Delegates to the Conference on Limitation of Armament* (Washington: Government Printing Office, 1922), p. 31; U. S., Inter-departmental Committee on the Philippines, *Report on Philippine-United States Trade Relations,* 2 vols. (Washington: Government Printing Office, 1935), II, 288-91.

Since the promises of trade and profit were received with mixed feelings in business-conscious America, the group around General Wood usually appended a moral argument to its market quotations. Men like Bishop Charles A. Brent, the Episcopal leader in the Philippines, emphasized the necessity of remaining in the islands because the Filipinos needed the steadying hand of Christianity. He said publicly, "The people of the Philippines require our rule. We are not in the Philippines for our pleasure or profit. If we were it would be the most natural thing in the world to say that the game is not worth the candle . . . and leave the Philippines to go to perdition in their own way. But we cannot do that."[37] Wood himself was quite conscious of the religious needs of the Filipinos and spoke of the connection between trade and Christianity in the Far East:

> [The islands are] the base from which we must work for the Open Door and the maintenance of our influence in the Far East. It is also the center and spearhead of the great Christian effort. If we can build up here a strong well-trained, well-disciplined people who are Christians, we shall have established a most powerful instrumentality for the extension of Christianity in the Orient, and on its extension and the extension of what is best in western civilization we must depend for the true advance to higher deeds and a better life on the part of the Oriental people.[38]

A year later, and just a year before he became governor-general to replace Wood, Henry L. Stimson wrote, "I am against removing wholly our sovereignty now or at any time. I believe its retention to be equally necessary for their welfare and protection and for our ultimate trade relations to the Orient."[39]

Underlying the views of General Wood and his associates was the premise that the Filipino *tao* (peasant) did not really want independence. The General and the Administration in Washington felt that

---

[37]Quoted in W. Cameron Forbes, *The Philippine Islands,* 2 vols. (New York and Boston: Houghton Mifflin Company, 1928), II, 383-84. See also memorandum of a conversation with Bishop Burney, Methodist bishop from China, Washington, September 8, 1924, Leland Harrison Papers, Box 46, LCMD.

[38]Wood to Hermann Hagedorn, Manila, July 8, 1925, Leonard Wood Papers, Box 179, LCMD.

[39]Henry L. Stimson to Wood, at sea, October 11, 1926, Leonard Wood Papers, Box 182, LCMD.

the politicos like Manuel Roxas, Manuel Quezon, and Sergio Osmeña used the independence issue as a means of garnering votes for themselves. Men who visited the Philippines reported that in private conversations the party leaders admitted they were not genuinely interested in independence.[40] Yet, when the Filipino legislature passed an act providing for a plebiscite of the people on the independence issue, Wood vetoed the bill, and Coolidge later vetoed it again when it was repassed by the Filipinos. In his message President Coolidge declared, "A plebiscite on the question of immediate independence would tend to divert the attention of the people towards the pursuit of mere political power rather than to the consideration of the essential steps necessary for the maintenance of a stable, prosperous, well-governed community."[41] Working within this viewpoint, Henry L. Stimson in late 1926 came to the conclusion that a form of semidominion status would suit the Filipinos admirably, provided the United States would maintain the power of veto and inspection. He wrote to Wood that he had been able to sell his views to Root, Hughes, Taft, Coolidge, and

---

[40]Secretary of War Weeks wrote to a friend: "As advised, we believe that the Philippine people desire to continue under the American flag and that those politically active among the Filipinos desire a greater present degree of autonomy with complete autonomy at a relatively early day. . . ." John W. Weeks to Charles G. Washburn, Washington, November 15, 1923, U. S., Interior Department, File 364-467, Archives.

The President wrote to the leader of the Philippine independence mission for 1924: "The extent to which the grievances which you suggest are shared by the Filipino people has been a subject of some disagreement. The American Government has information which justifies it in the confidence that a very large proportion at any rate, and possibly a majority of the substantial citizenry of the Islands, does not support the claim that there are grounds for serious grievance. . . ." Coolidge to Manuel Roxas, Washington, February 21, 1924, Calvin Coolidge Papers, Box 400, Philippines: 1, LCMD.

A Navy captain with years of Asiatic Fleet experience wrote to his brother: "The Philippines are an ungrateful child whose politicos will continue to agitate independence from the United States, but commercial independence is farthest from their desires. The protection they receive from our flag gives them more real independence than they can hope to enjoy, were we to cast them aloose." Captain Adolphus Staton to Henry Staton, San Diego, March 19, 1930, Adolphus Staton Papers, Box 3, Folder 51, Southern Historical Collection, University of North Carolina.

[41]Quoted in Kirk, *Philippine Independence,* p. 53.

even Alfred E. Smith.[42] Upon his return to the Philippines as governor-general, Stimson had a maximum of cooperation from Osmeña and Quezon; the latter told him that the Filipinos would accept dominion status were free trade advantages continued. To his old friend Elihu Root, Stimson confided: "It is a curious reversal of the current understanding of the Wood regime, that my chief and most loyal support should now be coming from the very political leaders who so viciously fought and vilified him! But it is so."[43] Time, however, was running out for Stimson, and independence was closer than he or Quezon imagined.

The final argument used by General Wood to support his view that the United States should not scuttle the Philippines was that independence would upset diplomatic balances in the Far East. The years of sullen relations with Japan caused Wood and many others to feel that the Philippines would become another Japanese prefecture or colony were the United States to grant them independence. He felt this likelihood was dangerous not only to America, but "Our withdrawal from the Philippines would probably be a cause for grave apprehension on the part of all Western nations with colonial possessions in the Far East. . . ." Wood summed up the problem when he wrote to Secretary of War Weeks:

> . . . In their heart [the Filipinos] have a genuine fear of Japan, and in considering the Philippine problem we cannot disregard the Japanese position, interests and possible action. . . .
>
> The natural resources of the Philippines supplement most of the shortages of those of Japan. We have unlimited iron, unlimited timber, great fisheries, vegetable oils without end, hemp, sugar, great possibility in cotton, enormous possibilities in tobacco, and we extend in a direction which, were the islands in Japanese hands, would give secure control over the great commercial routes from India, Europe and Australia. . . .
>
> The ambitions of Japan from her standpoint are legitimate. She is an Asiatic power. These islands are inhabited by an Asiatic race.

---

[42]Henry L. Stimson to Wood, New York, December 24, 1926, Leonard Wood Papers, Box 182, LCMD.

[43]Henry L. Stimson and McGeorge Bundy, *On Active Service in Peace and War* (New York: Harper and Brothers, 1947), p. 147; H. L. Stimson to Root, Manila, November 24, 1928, Elihu Root Papers, Box 233, LCMD.

Wood did not feel that war was close at hand, but he felt that the economics of the situation and not sentimentality would govern the Japanese attitude.[44]

At a time when British policies were being questioned at every turn in Congress, General Wood was most solicitous of the empire's well-being in the Far East. His vigorous assertion in the Wood-Forbes report that the United States must remain and further uplift the Filipinos was applauded generously in the British press. An ex-governor of the Punjab was grateful that America was turning its back on the dangerous doctrine of self-determination—"a doctrine which is sometimes exploited to cover moral cowardice and the shirking of responsibility." The London *Times* described the Filipino as incapable of self-rule as yet: "General Wood realized this, and to him are due the thanks not only of his own countrymen, but of the British people, for his emphatic assertion of the necessity for preserving the white man's power and the white man's prestige in the Pacific. . . ."[45] Though Wood and his coterie were not consciously aping the British in their imperial methods, it is interesting that one of Wood's military aides wrote to a friend who was a member of Parliament:

> General Wood has told me quite recently, that the United States is bound to hold the Philippines "indefinitely." . . .
>
> The Philippine question cannot be safely treated as one of purely local and domestic concern, affecting only Filipino and American interests. It vitally concerns British interests in Australia, Singapore, and India; Dutch interests in the Netherlands East Indies; French interests in Indo-China. . . .
>
> On the disposition of the Philippines hinges, I believe, the whole scheme of Christian civilization and Western culture and progress throughout the Orient. The United States has a huge stake in these

---

[44]Wood to John W. Weeks, Manila, March 31, 1922, Leonard Wood Papers, Box 162, LCMD. Nine years later a similar view was quite current. In the spring of 1930 an American withdrawal from the Philippines was considered a threat to the naval stability established at the London Naval Conference. Nicholas Roosevelt, "Philippine Independence and Peace in the Pacific," *Foreign Affairs* (April, 1930), p. 409.

[45]Sir Michael O'Dwyer, "Self-Government in the Philippines and in British India," *The Living Age,* May 6, 1922, pp. 331-35; "Filipino Ire at Uncle Sam," *The Literary Digest,* October 28, 1922, p. 18.

developments, and a tremendous responsibility in seeing them through. . . .[46]

And so it went through the years of the 1920's. The United States had to keep the Philippines because the Filipinos were incapable of governing themselves; they needed western-style Christianity to save them from perdition; they needed American manufactures to make them happy; they would fall prey to the Japanese or would be overrun by the Chinese shopkeepers; America owed it to the British, the French, the Dutch, and all other colonial Powers not to create new nationalistic urges in dependent territories; and finally, the Philippines were a foot in the Open Door, a means of preserving Chinese territorial integrity, and above all, a positive commitment in Far Eastern affairs. Yet the protection given this all-important area was not a strong Asiatic fleet and a heavily garrisoned Luzon, but a diplomatic guarantee, the Four-Power Treaty of December 13, 1921, which solemnly promised that the signatory powers would "respect their rights in relation to their insular possessions and insular dominions in the region of the Pacific Ocean." And if a Power should become recalcitrant, then the Powers "shall invite the other high contracting parties to a joint conference to which the whole subject will be referred for consideration and adjustment."

Thus American policy toward the Philippines was anomalous. Men like Theodore Roosevelt and General Leonard Wood recognized the danger of retaining the islands in the face of an aggressive Japan; yet when faced with dependence only upon diplomatic guarantees, they preferred to hold the islands. When Woodrow Wilson had the power in Congress to cut the islands adrift, he hesitated until war was at hand and then turned to more urgent matters. Possibly General

---

[46]Colonel Duckworth Ford ended his letter with the note, "It is unimportant that I have long held these views. But it may be momentous that General Wood has voiced them even informally. . . . Anglo-Saxonism must at all costs be maintained and developed in the Western Pacific, in the Far East, in India, so that if (or when) the next world war is fought out in the Pacific, Anglo-Saxonism will prevail. We Anglo-Saxons owe that much to the children of our great-grandchildren. We owe that much to humanity." (Copy) R. A. Duckworth Ford to Admiral Sir Guy Gaunt, K.C.M.G.,M.P., Manila, August 2, 1925, in Leonard Wood Papers, Box 179, LCMD.

Douglas MacArthur was correct when he evaluated the situation during the twenties:

> The whole country is engrossed in the business of making money and spending it. Nothing else interests or attracts public attention. The great events of the Far East attract absolutely no audience here. The Philippine issue is probably of less interest now than ever before, and, as you know, the country was always indifferent to it.[47]

The American attitude toward China and the Philippines in the 1920's had a certain uniqueness to it. The nation was definitely interested in the Open Door and the territorial integrity of China, and it was committed to keeping the Philippines. Yet force was not to be applied in support of these Far Eastern commitments. When American lives were directly threatened, as at Nanking in the turbulent spring of 1927, a naval bombardment and *ad hoc* collective action would be used for protective purposes, but American troops would not cooperate with the garrisons of other countries to head off trouble or take punitive action. While the United States would undoubtedly have acted to defend the Philippines from any direct aggressions, the response would of necessity have been ineffective. The Asiatic Fleet was entirely too weak to do much more than show the flag and meet small-scale crises in Far East waters. Essentially, the United States was depending on the Nine-Power Treaty of 1922 to protect its China interests and on the Four-Power Treaty of 1921 to shield the Philippines. It is a bit ironical that Americans could place such faith in paper defenses for their Far Eastern commitments and at the same time so pointedly ignore that major "scrap of paper" designed to keep the peace of the world—the Covenant of the League of Nations.

---

[47]General Douglas MacArthur to Wood, Atlanta, June 30, 1925, Leonard Wood Papers, Box 177, LCMD.

2

The Problem of Japan

THE PRESENCE of Japan in the Far East infinitely complicated American Far Eastern policy. Maintaining the Open Door and defending the Philippine Islands became increasingly complex with the growth of Japanese hegemony in eastern Asia. In view of this growth the success or failure of the China or Philippine policies of the United States depended on the nature of Japanese-American relations.

American foreign policy, Japanese foreign policy, or the external policy of any country is formulated to insure the safety of the nation and its inhabitants and to promote their welfare. To realize these great national objectives there are such subsidiary policies as determination to protect the nation by military force and to help the commerce and business of the nation find suitable trade outlets. It was at this all-important subsidiary policy level that Japanese and American interests clashed.

During the years 1922 to 1931, in the absence of air power as we know it today, both countries relied upon their navies as the first line of defense. The Japanese strategists viewed their problem as similar to that of Great Britain. They were an insular nation, they had no great continental depth into which they could retreat, they had potentially powerful neighbors nearby; thus a battle fleet capable of meeting and destroying an enemy expeditionary force was a vital necessity. For the United States a similar naval problem existed, but the American public put almost as much faith in the width of the two oceans as it did in the fleet.[1] Had both Japan and the United States needed navies for coastal defense purposes alone, there would have been no problem, but the United States had to consider the defense of the Philippines as well as the security of the continental littoral. The more obvious solution to American naval needs would result in a new dilemma: If the United States had a fleet large enough to defend the mainland and the Philippines, then the fleet menaced Japan; if Japan had a navy large enough to meet the United States Fleet, then the Japanese navy was a direct menace to the Philippines.[2] The proposed solution led to the Five-Power Naval Treaty of February, 1922. The Japanese accepted capital ship inferiority to the United States at the ratio of five to three, and the United States agreed to no additional fortifying of her Asiatic possessions. This treaty soon provoked further ill-feeling between the United States and Japan in naval matters.

The governments of Japan and the United States also collided in promoting their commercial interests. The Department of State felt that insistence upon maintaining the Open Door and the territorial integrity of China would best serve American commercial needs. Basically, this policy assumed that no nation had a greater interest in Far Eastern trade than the United States, but unfortunately for America, the Japanese rejected this premise.

The China market, for the American businessman, remained in the potential stage throughout the 1920's. Industrial jeremiads at the turn of the century had created what was to become a permanent conviction that American business was producing a heavy surplus that required new markets, and out of this conviction arose the belief that China, which still had relatively low tariff due to the unequal treaties, could absorb that surplus. Yet despite China's comparative freedom from the economic nationalism that had gripped most of the nations of the world at this time, American exports to China remained quite low. In the years 1923 to 1931, exports to China by American firms did

---

[1]George A. Grassmuck, *Sectional Biases in Congress on Foreign Policy*, The Johns Hopkins University Studies in Historical and Political Science, Series LXVIII, No. 3 (Baltimore: The Johns Hopkins Press, 1951), pp. 49-52.

[2]Gordon C. O'Gara, *Theodore Roosevelt and the Rise of the Modern Navy* (Princeton: Princeton University Press, 1943), pp. 5-6.

not rise above an average of 3 per cent of all American exports, a figure which represented 18 per cent of China's total imports.[3] A glance at the American export figures to Japan shows that the United States was exporting approximately twice as much to Japan as to China during the period.[4] A very rough approximation shows that American exports to China and Japan were about 9 to 10 per cent of total American exports. The superior level of economic development in Japan, its greater urbanization, and its sounder trading practices accounted in part for the higher Japanese imports of American goods. Thus the Japanese interest in China, commercially speaking, was considerably greater than that of the United States. The Japanese exported an average of 22 per cent of their total exports to China in the years 1923-31, or 27 per cent of China's total imports.[5] The figures (3 per cent of America's exports as compared to 22 per cent of Japan's) show the relative importance of the Chinese market to each nation.

In the field of investments in China, there was an even greater disparity between Japanese and American interests by 1931. Of an estimated $3.2 billions invested in China by all nations, Japanese businessmen had invested 35.1 per cent of the amount as compared to American investments of 6.1 per cent. In terms of percentages of total foreign investments of each country, the Japanese had invested 81.9 per cent of their total in China, whereas Chinese investments represented a mere 1.3 per cent of American investments abroad.[6]

When these figures are viewed with the realization that Japan did not attempt agricultural self-sufficiency in the 1920's, their importance increases somewhat. Japanese concentration on industry had created an urbanized economy that bought imported food and raw materials with exported manufactured goods. A sudden change in the China market could mean possible starvation in Japan, or at the least a heavy government program of agricultural importing. These economic facts of life caused increased pressures on the Chinese to keep

---

[3]Philip G. Wright, *Trade and Trade Barriers in the Pacific* (Stanford: Stanford University Press, 1935), p. 482, Table 185; p. 514, Table 211.

[4]*Ibid.,* pp. 514-15, Table 211.

[5]*Ibid.,* p. 484, Table 187; p. 482, Table 185.

[6]C. F. Remer, *Foreign Investments in China* (New York: The Macmillan Company, 1933), pp. 74-80.

them within the Japanese economic orbit, and Japanese interference in Chinese affairs to assure that internal chaos did not ruin an all-important market.[7]

The Japanese did not place full reliance on the China market alone; the 1920's found them vigorously casting about for other outlets in the Far East and western Pacific area. As early as 1908 the Oriental Development Company had been incorporated to exploit Chosen, and it later established subsidiary agents to develop markets and businesses in the Dutch East Indies, Hainan, the Philippines, and the South Sea Islands. American consuls throughout the Far East noted Japanese economic pressure on the Dutch East Indies and the Philippines and observed how this activity was generally accompanied by anti-American propaganda. From Formosa the American consul, Henry B. Hitchcock, commented, "Formosa is frankly spoken of by the Japanese as their outpost in the commercial conquest of the South Seas. . . ."[8] The Dutch Indies were visited annually by Japanese naval vessels and business missions, all desiring to impress the Dutch with the value of close trade connection with Japan. Yet the American consul at Batavia wrote that the Dutch took pains to treat him as well as they did the Japanese, if not better. He felt the islanders were worried about Japanese "peaceful penetration" and its ramifications.[9] In the Philippines the Japanese established themselves in such numbers that some caustic American writers were referring to the province of Davao in Mindanao as "Davaokuo." By 1930 they held approximately one-fifth of the cultivated land in Davao and in the years 1918 to 1930 had increased

---

[7]In view of Chinese boycotts, the Japanese defended their actions in China with the rationalization that "the loss of our economic opportunities in China signifies *ipso facto* the loss of our right to exist, the anti-Japanese movement presents a grave danger to the national existence of Japan." Japan, Foreign Office, *The Present Condition of China: With Reference to Circumstances Affecting International Relations and the Good Understanding Between Nations Upon Which Peace Depends,* "Document A" (July, 1932), p. 74.

[8]Jerome B. Cohen, *Japan's Economy in War and Reconstruction* (Minneapolis: The University of Minnesota Press, 1949), pp. 34-35; U. S. Department of State, File 894.5611/1, Taihoku, Taiwan, March 23, 1921, Archives.

[9]D/S, Files 894.20256d/2, Batavia, Java, July 16, 1923; 894.20256d/1, Batavia, Java, June 27, 1924; 856d.911/–, Soerabaya, Java, August 28, 1925, Archives.

their population from 2,000 to 5,000. To the Chief of the Bureau of Insular Affairs these statistics were ominous. Yet, though the Japanese Government was interested in overseas markets and in exporting some of its surplus population, the oft-repeated arguments for emigration in Japanese newspapers suggest that the Japanese preferred to remain at home. By 1928 Japanese government officials recognized this trend and merely encouraged investments in rather than emigration to foreign areas.[10]

Simply stated, Japanese and American national policies, though basically pointing toward similar national objectives, *i.e.*, capturing the Far Eastern markets, clashed due to the relative importance of subsidiary policies. Their Far Eastern markets were a matter of life or death to the Japanese, and as a result of this realization they built a navy capable of supporting their policies in Far Eastern waters. This navy, unfortunately, was strong enough to menace American possessions in Guam and the Philippines. The United States, on the other hand, demanded absolute equality with the Japanese in the Far East, though its interests were in no way equal. While this demand was often expressed, the United States was very slow to build a navy equal to the task of supporting its policy declarations. The American Congress put its faith in multilateral treaties limiting naval armaments, and looked approvingly and hopefully upon the development of air power, which many believed would eliminate the expensive battleship line and provide better security for American shores.[11] The Japanese, however, since 1894 had tasted the rewards of "blood-and-iron" policy in the Far East and thus were willing to place more faith in a sound naval program than in a pious treaty system.

The 1920's represent a period when an American-Japanese war was theoretically possible in the light of such national policy conflicts. It never came off; the Japanese were unable to muster the financial strength to meet the challenge. Years of tension ensued, during which

---

[10]Memorandum, F. Lej. Parker to the Secretary of War, Washington, April 28, 1930, U. S., Interior Department, File 364-713, Archives; D/S, File 894.00 P.R./11, Tokyo, November 19, 1928, Archives.

[11]Ashbrook Lincoln, "The United States Navy and Air Power, A History of Naval Aviation 1920-1934" (unpublished Ph. D. dissertation, University of California, 1946), pp. 12-13.

31

time minor matters such as immigration laws or fleet maneuvers served as escape valves for the heat created from the more basic problem of America's frustrating Japan's desires in Asia.

When the curtain was run down on the Washington Conference in February, 1922, many felt that all problems involving Japan and the United States had been laid to rest. The capital ship race had been halted, the Sino-Japanese situation had reached a reasonable resolution, and a new era was surely dawning. Elmer Davis cheerfully commented in the *New York Times,* "much of the important provocation that might lead to trouble between Japan and the United States has disappeared. There are still, of course, the Japanese in California . . . in Manchuria and Siberia. But a little wisdom and common sense can make it very unlikely that trouble should ever arise from those problems." Davis was obviously too hopeful.

In the early 1920's those Japanese aliens in California became a critical problem in Japanese-American relations. Once again California passed legislation designed to discriminate against aliens "ineligible for citizenship," and such activity was emulated by other coastal states. By December, 1923, the urge to do something about the Japanese reached the national level. Representative Albert Johnson of Washington introduced a new "national origins" immigration bill designed to replace the immigration act of 1921. For inhabitants of the Pacific slope it had special significance; it excluded completely, by the device of denying a quota, immigrants from countries whose citizens were ineligible for citizenship.[12] Without naming them, the Johnson bill was

---

[12]The privilege of naturalization was limited by the Naturalization Act of 1906. In this act naturalization was limited to "free white persons" or persons of "African nativity or African descent." The Supreme Court declared that a Japanese could not fit either of these categories and that the 1906 Act was constitutional and applicable. *Ozawa* v. *U.S.,* 260 U.S. (1922), pp. 178-99. An excellent summary of Japanese-American relations in terms of immigration can be found in A. Whitney Griswold, *The Far Eastern Policy of the United States* (New York: Harcourt Brace & Company, Inc., 1938), pp. 340-79, particularly pp. 370-79 for the 1924 Act. See also Yamato Ichihashi, *Japanese in the United States* (Stanford: Stanford University Press, 1932), pp. 298-310; Rodman W. Paul, *The Abrogation of the Gentlemen's Agreement* (Cambridge, Massachusetts: Phi Beta Kappa Society, 1936), pp. 13-97; Eleanor Tupper and George McReynolds, *Japan in American Public Opinion* (New York: The Macmillan Company, 1937), pp. 170-97.

designed in part to halt further immigration of the Japanese to the United States. Though Secretary of State Hughes and the President were opposed to its passage so long as the exclusion clause was included, the Johnson bill was approved by the House of Representatives 308 to 62, and by the Senate 69 to 9, and on May 26, 1924, it was signed by President Coolidge. In signing the bill the President stated formally his regret that he was unable to exercise an "item veto" and thus eliminate the exclusion clause. As the President signed the bill, Secretary Hughes wrote a dignified letter to Ambassador Masanao Hanihara and in it stated that both he and the President were opposed to the exclusion provision, but they could do nothing in the face of a determined Congress. Hughes reminded Hanihara that a Presidential veto would merely cause additional acrimonious debate, and this would undoubtedly convince the average Japanese citizen that the Congress of the United States was prejudiced completely against him. Sincere as they were, Hughes's letter and the President's statement were poor sops to the outraged Japanese.[13]

Had the issue of immigration remained completely free of outside pressure on the Japanese and American governments, there is little likelihood that the matter would have taken on the serious proportions that it assumed. However, the press in both countries took up the issue. In the United States there was a great deal of editorializing on whether the Japanese protest before the immigration act was passed constituted unreasonable meddling with a sovereign right of the United States, and later whether it was a veiled threat.[14] Once the bill was signed by President Coolidge, it ceased to be an important matter for American newspapers, but not so in Japan. The newspapers that had been remarking a year before that "it seems almost incredible that people of intelligence could have been seriously concerned . . . that there was to be a war between Japan and America . . ." were now printing scare headlines. A few newspapers attempted to rationalize in favor of the United States, but most agreed with the Osaka *Mainichi,* Tokyo *Nichi Nichi,* Tokyo *Hochi,* and Tokyo *Kokumin* that the immigration act

---

[13]Memorandum (confidential) of an interview with the Japanese Ambassador, Washington, May 23, 1924, Charles E. Hughes Papers, Box 176, LCMD.

[14]"Exclusion or Quota for Japanese?" *The Literary Digest,* March 1, 1924; "Congress for Japanese Exclusion," *ibid.,* April 26, 1924.

was an insult, deliberately perpetrated, and that to accept it would cause Japan to lose face in the Far East.[15] July 1 became "national humiliation" day, upon which for a few years mass meetings were held to protest America's action; but by July, 1928, the chargé in Tokyo was able to observe that the Japanese had passed the "blind resentment" stage. He felt that the people as a whole were able to appreciate the immigration issue and its significance to America, but he warned that the Japanese had not dropped the matter completely.[16] Occasionally Japanese leaders capitalized on antiexclusion sentiment to obtain support for internal programs; but on the whole the Government accepted Prime Minister Wakatsuki's view that the Japanese should not immigrate to areas where they were not welcome, that the solution to overpopulation was further industrialization.[17]

Though official relations remained outwardly friendly, evidence soon appeared after the passage of the immigration bill that the Japanese were going to use it to weaken the American position in the Far East. Ambassador Jacob Gould Schurman in Peking had already warned Secretary Hughes that Japan would attempt to replace the United States as China's friend. If Japan were alienated by an exclusion act, then America could expect the Japanese to assume leadership in a Pan-Asiatic movement.[18] Japanese-owned newspapers in China began to emphasize that they were shouldering the burden of defending Asiatic rights, and Japanese consulates through the Far East became

---

[15]*Japan Weekly Chronicle,* June 14, 1923, cited in: George H. Blakeslee, *The Recent Foreign Policy of the United States: Problems in American Cooperation with Other Powers* (New York and Cincinnati: The Abingdon Press, 1925), pp. 217-18. For views a year later see: "Japanese Rage at Exclusion," *The Literary Digest,* May 31, 1924, pp. 18-19.

[16]D/S, File 711.945/1309, Tokyo, July 11, 1928, Archives.

[17]D/S, File 894.30/52, Tokyo, June 28, 1926, Archives. In January, 1929, the embassy in Japan noted that Baron Tanaka had addressed the Diet and assured the members that Japanese inactivity concerning the American immigration act did not mean that the Government was reconciled to exclusion. The Osaka *Mainichi* of January 25, 1929, heartily applauded Tanaka's stand. D/S, File 711.945/1312, Tokyo, January 26, 1929, Archives.

[18]D/S, File 711.945/1071, Peking, April 30, 1924, Archives. See also clipping from *The Shanghai Times* for April 15, 1924, enclosed in D/S, File 711.945/1093, Shanghai, April 16, 1924, Archives.

information centers for the distribution of anti-American literature. American consuls from Calcutta to Melbourne saw the alarmed reaction of the English to the exclusion act. Englishmen feared it would turn the Japanese toward Australia and New Zealand, yet it was difficult for them to condemn what was clearly the Commonwealth's national policy. From Melbourne, Consul General Maxwell Blake surmised that Australians were upset not by the act but by the clumsy manner in which it was handled. He enclosed an editorial from the Melbourne *Herald* for April 30, 1924, predicting "America's action must sooner or later lead to war between the two countries. Those who dwell in the Pacific and especially those who declare the trespassing Asiatics will be prosecuted, must look to their defences."

It is difficult to generalize further in regard to the effects of the immigration act upon Japanese-American relations without chronicling the many inevitable and unpleasant incidents resulting from that ill-considered law. What is significant is that Secretaries of State Hughes, Kellogg, and Stimson were saddled with the problem and were unable to offer any hope of remedy. In his instructions to Ambassador Edgar A. Bancroft in February, 1925, Secretary Hughes warned of the inutility even to hint to the Japanese that the act might be modified. Rather, he expected the Ambassador to treat with the Japanese in a friendly, cordial manner, without brusqueness but also without subserviency. He hoped that time would heal the wound, but he realized the Japanese had been deeply hurt. Secretary Frank Kellogg adhered to this policy, and only at the time of the London Conference was even the possibility of modifying the exclusion act opened to carefully guarded consideration.[19]

The exclusion act was to prove of lasting importance. Secretary Hughes predicted with terrible accuracy what was to be the Japanese attitude when he wrote to an old friend:

It is a sorry business and I am greatly depressed. . . . Of course, there is no danger of war. Japan cannot threaten anybody. She is overwhelmed with her economic difficulties as a result of the earthquake. . . . That makes the situation all the worse because she feels

---

[19]D/S, File 711.945/1215, Washington, February 19, 1925, Archives; also Secretary of State to President Hoover, London, February 17, 1930, D/S, File 500.A15A3/708½, Archives.

that we have chosen to affront her at such a time. The question is not one of war but of the substitution of antagonism for cooperation in the Far East, with all that that involved. Our friends in the Senate have in a few minutes spoiled the work of years and done a lasting injury to our common country.[20]

The winter and spring of 1924-25 found Japanese-American relations additionally burdened by a particularly thorny problem. The Navy Department planned to hold extensive maneuvers in the Pacific around Hawaii and to climax the maneuvers with a cruise to Australia, involving a good portion of the Pacific battleship fleet and supporting units. The Pacific maneuvers and their tactical exercises were the climax of a four-year training cycle, and the department had been planning the Australian cruise since late 1923 as a means of testing Battle Fleet capabilities.[21]

The Japanese press in the summer of 1924 began to balloon the issue—particularly in the vernacular newspapers. Emphasized were the apparent inconsistencies between American interest in naval disarmament and Pacific naval maneuvers. By winter the Japanese press was almost rabid. The English-language edition of the Osaka *Mainichi* for December 14, 1924, broadened the issues involved:

> The United States is going to carry out in the Pacific Naval manoeu-vres, the scope of which is so gigantic that no excuse will be of avail against a contention that the American Navy is a menace to the Japanese Navy. *Unless the United States will modify the Immigration Act* and refrain from such action as to engage in such gigantic Naval manoeuvres as planned by the American Navy, the establishment of a truly friendly relation between the two countries will be out of the question.

---

[20]Charles E. Hughes to Frank H. Hiscock, Washington, April 24, 1924, quoted in Merlo J. Pusey, *Charles Evans Hughes,* 2 vols. (New York: The Macmillan Company, 1951), II, 516.

[21]U. S., Congress, House, Naval Subcommittee of the Committee on Appropriations, *Hearings on Naval Appropriation Bill for 1926,* 68th Cong., 2d Sess., November 17, 1924, H. R. 10724, pp. 46-51; *Hearings fiscal 1925,* 68th Cong., 1st Sess., December 20, 1923, H. R. 6820, pp. 92-93; Robert E. Coontz, *From the Mississippi to the Sea* (Philadelphia: Dorrance and Company, 1930), p. 429. For an account of the 1925 maneuvers by the Commander, Battleships, Battle Fleet, see Henry A. Wiley, *An Admiral from Texas* (Garden City, New York: Doubleday, Doran & Company, 1934), pp. 251-67.

In an earlier issue the Osaka *Mainichi* had predicted that "the cruise of the American fleet to the Hawaiian Islands in fighting trim will make the breaking out of war inevitable."[22]

The reaction to the Japanese press attack was equally strong in the United States. On December 19, 1924, the House of Representatives rejected a resolution asking the Navy Department to call off its maneuvers, with floor comment against appeasement of Japan. A few months later, Secretary of State Hughes wrote to Ambassador Cyrus E. Woods in Tokyo, opposing cancellation of the exercises. "To change the Navy's plans because of ill-advised agitation would only postpone trouble and make it more difficult in the future to do the ordinary thing. It is better that the agitation should quiet down and such matters should be regarded on their merits. It was the general opinion that it was in the best interests of our relations with Japan that our Navy should go on with its plans."[23]

Once American determination was clear, the Japanese leadership helped to cool the heated atmosphere. Foreign Affairs Minister Baron Shidehara publicly declared that the Japanese Government could see no harm in the maneuvers, and asked that his people be excused because of their naturally suspicious character. In the lower house of the Diet Mr. Nakamura commented in January, 1925, that the American maneuvers in no way endangered Japan or violated the Four-Power Treaty. Once the Government had spoken, the Japanese press returned to quiescence. Occasional articles did appear reaffirming the Government's view that the maneuvers were no menace, yet expressing hope for cancellation of the exercises.[24]

It is obvious from the timing and the character of the comment that the Japanese protests amounted to less than token resistance. Yet the excitement created helped to maintain the anti-American spirit, still strong as an aftermath of the immigration act.

[22]D/S, File 711.94/531, Tokyo, December 19, 1924, Archives (my italics); "Pacific (?) Naval Maneuvers," *The Literary Digest,* December 27, 1924, pp. 7-8.

[23]Hughes to Cyrus E. Woods, Washington, March 4, 1925, Charles E. Hughes Papers, Box 76, LCMD.

[24]D/S, Files 711.94/533, Tokyo, January 5, 1925; 711.945/1262, Tokyo, January 17, 1925, Archives; "The Troublous Pacific," *The Literary Digest,* May 30, 1925, p. 17.

The Immigration Act of 1924 and the florescence of Japanese interest in the American Battle Fleet maneuvers of 1925 colored to some extent the total milieu in which Japanese-American affairs were conducted; but the clearest picture of conflicting national interests results from an examination of business relationships between the two nations. If international trade and finance can be an agency for promoting friendship, there was ample opportunity to solve all problems between the countries; but efforts aimed at closer economic relationships were not wholly successful.

In December, 1922, the State Department was approached by representatives of several prominent American banking houses who desired the views of the department on a proposed loan to the Oriental Development Company of Japan. The course of the conversations revealed the information that the money would probably finance various projects outside Japan in such areas as Singapore, the Straits Settlements, Manchuria, Mongolia, and the South Seas. The answer given to the banking representatives was based on the principle that "this Department will not view with favor the use of American money to provoke [promote?] competition with American enterprises in third countries. . . ." The banking group (National City of New York, Riggs of Washington) was not easily discouraged and returned on January 3, 1923, for further consultation with Secretary of State Hughes, but again it was turned away without department approval of the loan.[25]

In a confidential memorandum, the Economic Adviser stated the principal reason for denying approval of the loan. He believed that "to strengthen Japan's hand in Manchuria and Mongolia would seem to be borrowing both economic and political trouble for the future." Stanley K. Hornbeck, Chief of the Division of Far Eastern Affairs, concurred heartily. He stated, ". . . the funds in question, if advanced, would contribute either directly or indirectly to the promotion of

---

[25]Memoranda, December 16, 1922, D/S, File 894.51 Or4/1,2,3; memorandum of a conversation, January 3, 1923, File 894.51 Or4/5, Archives. The State Department policy was not to go on record as approving a loan flotation in the United States as being a good risk, but merely to refrain from offering objections. Secretary Hughes felt the State Department had to be notified of possible flotations in order to prevent conflicts with larger policies. Herbert Feis, *The Diplomacy of the Dollar, First Era 1919-1932* (Baltimore: The Johns Hopkins Press, 1950), p. 9.

Japan's special economic program on the continent and the department has a perfect right to withhold its approval if and so long as it feels that the prosecution of that program is inimical to American interests."[26] Heavy pressure from the embassy in Tokyo and the National City Bank, plus assurances from the president of the South Manchurian Railroad, resulted in a department reversal in February, 1923. The Oriental Development Company received its loan.

The policy that emerged from the Oriental Development Company loan became one of the guides for the State Department during the 1920's. By stating "it is not desirable that American credit be made available to foreign interests for investments or enterprises in third countries in cases in which the use of such American credit would tend to prejudice or circumscribe the opportunities for American enterprises," the department put itself in step with the business-conscious Administration.[27] In assuming the right to pass on loan flotations, the State Department consciously made use of the American market as a lever in its conduct of foreign affairs. With respect to Japan, the general policy of not sanctioning loans for use in third countries (though the Oriental Development Company loan was an exception) placed the United States at the side of China as a guardian against Japanese economic penetration and the control that would follow. This policy, though consistent with our China program, continuously annoyed bankers who realized that the Japanese were a better financial risk than their neighbors to the west.

An opportunity to use the American bond market as a means of improving Japanese-American relations came in September, 1923. The Japanese archipelago, particularly the Tokyo-Yokohama area, was violently shaken by a series of earthquakes which left Japan stricken and paralyzed. In the United States and Japan bankers quickly foresaw the need for reconstruction loans. The governor of the New York Federal Reserve Bank suggested to Secretary Hughes that America take advantage of this opportunity to improve Japanese-American

---

[26]Memorandum by A. N. Y[oung], January 5, 1923, D/S, File 894.51 Or4/7; memorandum by S. K. H[ornbeck], January 6, 1923, File 894.51 Or 4/8, Archives.

[27]*Foreign Relations, 1923,* II, 508.

relations and thus head off any embarrassingly opportunistic consortium formation.[28]

The Japanese sent financial missions abroad to seek loans, and the Japanese Ambassador in Washington talked with State and Treasury Department officials along similar lines. Ambassador Hanihara estimated the Japanese needs at Yen 100,000,000 ($50,000,000) in 1924 and possibly as much in 1925. In Tokyo the *Asahi Shimbun* spoke in terms of a billion Yen. In January, 1924, J. P. Morgan and Company sought Secretary of State Hughes's attitude toward a $150,000,000 loan to Japan. The Secretary could see no basis for objection and concluded, in his letter of approval, "I may add that it would be a source of great satisfaction if, at this time of their courageous effort to overcome the devastating effects of the recent disaster, it should be found possible to make this market available to the Government and people of Japan on the most favorable terms possible."[29]

The loan was made by issuing bonds paying 6½ per cent interest, and these were very quickly sold in the American market. The Japanese partisan press exploded, and public sentiment briefly flared when it was realized that such a high interest rate had been accepted by the Japanese Government, especially in view of the oversubscription in America. Thus the fortuitous financial situation created by a great natural disaster, which might have paved the way for better relations, in the end contributed to a deteriorating situation. The Government of the United States could of course offer no aid because it had pledged itself against foreign loans, particularly when ready capital was available from private sources.[30]

By the winter of 1927-28 American bankers again requested the Department of State to consider a prospective loan to Japan. The South Manchurian Railway Company desired to undertake new construction and to refinance some old obligations and was therefore look-

---

[28]Benjamin Strong to the Secretary of State, D/S, File 894.51/176, New York, October 7, 1923, Archives.

[29]Secretary of State to Thomas W. Lamont, Washington, January 28, 1924, D/S, File 894.51M82/–, Archives.

[30]D/S, Files 894.51/191, Tokyo, February 14, 1924; 894.51/193, Tokyo, February 29, 1924; 894.51/194, Tokyo, February 18, 1924, Archives; Feis, *Diplomacy of the Dollar*, p. 6.

ing to the American money market. Thomas W. Lamont of Morgan and Company again did the contact work, both in Japan and with the State Department. In a personal letter to Assistant Secretary of State Robert E. Olds, Lamont said that approximately $200,000,000 had been loaned to the Japanese Government and various municipalities since the earthquake, and that Secretary Kellogg had as recently as September, 1927, requested that Morgan and Company continue its aid to the Japanese. Lamont now stated that more financing was desired by the Japanese and requested an interview at the department. Kellogg told his subordinates that the policy concerning loans for third-country developments would be continued; but at the conference with Lamont on November 17, 1927, no specific loan was mentioned, and thus the department had nothing on which to act.[31]

In the Far East the prospects of a Morgan loan to the South Manchurian Railway created unusual interest. In Shanghai General Chiang K'ai-shek and other Kuomintang leaders met with Admiral Mark L. Bristol, Commander-in-Chief of the Asiatic Fleet, to discuss Lamont's intentions. Bristol denied any knowledge of the purposed loan. Without pressing the matter, H. H. Kung commented, "This loan, although made to the Japanese Government, will be used by the South Manchurian Railway to strengthen Japan's hold in Manchuria, close the open door, and endanger the peace in the Pacific. . . ."[32] In Peking Ferdinand Mayer, the chargé ad interim, received similar advice from the headquarters of General Chang Tso-lin. The General felt that any aid to Japan would merely increase her economic grip on the Manchurian provinces. Chang suggested that he would certainly welcome American capital for investment in Manchuria, an area in which he could exert the greatest amount of control. But from Tokyo Ambassador Charles MacVeagh warned of the danger to Japanese-American relations that would arise from United States suspicions of Japan's intentions in Manchuria and of American lack

---

[31]Thomas W. Lamont to Robert E. Olds, New York, November 11, 1927, D/S, File 894.51So8/48; memorandum by Arthur N. Young, November 1, 1927, D/S, File 894.51So8/–; memorandum by N. T. J[ohnson], January 14, 1928, D/S, File 894.51So8/54, Archives.

[32]Resumé of a conversation between Admiral Bristol and Chiang K'ai-shek at Shanghai on November 14, 1927, D/S, File 811.30 Asiatic Fleet/16, Archives.

of faith in the Washington treaties, in which all participants had pledged respect for the Open Door and China's territorial integrity.[33]

On the basis of the information received from the Far East, and with the Government's loan policy in mind, Assistant Secretary Olds decided:

> . . . it would be far less serious to refrain from objection than deliberately to interpose it and defeat the transaction. The charge of intervening on one side of the controversy would come with considerably more force if we objected than if we refrain and treat the matter as one of simple routine, regarding the loan as made on the guaranty of the Japanese Government to a corporation whose ownership at this time cannot be, and is not, disputed. The fact that our bankers do not propose to take on the property any lien which would run beyond the period of Japan's undisputed ownership [1936-37] is rather important in this connection.[34]

Despite Secretary Olds's views, the legation in China brought enough pressure to bear that by the second week in December it had become evident to the Japanese that they would not get their loan—not immediately, at least.[35] Dr. Takuma Dan, the head of the Mitsui interests, and probably the most important financial figure in Japan, told Ambassador MacVeagh of the Japanese disappointment over the transaction. He felt the State Department had killed the loan because of Chinese propaganda. Kellogg advised MacVeagh to adhere to the State Department story that no loan proposal had been made, and therefore the department had absolutely no comment. In strictest

---

[33]D/S, Files 894.51So8/1, Peking, November 19, 1927; 894.51So8/1a, Washington, November 19, 1927; 894.51So8/2, Tokyo, November 21, 1927, Archives.

[34]Memorandum by R. E. O[lds], November 21, 1927, D/S, File 894.51So8/49, Archives.

[35]See particularly the exchange of cablegrams between the chargé at Peking, Ferdinand Mayer, and the State Department in D/S, Files 894.51So8/49, Peking, November 22, 1927, and 894.51So8/8, Peking, November 25, 1927, Archives. The naval attaché in Peking wrote to Admiral Bristol that Mayer had polled the whole legation, then advised the State Department against allowing the South Manchurian Railway loan. Mayer felt that both the Kuomintang and Chang Tso-lin's government would react quite violently were the loan concluded. [Cdr.] H. Powell to Bristol, Peking, December 1, 1927, Mark L. Bristol Papers, Box 83, MLB 145-27, LCMD.

confidence he advised MacVeagh of concern on the part of American bankers set off by the vigorous Chinese clamor; it had been decided, he said, to let the situation settle down before making the loan. In the summer of 1928 Morgan and Company floated a $20,000,000 bond issue for the Japanese Government to refinance two loans made to the South Manchurian Railway. The State Department could find no grounds for opposition, though the money was to be spent in a third country and used against China's interests.[36]

The delays in granting the South Manchurian Railway loan left a definite feeling of resentment among the Japanese. The State Department's reluctance to use American capital for Japanese exploitation in Manchuria was obvious. It was likewise clear that American Far Eastern policy, at least in terms of loans, was entirely consistent with its traditional policy to protect the Open Door and maintain the territorial integrity of China. In broader outline the Japanese saw that the United States would willingly approve loans to be spent for developments in Japan, but America was quite unwilling to see Japan expand, even financially, onto the continent of Asia, and particularly in China.

While investigating the relationships between the United States and Japan it is pertinent to look at the host of minor irritants that formed a substratum to the major problems. The State Department files are interesting in this regard because of their topical arrangement. The most cursory glance through the records reveals a plethora of letters, reports, and memoranda covering every point of mutual contact from espionage to trademark infringements. When considered by source, geographically and socially, it can be seen that all types of Americans, from Federal Bureau of Investigation agents to small businessmen, took the opportunity to comment on the Japanese and their activities.

American manufacturers found many grounds for complaints against the Japanese about trademark, copyright, and patent violations. To a certain extent it was fruitless to protest to the State Department or to the Japanese Government. The laws covering such areas in Japan were not similar to those of the United States, and few suits,

---

[36]D/S, Files 894.51So8/20, Tokyo, December 9, 1927; 894.51So8/20, Washington, December 10, 1927; 894.51So8/28, Washington, April 19, 1928; 894.51So8/28, Peking, April 24, 1928, Archives.

once begun, could be fought to a satisfactory conclusion. Trademark infringements constituted a large body of official complaints. The Japanese manufacturers had early realized the value of American names on their products for prestige purposes. Violations became ludicrous when the Japanese began manufacturing "Wright Whirlwind" [aircraft engines] wearing apparel, "Willys-Knight" wireless apparatus, or "Hudson" overshoes.[37] The results were to camouflage cheap Japanese merchandise with an American label and thus decrease the appeal of the American brand over a period of time.

Since copyright law was extremely vague in Japan, Japanese motion-picture exhibitors often appropriated American films. During the years 1924-25 at least seven major productions, among them "Babylon," "Camille," and "Greed," were stolen by the Japanese. The mere change of title or deletion of a scene was enough to convince a Japanese court that the film had not been pirated and was actually a Japanese creation.[38]

Patent infringements were a similarly vexatious problem, yet little justice could be obtained for the American inventor, manufacturer, or patent owner. Powerful American firms like the Standard Oil Company found they could get their cases taken to the ministry level but without satisfaction.[39] The end result of these business irritations was the creation of a body of American businessmen, increasingly vocal in their complaints, which affected ever-widening circles through membership in business associations and clubs. It was undoubtedly serious to have such an important element in American society prejudiced against Japan.

One could hardly leave the subject of Japanese-American relations as seen from the grass roots without commenting upon the State Department file of reports on individuals. It contains hundreds of letters and reports concerning suspicious activities of Japanese in the United States. The letters run from unverified rumors and crank letters

[37]Perry J. Stevenson to Wilbur J. Carr, Washington, August 22, 1928, D/S, File 894.543/19, Archives.

[38]D/S, Files 894.544/- and 894.544B11/-, Archives, are particularly rich in this type of complaint.

[39]D/S, Files 894.542/- (N87, St2, and Se4), Archives, are but a very small portion of the company files dealing with patent complaints.

to dossiers on certain Japanese agents prepared by the Federal Bureau of Investigation. The heaviest number of letters came from the Pacific Coast area, where the inhabitants were somewhat predisposed to see a Japanese spy in every sukiyaki shop. Tourist bureaus and state information centers were particularly suspicious, and some reported Japanese for buying road maps or requesting information about roads in the national parks. The number of communications is impressive in that it shows the continued dislike and suspicion of the Japanese in the western states during the years after 1924.[40]

America's Far Eastern policy in the years between the Washington Conference of 1922 and the Manchurian episode of 1931 was increasingly China-centered. The administrations of Harding, Coolidge, and Hoover, which had looked upon China as a potential outlet for American industries in the 1920's, exhibited a persistently friendly concern for China's territorial integrity and a dogmatic devotion to the Open Door policy. Many other considerations kept the United States Government firmly on the side of the Chinese, among them the pressure from the churches with missionaries in China. But the guiding principle was the Republican belief that "the business of government is business."

American possession of the Philippine Islands complicated that Far Eastern policy. The Wilsonian trend toward independence for the former Spanish Isles was quickly reversed in 1921, and in the following ten years the Presidents gave no encouragement to the Filipinos and their movement for autonomy. The White House informed them that they were politically immature and should be grateful that the United States had prevented their falling into the hands of some predatory neighbor. Yet in this same period the American Government made Philippine defense virtually impossible by limiting fortifications to those existent before 1922 and by assuring bare equality of the United States Navy and the Japanese in Far Eastern waters. Philippine defense hinged completely on having a navy five-thirds the size of Japan's, the funds for which Congress failed to provide. Thus the Philippines became, to some extent, a hostage of the Japanese Empire.

During this period, when the United States was pursuing a con-

---

[40]Reports on Japanese individuals in the United States can be found in the State Department's 894.20211 file at the National Archives.

sistently friendly policy toward a slowly uniting China, much was done to harm Japanese-American relations. Basically the Government of the United States assumed that it had as great a stake in the Far East as Japan, and it therefore pursued a policy of blocking any attempt at Japanese economic hegemony in China. While consciously attempting to check the Japanese in order to assure fair competition for American interests, the United States did little in other areas to improve the state of affairs between the two countries. The Japanese considered the Immigration Act of 1924, with its exclusion clause, a gratuitous insult, and spectacular, though minor, incidents such as the 1925 naval maneuvers and the temporary discouragement to the South Manchurian Railway loans led the Japanese nation to believe that the United States was the national enemy.

The defense of American commitments in the Far East of necessity rested with the Navy Department. The United States Army was too small to do the job, and dependence upon strategic air power to support national policy was little more than a projection of Colonel "Billy" Mitchell's active imagination. In assuming the responsibility for upholding America's Far Eastern policy in the 1920's, the Navy did so with complete realization that the task would be extremely difficult. In September of 1921 the General Board of the Navy had drafted a position paper for the American delegates to the Washington Conference on the Limitation of Armament. In it the Board concluded that Japan's foreign policy consisted of three basic points: (1) Territorial expansion, by peaceful means if possible, by conquest if necessary; (2) Commercial domination of the Orient; (3) Eventual political control of the Far East.[41] If the Navy's estimate of Japan's intentions was correct, American Far Eastern policy stood athwart the path Japan would be taking in the years ahead. From its studies the General Board believed that only a preponderance of American sea power in the western Pacific would deter Japan's ambitions. Facing the future, the American admirals seized upon that famous aphorism attributed to Admiral Heihachiro Togo after the Battle of Tsushima Straits:

> In the hour of Victory
> Tighten your helmet strings.

---

[41]U. S., Navy Department, *Report of the General Board on Limitation of Armaments* (Washington, 1921), p. 8.

46

3

The United States Navy and the Japanese "Enemy"

I N THE YEARS between the Spanish-American War and the Washington Conference on the Limitation of Armament, 1921-22, those charged with the creation and implementation of United States naval policy gradually accepted the premise that Japan was America's national enemy.[1] This was a critical assumption, for it controlled the Navy's outlook on a number of questions concerned with national defense: Where should the United States Fleet normally be based? What, if any, new naval bases needed to be constructed? What types of naval vessels deserved first priority in construction planning? Which war plans needed to be developed or revised? What positions should the Navy take when naval limitation questions were discussed? Should the nation withdraw from any of its commitments abroad, particularly in the Far East? These were not easy questions; fortunately the Navy did not have to meet them all at once. Yet as each problem was studied, the President, or the Secretary of the Navy, or the Navy's General Board, or possibly a delegation to a naval conference had to approach it with another question even more basic: Will this solution strengthen or weaken American naval power in the Pacific? Or, put another way, could the Navy meet its hypothetical enemy in the Far East with reasonable assurance of victory at sea?

The United States Navy's responsibilities in the Far East began with the organization of the East India Squadron in the 1830's. In

---

[1]See the author's "The United States Navy and the Japanese 'Enemy': 1919-1931," *Military Affairs,* XXI (Summer, 1957), 61-74.

subsequent years, with certain major actions excepted, such as Perry's mission to Japan, the Navy displayed little more than sporadic interest in the island kingdom. The results of the Sino-Japanese War of 1894-95 ended this passiveness. The relative ease with which Japan defeated China was surprising; the dispatch with which Admirals Tsuboi and Ito decimated the Chinese navy in the battle at the Yalu was an eye-opener for naval strategists. Very obviously a new sea power had been born at the close of the nineteenth century.[2]

A steady growth in Japan's political ambitions paralleled the development of her naval might. The Sino-Japanese War saw China displaced as Korea's suzerain. Japanese designs on the Liaotung Peninsula and the Manchurian hinterland were frustrated only through active intervention by Germany, France, and Russia. But Japan's objectives were clear: She intended to share in the predicted partition of China; she would soon rid herself of the encumbering unequal treaties; and she would assume control over Korea despite Russia's interests there and in Manchuria to the north. In 1895 none of these ambitions directly affected the United States, though the threatening break-up of China was soon to absorb this country's attention.

In 1897 the Japanese Government did intrude itself into a matter of some moment to America. On June 19, 1897, Japan officially protested the newly signed treaty of annexation between the Republic of Hawaii and the United States. A few weeks of tension ensued, but Hawaiian and American assurances that Japanese immigration rights into the Hawaiian Islands would be respected led to a dissipation of the crisis. The Japanese withdrew their protest on December 22, 1897.[3]

During those summer months of excitement the Navy and its new assistant secretary, Theodore Roosevelt, actively studied the question of whether the United States could defend its interests in

[2]The best general history of the development of Japanese and American sea power can be found in E. B. Potter and Fleet Admiral Chester W. Nimitz, *Sea Power: A Naval History* (Englewood Cliffs, New Jersey: Prentice-Hall, Inc., 1960), 932 pp.

[3]Hilary Conroy, *The Japanese Frontier in Hawaii, 1868-1898* (Berkeley and Los Angeles: University of California Press, 1953), pp. 131-38; William R. Braisted, *The United States Navy in the Pacific, 1897-1909* (Austin: University of Texas Press, 1958), pp. 11-16.

Hawaii. The answer was yes, but it would be difficult. This brief tempest concerning Hawaii demonstrated to those who were inclined to study the question that the nation needed more battleships, drydocks, and better-equipped navy yards. Of necessity the United States was deeply concerned about events in the Hawaiian Islands in 1897, but it was also definitely committed to upholding the Monroe Doctrine in the Caribbean against any challenges. Germany, with a growing navy, was a problem there. Thus, while the American Navy had been alerted to the potential menace of Japan, it had more important interests to protect nearby.

The settlements of the Spanish-American War and the crushing of the Boxer Rebellion in China further enlarged the responsibilities of the United States Navy. The Philippine Islands and the newly proclaimed Open Door policy had to be defended in a period when relations with Germany had deteriorated noticeably. Fortunately for America, balance of power politics among the Great Powers provided the necessary protection for this country's interests. Japan, with Great Britain as an ally, was readying herself to check Russian ambitions in northeast Asia. Great Britain and France were steadily moving toward an entente that would hold Germany at bay. Behind this screen of diplomatic intrigue and concomitant developing hostilities among the Great Powers, the United States suppressed the Filipino insurrection and began a policy of positive control in the Caribbean based on the Roosevelt Corollary to the Monroe Doctrine. The Navy was given time to acquire more modern battleships and to begin the development of naval bases at Pearl Harbor and in the Philippine Islands.

On February 8, 1904, Japan opened war on Russia with a naval attack on the Russian fleet at Port Arthur. Though resisting bitterly on land, the Russians were no match for the Japanese at sea. The disastrous defeat of Admiral Rojdestvensky's Baltic Fleet at Tsushima Straits in May, 1905, led directly to the Treaty of Portsmouth and Russia's capitulation. The combination of "Nogi by land and Togo by sea" convincingly demonstrated that Japan had learned well from the writings of Clausewitz and Mahan.

The conclusion of the Russo-Japanese War ushered in a new period of uneasiness within the American Navy—a general suspicion of

49

the Japanese and their battle-tested navy. The war scare of 1907-9 and the world cruise of the battleship fleet were to some extent results of this clouded relationship.[4] Superimposed upon this foundation of distrust at the opening of the World War was a feeling of apprehension caused by Japan's seizure of the German islands in the north Pacific. Evidently Japan's control of those islets would endanger any conjectural American advance to the defense of the Philippines.[5] By the close of the World War the Navy recommended that the islands in question be internationalized, but not under Japanese control, and warned most emphatically against permitting any Power, unless it be the United States, to have possession of the other Mariana Islands:

> Their position within the immediate vicinity of Guam is capable of development into submarine bases within supporting distance of Japan, and, in the event of war, this would make their continued possession by that country a perpetual menace to Guam, and to any fleet operation undertaken for the relief of the Philippines.[6]

Nevertheless the Paris Peace Conference resulted in Japanese retention of the German islands under a mandate from the League of Nations.[7] Navy Department realists could do little more than accept the situation, but they did suggest that the United States try to offset

---

[4]*Ibid.*, chap. v; George T. Davis, *A Navy Second to None: The Development of American Naval Policy* (New York: Harcourt, Brace & Company, Inc., 1940), pp. 131-34. The war scare of 1907-9 is fully treated in Thomas A. Bailey, *Theodore Roosevelt and the Japanese-American Crises* (Stanford: Stanford University Press, 1934), chaps. xi and xii; Louis Morton, "Military and Naval Preparations for the Defense of the Philippines during the War Scare of 1907," *Military Affairs,* XII (Summer, 1949), 95-104.

[5]Earl S. Pomeroy, *Pacific Outpost: American Strategy in Guam and Micronesia* (Stanford: Stanford University Press, 1951), pp. 51-53.

[6]"Findings of the General Board, 1/24/1918," quoted in U. S., State Department (Confidential) *Papers Relating to Pacific and Far Eastern Affairs Prepared for the Use of the American Delegation to the Conference on the Limitation of Armament, Washington, 1921-1922* (Washington, 1922), p. 1074. Hereafter, D/S, *Papers Relating to Pacific and Far Eastern Affairs.* Also U. S., Navy Department, *Report of the General Board on Limitation of Armaments— Confidential* (Washington, 1921), letter of December 2, 1918.

[7]Russell H. Fifield, "Disposal of the Carolines, Marshalls, and Marianas at the Paris Peace Conference," *American Historical Review* (April, 1946), 472-79.

the Japanese gains. Admiral Albert Gleaves, Commander-in-Chief of the Asiatic Fleet, believed France, in payment of her war debt, could be persuaded to cede the United States certain islands south of the equator. With these a line might be established from Panama to the Philippines by way of Samoa. "The greatest weakness in this line is from Panama to Samoa. The only way to strengthen it will be by developing bases at the Galapagos Islands, Tahiti, the Marquesas and Tuamotu Islands."[8] Here might have been a suitable remedy for the Navy's problem, but nothing came of it. By the time the Washington Naval Conference convened in November, 1921, the Japanese were firmly ensconced in their Pacific mandate.

The months from the close of the World War to the opening of the Washington Conference on the Limitation of Armament on November 12, 1921, may definitely be called a "war scare" period. The presence of the Japanese in the Pacific islands straddling the route between the Hawaiians and the Philippines worried American naval planners; there was a resurgence of anti-Japanese land legislation in the Western states; and the furious race in naval construction between Japan and America boded evil.[9] The files of the State Department further testify to considerable study both in the department and in the field to determine whether conflict was imminent. By war's end, the Director of the War Trade Board Intelligence Office had reported, on the basis of mail intercepted in Seattle and San Francisco:

> As much correspondence, originating both in Japan and in the United States, from both Japanese and Americans, continually refers to the possibility of war between the two countries, it seems probable that the subject is being widely discussed in Japan. These letters come from all classes of society. . . . Practically all of these express the opinion that Japan will some day be forced to wage a defensive war

---

[8]"Admiral Albert Gleaves to the Secretary of the Navy, October 16, 1919," quoted in D/S, *Papers Relating to Pacific and Far Eastern Affairs,* pp. 1074-75.

[9]A. Whitney Griswold, *The Far Eastern Policy of the United States* (New York: Harcourt, Brace & Company, Inc., 1938), pp. 368-70; Rodman W. Paul, *The Abrogation of the Gentlemen's Agreement* (Cambridge, Mass.: Phi Beta Kappa Society, 1936), pp. 10-15; Harold and Margaret Sprout, *Toward a New Order of Sea Power: American Naval Policy and the World Scene* (Princeton: Princeton University Press, 1943), pp. 88-121.

against the United States, because of the racial animosity shown by the latter against Oriental peoples, intensified by the restrictions against necessary territorial and industrial expansion which it endeavors to impose upon Japan in an arrogant manner.[10]

A State Department concerned about Japanese public opinion also took an interest in Japanese activities throughout the world. Japanese purchases of arms, nitrates, or war materials were dutifully reported by American consuls from Berlin to Iquique, Chile. The Japanese, according to persistent rumor, were hiring German naval officers—submariners—and British naval aviators expert in aircraft carrier techniques.[11] What becomes quite evident is that the Secretary of the Navy, as well as the Secretary of State, was concerned with the drift in Japanese-American relations.

Statesmen in the United States, Great Britain, and Japan recognized that the international tensions should not be allowed to continue unabated. If the naval and arms race among the European Powers had produced a war in 1914, there was always the possibility that history might repeat itself. Besides, the taxation required to support the new navalism was hampering economic recovery in all three nations and could easily lead to a revolt from the left in Japan. Within the British

---

[10]War Trade Board to Secretary of State, December 11, 1918, U. S., Department of State, File 894.00/149, Archives. The files of the State Department, particularly the 711.94P81 File, fairly bulge with the clippings sent by worried people, appalled at sensationalism in the daily press. From San Francisco, ironically, the President of the Chamber of Commerce sent in several clippings depicting the anti-Japanese trend in the reporting of the local *Bulletin*. Commenting on the serious problem involved in so insulting the Japanese, he concluded, "This occurs to us to be a most serious and flagrant case. . . . We are, of course, powerless to stop such sensational propaganda, but surely there must be some federal method of dealing with such matters if it is clear that our national interest is imperiled thereby." A. McBean to the Secretary of State, San Francisco, April 29, 1921, D/S File 711.94/389, Archives. Particularly offensive to Mr. McBean were the red-ink headlines "Annihilate Americans!" (April 23, 1921), and "Crush U.S.!" (April 22, 1921). The headlines called attention to an English-language translation of Major General Kajiro Sato's book, *America and Japan Fight*.

[11]See D/S, File 894.24, particularly serials /5 to /28 for information on raw materials and arms purchases. Concerning German aid to Japan see D/S, File 894.22/2,4,5. For information on British aid in the field of naval aviation see particularly D/S, File 894.24/21, London, April 6, 1921, Archives.

Empire there was restiveness over a possible renewal of the Anglo-Japanese Alliance, a move that would be most embarrassing to Canada were war to occur between Japan and America. And in the United States, Senator William E. Borah was pressing for action to terminate the naval race to which the country was a party. On December 14, 1920, the senator from Idaho introduced a concurrent resolution requesting the President to call a conference that would end naval competition. The resolution failed, but Borah was just beginning. When the new, Sixty-seventh Congress convened in April, 1921, Borah again pressed his resolution. Though Harding briefly blocked the Borah resolution, it was evident that the nation stood behind the doughty Idahoan. Really having no choice, President Harding did make sure that the credit for calling the Washington Conference on the Limitation of Armament was attributed to his administration.[12]

On July 8, 1921, Secretary of State Charles Evans Hughes informed Great Britain that the United States was interested in arranging an international conference to study the question of arms limitation. The British were agreeable; in fact they had actually taken the initiative, but their own invitation had been delayed by the American ambassador in London.

In preparation for the naval conference, Assistant Secretary of the Navy Theodore Roosevelt, Jr., in a precept to the General Board dated July 27, 1921, ordered its members to begin a study of American naval policy. He wanted to know what would be the naval strength necessary to support the nation's current diplomatic policies. As a guide he listed five general principles upon which American diplomatic practice was based:

---

[12]Many studies have been made of the Washington Conference, the most important being: Sprout and Sprout, *Toward a New Order of Sea Power;* Merlo J. Pusey, *Charles Evans Hughes* (New York: The Macmillan Company, 1951), II, 445-522; Pomeroy, *Pacific Outpost,* pp. 75-115; Capt. Dudley W. Knox, *The Eclipse of American Sea Power* (New York: The Army and Navy Journal, 1922); Yamato Ichihashi, *The Washington Conference and After* (Stanford: Stanford University Press, 1928), pp. 3-152; Raymond L. Buell, *The Washington Conference* (New York: D. Appleton & Company, 1922); John Chalmers Vinson, *The Parchment Peace* (Athens, Georgia: The University of Georgia Press, 1955), and *William E. Borah and the Outlawry of War* (Athens, Georgia: The University of Georgia Press, 1957), pp. 31-47.

1. The United States will not consent to the limitation of its sovereign power.
2. The United States will continue to maintain the Monroe Doctrine.
3. The United States will not consent to any limitations of its Navy that might imperil any part of its territory or the citizens thereof.
4. The United States must have at all times a sufficient force to insure unimpeded lanes of communication for its commerce.
5. The United States must be in a position to maintain its policies and the rights of its citizens in any country where they may be jeopardized.[13]

The report of the General Board in response to the Secretary's order, published under the date of September 12, 1921, is an interesting exposition of all aspects of American foreign policy and naval power. The board examined the foreign policies of the five principal naval powers invited to the conference, particularly the policy of Japan. And in addition to its foreign policy, the naval board analyzed Japan's institutions (social and political) and the uses to which the Japanese put the imperial navy. The sources for General Board information were naval attaché reports, personal experiences of the board members, and extensive closed hearings.

In considering the goals of Japanese foreign policy the board concluded that Japan was aiming for eventual commercial and political domination of the Far East, to be accomplished by territorial expansion, supported by naval preponderance in the "Yellow Sea, China Sea, Japan Sea, and the waters of the western and southern Pacific with the islands lying therein." This hegemony in the Far East would be further promoted, the board predicted, by regional understandings, an attempt to continue the Anglo-Japanese Alliance, and active propaganda through control of home newspapers and subsidization of Japanese newspapers in foreign countries.[14]

The General Board took a studied look at Japan's institutional structure. In view of Japan's monarchical government, the board believed the "Japanese governing classes [were] militaristic with feudal traditions; consequently the Japanese Government [was] aggressive."

---

[13]The Secretary of the Navy to the General Board, July 27, 1921, U. S., Navy Department, *Report of the General Board on Limitation of Armaments* (Washington, 1921), pp. 4-5.

[14]*Ibid.*, pp. 8-9.

54

These characteristics were of extreme importance in governing relations between Japan and America because

> In controversies arising between Governments of dissimilar foundations, as between constitutional governments and monarchies, the differences are far more difficult of solution as they involve questions of national character as expressed in forms of government. . . . On the one side will be a government representing free individuals controlled by constitutional law; on the other a government dominated by a centralized class control, and looking at world problems with different eyes from ours. *The permanent adjustment of controversial problems with governmental planes so wide apart is difficult, can not be permanent, and will be maintained only by force.* . . .

Any trouble with Japan would necessarily take place in the Far East, and mere equality in sea power with Japan would render the United States incapable of action in Oriental waters. Thus "Great Britain's former ratio of 2 to 1 is the only safe ratio for the United States to maintain now as toward Japan until such time as she adopts a government similar to ours and is actuated by ideals in harmony with our own."[15]

In accord with its stated views, a skeptical General Board recommended several plans concerning relative naval strengths for Japan and America, each one insuring the United States 40 to 50 per cent superiority over the Japanese Navy. The "Basic Plan" of October 8, 1921, calling for the completion of all ships whose keels had been laid,[16] envisioned an estimated ratio of 10 to 6 for the United States and Japan, with approximately 1,000,000 tons of capital ships for the American Navy. The General Board modified this plan a week later, reducing American tonnage to 820,000 tons of mostly post-Jutland

---

[15]*Ibid.,* pp. 8, 14 (my italics).

[16]Fifteen capital ships were under construction in October, 1921. They included the battleships *Colorado* (BB45), *Indiana* (BB50), *Iowa* (BB53), *Massachusetts* (BB54), *Montana* (BB51), *North Carolina* (BB52), *South Dakota* (BB49), *Washington* (BB47), *West Virginia* (BB48), and the battle cruisers *Constellation* (CC2), *Constitution* (CC5), *Lexington* (CC1), *Ranger* (CC4), *Saratoga* (CC3), *United States* (CC6). After the Washington Conference, *Colorado* and *West Virginia* were completed, and *Lexington* and *Saratoga* were converted to aircraft carriers. The remaining eleven vessels were scrapped.

capital ships and cutting Japan to a 50 per cent ratio. Below this tonnage the General Board refused to go. When pushed by Secretary Hughes to compute the ratios on a "stop now" basis, the board returned the figures on October 26 with the warning that such a course of action was "fraught with probable dangerous results."

> 16. The proposition [Stop now plan] would probably be acceptable to Japan, as it reduces our Navy to a point where she would feel that the United States would be impotent to restrain her aggressive plans in the Far East. These fifteen capital ships (building) brought Japan to the Conference. Scrap them and she will return home free to pursue untrammeled her aggressive program.

> 17. The General Board believes that the peace of the Far East and the safety of China is absolutely dependent upon the ability of America to place a force of unquestioned preponderance in the Western Pacific. If these fifteen ships be stricken from the Navy list, our task may not be hopeless; but the temptation to Japan to take a chance becomes very great.[17]

Despite the General Board's unequivocal stand, the American delegation helped negotiate and then signed the Five-Power Treaty of February 6, 1922. From the naval viewpoint the most significant parts of this treaty were Articles IV, VII, and XIX. Articles IV and VII established a ratio of 5-5-3 among the United States, Great Britain, and Japan, respectively, in battleships and aircraft carriers. The treaty reduced capital ship strength (battleships and battle cruisers) for the United States to 525,000 tons, plus 135,000 tons of aircraft carriers. While there was a 5-to-3 ratio with Japan in the limited classes, the same was not true in the unlimited classes. Here the United

---

[17]Memorandum on Naval Matters Connected with the Washington Conference on the Limitation of Armament 1921-22, compiled by William Howard Gardiner, New York, October 25, 1924, Hilary P. Jones Papers, Box 1, LCMD. This remarkable paper was written from the confidential records of the General Board by Gardiner, who later became a president of the Navy League. It quotes at length from the many General Board reports concerning the Washington Conference and is all the more unusual because those same records were closely restricted for private researchers until very recent years. The paper was used by Admiral Jones and others to present the Navy's case for more cruisers in 1924-25, and as background for the various naval conferences through the years.

States was greatly superior to Japan in submarines and destroyers but decidedly inferior in modern postwar cruisers.[18]

But ships were not the whole story. Article XIX declared that naval bases in the western Pacific would be kept *in statu quo*. For the United States it meant no further base construction at Guam, the Philippines, the Aleutians, or any small islands held west of Hawaii. Of the three provisions enumerated, the Navy found Article XIX the most odious, basically because it felt it had been unnecessary, but more importantly because it weakened the Navy's ability to defend American interests in the Pacific.

Though the Five-Power Treaty was drawn with Navy Department advice and later defended by the men who participated in the conference,[19] perceptive attacks upon the treaty, particularly Article XIX, were made by retired officers, principally, and by such unofficial naval agencies as the Naval Institute, the Navy League, and the *Army and Navy Journal*. Soon after the conference ended, Captain Dudley W. Knox, a retired naval officer and naval adviser to the *Army and Navy Journal*, charged into print with his *Eclipse of American Sea Power*. In summarizing the losses to the United States from the Five-Power Treaty Captain Knox concluded:

---

[18] AUXILIARY VESSELS IN COMMISSION AFLOAT, JANUARY 1923

COUNTRY	MODERN CRUISERS	OLD CRUISERS	DESTROYERS	SUBMARINES
United States	0*/0	11*/11	295	126
Great Britain	2*/29	0*/11	193	65
Japan	2*/15	5*/5	98	57

*Heavy cruisers (8-inch guns) /Light Cruisers (less than 8-inch guns)
SOURCE: Oscar Parks and Francis E. McMurtrie (eds.), *Jane's Fighting Ships, 1923* (London, 1923), 401 pp.
The Five-Power Treaty of 1922 is in U. S., *Statutes at Large,* Vol. XXXXIII, 1655-85.

[19]Assistant Secretary of the Navy Theodore Roosevelt, Jr., wrote a defense of the treaties for the *Ladies Home Journal* of April, 1922; T. Roosevelt to Hughes, Washington, March 29, 1922, Charles E. Hughes Papers, Box 4B, LCMD. Admiral W. V. Pratt published several articles in the *United States Naval Institute Proceedings* defending the treaty, the principal one being "Some Considerations Affecting Naval Policy," in November, 1922. Pratt also defended the treaty in popular magazines such as *Current History* (April, 1923), and *North American Review* (May, 1922).

Of even greater importance than the loss to us in tonnage strength is the sacrifice we have made respecting Western Pacific Bases. . . . The difficulties of the long journey for our fleet to the Orient and of maintaining a large naval force there operating actively, under the conditions imposed by the treaty, will effectively reduce our initial strength at home to a decided inferiority in the Western Pacific. . . . Both Great Britain and Japan are assured of ample base facilities in the Orient while we are denied them, and in consequence we no longer possess the power to defend the Philippines or to support any other American Far Eastern Policy.[20]

The United States Naval Institute in its *Proceedings* followed Captain Knox's line and in many articles castigated the Five-Power Treaty and Article XIX—Japan had gained at America's expense. Typical was Captain (later Rear Admiral) Frank Schofield's acid

Had I been a [Japanese] naval strategist, I would have done all I could do to keep America from fortifying further her naval positions in the Philippines and Guam, and of operating her naval forces there. I would have tried to consolidate and strengthen Japan's hold in the Far East through making it difficult for America to interfere. I would have seen that America's weakness in the Far East was Japan's strength. . . .[21]

At the instigation of the Navy League's vice-president, the institute reprinted from the *Atlantic Monthly* Hector Bywater's disturbing essay, "Japan: A Sequel to the Washington Conference," which baldly accused the Japanese of rushing their Bonin Island fortifications to completion on the eve of the Washington Conference. The pessimistic comment on this piece in later issues was considerable, and repercussions were felt throughout the fleet, especially since Naval Institute policy of that day kept membership principally limited to active duty

---

[20]Knox, *The Eclipse of American Sea Power,* pp. 135-36.

[21]Captain Frank H. Schofield, "Incidents and Present Day Aspects of Naval Strategy," *United States Naval Institute Proceedings* (May, 1923), p. 782. Articles printed in the *Proceedings* go through a screening board consisting of six or so naval officers. The policy for publication is informal, but the general rule is that no article will appear that the Department of the Navy does not approve. From the formal viewpoint the institute is separate from the Navy, but the president of the institute is always a senior admiral on the active duty list, usually the Chief of Naval Operations.

and retired armed forces officers.[22]

At the Naval War College similar pessimism was expressed. The Class of 1923, graduating in September, 1922, submitted papers on "Policy—In Its Relation to War: with Special Reference to U. S. Policy in the Pacific." The unanimity of viewpoint on Article XIX expressed in these studies reflected fleet attitudes. "By this the possibility to exert the naval strength [of the United States] promptly and effectively in the Western Pacific was given up, in fact almost insurmountable difficulties were placed in the way of conducting a naval campaign in the Western Pacific." Japan, these senior officers wrote, had gained so much that the United States would have to keep the Philippines in perpetuity in order to checkmate Japan in the western Pacific.[23]

By the spring of 1923 the Navy had arrived at this position: Japanese naval policy as it applied to the Far East was basically aggressive; the United States was on the verge of exchanging ratifications limiting the ability of the American Navy to operate in the Far East to check aggression; the Administration had decided to continue holding the Philippines as an American possession; and the naval service at large, because it had identified Japan as the national enemy, was convinced of great evil inherent in the Five-Power Treaty. The only possible solution was to push a campaign of education designed to bring the Navy up to full treaty strength, maintained in perfect condi-

---

[22]Hector C. Bywater, "Japan: A Sequel to the Washington Conference," *United States Naval Institute Proceedings* (May, 1923), pp. 819-20.

[23]"Class of 1923 Thesis: Policy—In Its Relation to War: With Special Reference to U. S. Policy in the Pacific" (manuscript, Naval War College, September, 1922). In deference to the wishes of the War College Librarian, the authors of the theses cited are not directly identified in the body of the book. William Howard Gardiner published an article, "The Philippines and Sea Power," *North American Review* (August, 1922). He argued that with Article XIX limiting the Navy in the western Pacific, the United States would have to keep the Philippines to block Japanese expansionism to the south. Gardiner wrote to the chief of the Bureau of Insular Affairs in the War Department and offered to send as many reprints of the article to the bureau as it felt it would need. He noted, "in confidence," that he had been asked to send the Navy Department several hundred. William Howard Gardiner to Major General Frank McIntyre, New York, July 23, 1922, U. S., Interior Department, File 6144, Archives.

tion and supported by the people and Congress. The Navy Department undoubtedly hoped the American people would heed the warning of the defense-conscious Charleston *News and Courier*:

> The American people are not jingoes, but they know instinctively that someday there will be war between this country and Japan unless the Japanese understand that their prospects of success would be slender. An efficient Navy is therefore our best guaranty of peace with Japan and our only guaranty of peace.[24]

During the balance of the 1920's the Navy stood by its identification of Japan as the national enemy of the United States. A brief glance at the background papers prepared for the naval delegation to the Geneva Naval Conference of 1927 displays this rigidity of attitude. In a later chapter, where the London Naval Conference of 1930 is discussed, the same naval viewpoint is observable.

By the spring of 1927 pressure in the United States and from the world at large had resulted in the calling of another naval conference, to be convened in June at Geneva to consider limitation and possibly reduction in those classes of naval vessels not limited by the Washington Five-Power Treaty. Again the General Board studied American naval needs in the light of the foreign policies of the United States, Great Britain, and Japan. As we have seen, the relations between Japan and the United States had been strained by the Immigration Act of 1924 and the naval maneuvers of 1925, and these incidents undoubtedly influenced the conclusions of the General Board.

Examining the national policies of Japan and the United States, the board rather clearly showed no change in its opinion of Japanese aggressiveness. Japan's goal, the "political, commercial, and military domination of the Western Pacific," involved subordinate policies:

1. To render the military position of all other powers in the Western Pacific relatively weak.
2. To exploit China.
3. To extend Japanese political control over areas that are essential or desirable to supplement Japanese deficiencies in raw materials.
4. To maintain a navy strong enough successfully to combat in the Western Pacific the Navy of any other power.

---

[24]"Navy Plans Sunk by the Senate," *The Literary Digest,* June 21, 1924, pp. 15-16.

These subordinate Japanese policies ran counter to one of America's principal national policies—the Open Door.[25]

Turning to the subject of the naval policies of the three Powers, the General Board noted that at Geneva the Japanese were likely to ask for further limitations on Pacific Ocean naval bases and for a more favorable ratio than 5 to 3 for cruisers, destroyers, and submarines. Anticipating a demand for possibly a 5-5-3.5 ratio (70 per cent of the U.S. naval strength) in cruisers, the General Board commented, "The desire of Japan for security to her sea lines of communication is in conflict with the American desire for security of sea lines of communication to China and the Philippines, and the protection of the Philippines." The board believed the United States position in the Pacific was greatly weakened by the 1922 treaty with its 5-to-3 ratio; to "further weaken our position, . . . by changes in ratios unfavorable to us . . . would not conduce to peace but would have the opposite effect by giving greater security to Japan in the furthering of her policies and plans adversely affecting the United States."[26] On further limiting naval bases the General Board was most obdurate. Hawaiian fortifications could be restricted only if Japan were to reduce her fleet to a point of relative impotence against the Philippines. As matters stood, Japanese control of quondam German islands in the central Pacific and Japanese bases at Formosa and the Bonins made it simple for her

---

[25]U. S., Navy Department, General Board No. 438, Serial 1347-1 (a), dated April 21, 1927. This report is one of twelve compiled between March 11 and June 1, 1927. A file of these reports may be found in State Department File 500.A15A1/684 at the National Archives. Hereafter, "General Board 1927." In the April 21, 1927, report the General Board determined that the national policies of the United States were:

1. No alliances.
2. The Monroe Doctrine.
3. The Open Door.
4. Maintenance and strengthening of American merchant marine.
5. Exclusion of Asiatics.
6. Limitation of other immigrants by quotas.

[26]*Ibid.*

to menace the routes from Hawaii to the Far East. Further reduction of American base strength could not be considered.[27]

General Board views were colored by the thought that the United States would have to carry a Japanese war into Far Eastern waters, and therefore the Navy needed the strongest possible shore establishment in the Pacific.[28] American bases west of Hawaii were limited to their pre-1922 condition; hence the board paid some attention to the British base at Singapore, which was under construction and was completely unlimited by the naval treaties. Any move to limit the completion of the Singapore base was a matter for the British and Japanese alone, but the United States should consider certain facts:

> In its consideration of British-American relations, in connection with the general situation in the Far East, the General Board has given serious weight to the fact that *the two nations are in accord on most of the great problems of that area. Their interests there march together.* The methods used by Great Britain to obtain her objectives are irritating to us at times, and even from time to time cause friction between the two governments. The General Board believes, however, that the probability of any great differences arising between the two countries in the near future, that cannot be settled through diplomatic channels, is very remote, provided an equality in naval strength between the two countries is maintained. It considers, therefore, that British bases in the above region should not be brought into discussion by us. *The very existence of certain British bases in this region may well serve our interests there at some future time.*[29]

This statement found support at the Naval War College in the Class of 1927 project, in which student officers undertook a logistics study of an Orange-Blue (Japanese-American) war. "It is probable that England would be driven into active opposition against Japan

---

[27]"General Board 1927," study 11(j), dated May 7, 1927; study 3(h), dated April 22, 1927.

[28]"General Board 1927," study 10(d), undated. The General Board wrote: "In case of war with Japan, our strategical situation is very bad. In order to bring the war to a successful conclusion it would be necessary to carry the war to the Western Pacific and to bring such pressure on Japan as to make it intolerable to her nationals. Before extensive operations in that area could be undertaken by us it would be necessary to establish our fleet in that area."

[29]"General Board 1927," study 3(h), dated April 22, 1927 (my italics).

through Australia. This would surely happen if Japan should show a policy of expansion. Australia is very friendly to the United States and she could be counted on to assist in every way even to the extent of entering the war as an ally."[30] This view of British-American relations, despite frequent Congressional twisting of the lion's tail in the period, was not unique to 1927 but can be found in the papers and writing of many naval officers throughout the 1920's. As one English writer described it, the United States and Great Britain had a community of interests in the western Pacific particularly since Japan was the hypothetical enemy of both in that area.[31]

The 1927 study of American naval policies by the General Board is significant for several reasons. The many individual reports that made up the General Board guide for the naval delegates spelled out rather carefully that Japan was still the primary worry of the American Navy. The basic clash of interests still existed, with Japan attempting political and economic control in eastern Asia and the United States advocating the Open Door. Noteworthy are the General Board's exposition of the parallel existing between American and British policies in the Far East and the subtle suggestion that these policies were complementary where Japanese matters were concerned.

In its efforts to awaken Congress and America to the Navy's needs and to alert them to the menace of Japan, the department used several propaganda devices as the situation demanded. Hampered most of the time by the lack of a favorable press, the Navy did receive consistent support from the Hearst chain and several strong metropolitan papers such as the *New York Herald-Tribune* and the *San Francisco Chronicle*. Of all the newspapers sympathetic with the naval viewpoint, the *Herald-Tribune* was the most important. In the early 1920's it featured a column on service affairs written by "Quarterdeck," Rear Admiral (Retired) William F. Fullam, one of the most

---

[30]Class of 1927, "Class of 1927 Report of Committee on: A Logistic Study of the Pacific Area as a Theatre of Operations in an Orange-Blue War" (mimeographed, Naval War College, April, 1927).

[31]Sir Herbert Russell, "The Pacific Zone: British View of American Naval Policy," *United States Naval Institute Proceedings* (August, 1925), pp. 1480-88.

tempestuous of the Navy's controversialists.[32] The Navy, however, had worse problems than an unsympathetic press—a hostile Congress and an indifferent public. To Admiral Hilary Pollard Jones, Commander-in-Chief of the United States Fleet, Congressional animosity toward the Navy was "utterly incomprehensible," and he wondered "why individuals or Congress should assume the attitude of personal hostility to any man because he wears a uniform. . . ."[33] The Pulitzer Prize-winning biographer of Secretary of State Charles Evans Hughes summed up the preconference attitude of the nation, ". . . the revolt against navalism was running stronger here than in any of the other major powers. Many newspapers took up the cause, and the big-navy men encountered a veritable cyclone of opposition in Congress."[34]

Naval tactics through the years have a military consistency. The naval secretaries, their assistants, and the naval bureau chiefs appeared year after year before the House and the Senate subcommittees of the Appropriations committees or before the Naval Affairs committees to state their requests, and in the 1920's they consistently met the same legislators in the committee rooms. On the whole the Navy, perhaps unwittingly, fared better than the Army, but the relatively better naval position hardly reduced the apprehensiveness of the naval leaders.[35] The Secretary of the Navy generally set the pace at the hearings by reading statements on the condition of the Navy and then answering questions. The secretary's statements, and those of the men who followed, were often loaded with comparative data to show how the Navy was falling behind Japan's or Great Britain's navy. Almost

---

[32]The papers of Admiral W. F. Fullam at the Library of Congress Manuscripts Division contain several boxes of clippings and scrapbooks of his published writing.

[33]Admiral Jones to Rear Admiral M. L. Bristol, New York, March 9, 1922, Hilary P. Jones Papers, Box 1, LCMD.

[34]Pusey, *Charles Evans Hughes,* II, 454.

[35]Robert Greenhalgh Albion, "The Naval Affairs Committees, 1816-1947," *United States Naval Institute Proceedings* (November, 1952), pp. 1227-37. An interesting and valuable study devoted in part to Congressional legislation on military and naval affairs can be found in George A. Grassmuck, *Sectional Biases in Congress on Foreign Policy.* The Johns Hopkins University Studies in Historical and Political Science, Series LXVIII, No. 3 (Baltimore: The Johns Hopkins Press, 1951), 181 pp., especially pp. 32-52.

always the statistics of the country furthest ahead of the United States were used—for aircraft carriers Great Britain, for cruisers Japan or Great Britain, for submarines Japan, for naval bases the Japanese in Formosa and the southwest Pacific mandate. Occasionally a chairman would protest the use of the comparative method because of the effect it would have on relations with other countries. Representative Thomas S. Butler once interrupted a speaker with the terse comment, "You appreciate that what we say in this public hearing will be known rather widely outside and if we ourselves should read about the Japanese or the English comparing their fleets with ours and talking about getting ready for battle in a couple of years, we would become nervous, therefore, I think we ought to lay this talk aside. . . ."[36]

The Office of Naval Intelligence through these years was the principal source of statistical data for the department. An insight into the Navy's methods can be obtained by noting a letter from the Director of Naval Intelligence to the naval attaché in Tokyo. "We are preparing now for the shock of the next Congress, and you cannot send in too much information about the Japanese Navy."[37] The hearings of the winter of 1924 show Naval Intelligence at its best in presenting the danger of Japan and Great Britain to the United States. The hearings opened with a barrage of data presented orally and in printed tables for the convenience of the congressmen. Several construction bills were at stake, and the Navy was very much interested in gaining authorization to modernize and modify battleships and their guns. The British Navy was shown to be overwhelmingly powerful in cruisers, and thus the United States did not actually have parity. Japanese foreign policy was described as having as its purpose the domination of the East; therefore, the United States needed a larger and more modern navy to protect its interests.[38] These hearings had a

---

[36]U. S., Congress, House, Committee on Naval Affairs, *Hearings on Sundry Legislation Affecting the Naval Establishment, 1922-23,* 67th Cong., 2d, 3d, 4th Sess., February 16, 1922, p. 300.

[37]Captain Luke McNamee to Captain Cotten, Washington, May 21, 1923, Lyman A. Cotten Papers, Box 10, Folder 153, Southern Historical Collection, University of North Carolina.

[38]U. S., Congress, House, Naval Subcommittee of the Committee on Appropriations, *Hearings on Navy Department Appropriation Bill for 1926,* 68th Cong., 2d Sess., November 17-19, 1924, H. R. 10724, pp. 1-127.

little more than average interest because of the strident protests the Japanese press had been making since the passage of the Immigration Act of 1924 with its exclusion clause.

Throughout these years men speaking independently, as well as the officers of the Navy Department and the General Board, spoke out against the Washington settlements, attempts to extend the treaties, and what they considered dangerous pacifistic trends. They too were opportunistic, seizing upon the issue that suited their needs and using for comparative purposes the country that illustrated their problem best. Some were naval officers like Bradley A. Fiske, William L. Rodgers, Dudley W. Knox, or Charles P. Plunkett, and generally those naval officers who spoke out were on the retired list. However, officers were not alone in their criticisms and were joined, aided, and at times outshouted by writers like Hector C. Bywater, William Howard Gardiner, or William B. Shearer, who provided reams of arguments for big-Navy proponents regardless of their reasons for desiring a larger fleet.

Of the professional writers Hector C. Bywater appears to have been the most influential and most widely read. He published broadly in every vehicle of communication from the *Atlantic Monthly* to the Naval Institute *Proceedings,* besides being a correspondent for the Baltimore *Sun.* As a prelude to the Washington Conference his *Sea Power in the Pacific* created widespread interest and drew attention to the strategical problems of the Pacific as they might relate to an American-Japanese war. On the heels of the 1924 Japanese exclusion act he published *The Great Pacific War,* a study of the problems involved in a war between the two nations. His newspaper articles showed his intense interest in Japanese naval developments, and their reprinting in the "Professional Notes" section of the Naval Institute *Proceedings* made them available to the American Navy at large. Bywater had little faith in the ability of the Japanese to control their political system and often predicted that Japan's leaders would precipitate a war as a means of preserving national unity.[39]

---

[39]Hector C. Bywater, *Sea-Power in the Pacific: A Study of the American-Japanese Naval Problem* (2d ed.; Boston and New York: Houghton Mifflin Company, 1934), pp. 316-18; *The Great Pacific War: A History of the American-Japanese Campaign of 1931-33* (London: Constable & Company, Ltd., 1925), pp. 1-14.

William Howard Gardiner, like Bywater, was a professional writer and publicist. Throughout the 1920's he was closely connected with the Navy League of the United States as either vice-president or president, and through his enthusiasm for naval matters had access into the inner circles of Navy officialdom. He traveled widely and lectured constantly on the same theme: America was not a self-contained continent, had to paddle in the stream of international politics, and therefore needed a powerful navy as its representative. He was often invited to speak before the General Board, the Naval War College, and the Foreign Service School of the State Department. Because of his close connections with the Navy, Gardiner was frequently called upon to supply interpretations or accumulate technical data to be presented to Congress by the Navy. Probably his greatest tour de force was a 1924 study made from the General Board records of 1921, showing that the Navy, after the Washington Conference, was not adequate to meet Japan in combat. This study was used as background to brief officers appearing before Congressional committees in the winter of 1924-25. Gardiner's propaganda line seldom changed in reference to Japan—a showdown by force was in the offing, he insisted.[40]

Although Bywater and Gardiner were fairly subtle in their publicizing of American naval problems, others were not. In a series of public speeches in 1924 Rear Admiral Bradley A. Fiske spoke of potential Japanese aggression in the Far East; Rear Admiral William L. Rodgers told the Institute of Politics at Williamstown, Massachusetts, that Japan was bent on war with America; and Secretary of the Navy Curtis D. Wilbur warned in San Francisco that Japanese wrath was no menace for "There is nothing so cooling to a hot temper as a piece of cool steel."[41] In 1928 Rear Admiral Charles P. Plunkett joined President Coolidge's "Papa Spank Club" by publicly predicting inevitable war with England or some nation due to international trade

---

[40]William Howard Gardiner to Rear Admiral Gleaves, New York, November 23, 1923, Albert Gleaves Papers, Box 16, LCMD. Two lectures to the Foreign Service School can be found in mimeographed form in D/S LNC Gardiner/3, 4, Box 23, Archives; Memorandum on Naval Matters, compiled by Gardiner, Hilary P. Jones Papers, Box 1, LCMD.

[41]Miriam Beard, "Our War-Advertising Campaign," *The Nation,* March 25, 1925, pp. 322-23.

conflicts. Secretary Wilbur's assistant secretary, T. Douglas Robinson, had to endure a Coolidge lecture for criticizing naval economies in the face of world unsteadiness.[42] Yet Congress maintained its equanimity, refused to be stampeded into heavy naval appropriations, and on the whole probably agreed with Senator Thomas J. Walsh, Democrat of Montana, in his views to a constituent:

> I am not only against a navy greater than is essential for the defense of the United States against the attack of a foreign foe, but I am not disturbed by the idea that we are going to be attacked next week or next year. . . .
>
> Twenty years ago, I was a delegate to the National Convention at Denver and listened as a member of the Committee on Resolutions to a two hours' harangue by Capt. Richmond Pearson Hobson, urging an appropriation for a big navy to meet impending war with Japan.
>
> That war is as remote today as it was then; indeed, since a visit to that country some five years ago, I am convinced that a war with Japan is about as likely as a war with Mars.[43]

To a certain extent the decade represents a study in frustration for the Navy. The General Board, with years of experience represented by its membership, as early as 1921 decided upon Japan as the future naval enemy and calculated that it needed a fleet twice the size of Japan's if called upon to defend American interests in the Far East—the Philippines and the Open Door in China. Yet in the end only Guam, with the most primitive defenses, and the Philippines, incapable of handling the attenuated battleship fleet, remained west of Hawaii. And so, in necessarily sounding the call to general quarters, the board was aided by propagandists within and outside the naval service. Japan was seldom emphasized as the hypothetical enemy (especially to the public), except by the careless or the reckless, because diplomatic relations between Japan and America had been anything but placid. Indeed, Great Britain was portrayed as the bête noire, and

---

[42]"Admiral Plunkett's War With England," *The Literary Digest,* February 11, 1928, pp. 7-9; Everett Sanders to T. Douglas Robinson, Washington, November 20, 1926, Calvin Coolidge Papers, Group 18, Box 58, LCMD; Robinson to Sanders, Washington, November 22, 1926, *ibid.* Sanders was Coolidge's secretary.

[43]Walsh to Reverend W. P. Jinnett, Washington, February 23, 1928, Thomas J. Walsh Papers, Box 295, LCMD.

hyphenate-vote-conscious congressmen seldom missed an opportunity to accuse the British of perfidy in their adherence to the Washington treaties. But the careful paralleling of British and American naval interests cannot go unnoticed even in the face of occasional Anglophobic blasts by highly placed officers. The 1927 analysis by Hector Bywater demands consideration, for he drew attention to what was probably unconsciously felt throughout the American Navy.

America's chief concern is to possess a fleet which shall be capable of neutralizing Japanese naval power and so ensuring the integrity of her Pacific possessions. There are, no doubt, people in the United States who sincerely believe in the possibility of war with Great Britain, and are therefore anxious that their navy should be in all respects equal, if not superior, to our own [Britain's]. . . . This belief is shared even by certain American naval officers, but it is certainly not reflected in the policy of the Washington administration. On the whole, it seems more probable that the American demand for naval equality is prompted mainly by a desire to uphold the *status quo* in the Pacific; in other words, *although the British navy is officially represented as the standard of power which must be achieved, America's true object is to maintain a two-fifths superiority over Japan, because Japan is regarded as the most probable antagonist of the future*. . . .[44]

[44]Hector C. Bywater, *Navies and Nations: A Review of Naval Developments Since the Great War* (London: Constable & Company, Ltd., 1927), p. 267 (my italics).

4

The Navy Tightens Its Helmet String:

Fleet Reorganizations and War Planning

ON DECEMBER 6, 1922, the Secretary of the Navy's General
Order No. 94 reorganized the United States Navy. The United
States Fleet was created, made up of two principal fleet subdivisions,
the Scouting Fleet based on the Atlantic Coast and the Battle Fleet
based on the Pacific, supported by two minor forces. Of the eighteen
battleships allowed by the Washington Conference, twelve were to form
the heart of the Battle Fleet, with the remaining ships, the oldest and
slowest at that, being assigned to the Scouting Fleet.[1] If there was any
question in the minds of Americans or Japanese about which ocean
was the more important, this Pacific orientation given to the Navy
removed all doubts. And if some pacifists felt squeamish about a
"battle" fleet being in the Pacific, the Navy did not feel similarly
uneasy, for it is more than probable that the name and location of the
fleet was deliberate. This new focus of American naval power was
certainly consistent with the views of the General Board.

Prior to 1919 the Navy had resisted attempts to split the fleet,
largely owing to the urgings of Admiral Mahan and the executive
actions of Theodore Roosevelt. The Russo-Japanese War had convinced Mahan that it was folly to divide a navy to the point where any
division could be overwhelmed by enemy naval forces. Accordingly
President Roosevelt, during the 1908-9 war scare, withdrew the

---

[1]U. S., Congress, House, Naval Subcommittee of the Committee on Appropriations, *Hearings on Navy Department Appropriation Bill for 1925*, 68th
Cong., 1st Sess., 1924, H. R. 6820, p. 82.

principal units from the Asiatic station and left only a cruiser squadron to face the Japanese fleet. On the eve of his retirement Roosevelt advised his successor, "Under no circumstances divide the battleship fleet between the Atlantic and Pacific Oceans prior to the finishing of the Panama Canal. . . ." And on the same day Roosevelt assured Mahan, whose views were never modified, that the fleet would never be divided.[2]

But the completion of the Panama Canal in August, 1914, resulted ultimately in a changed view within American naval circles. Throughout the World War the Navy had remained in the Caribbean and Atlantic. But at war's end, with the danger from Germany removed and with the Japanese tension steadily developing, plans were made for the creation of a Pacific Fleet. In the eyes of many, the size of the American Navy made it possible to transfer half of the fleet to the Pacific, though others believed, equally strongly, that such a move was an invitation to disaster.[3] It should be noted parenthetically that in January, 1917, the General Board had declared that the Navy should be twice the size of Japan's to operate successfully in the Far East, but this estimate would apply equally to any Japanese attempt to operate against the Pacific Fleet in American waters.[4] The business was settled when the Pacific Fleet, under the command of Admiral

---

[2]Roosevelt to William H. Taft, Washington, March 3, 1909; Roosevelt to A. T. Mahan, Washington, March 3, 1909; Elting E. Morison (ed.), *The Letters of Theodore Roosevelt* (Cambridge, Mass.: Harvard University Press, 1951-1954), VI, 1543. In 1906 Mahan had written: "But among the most important lessons of this war [Russo-Japanese]—perhaps the most important, as also one easily understood and which exemplifies a principle of warfare of ageless application—is the inexpediency, the terrible danger, of dividing the battle fleet, even in times of peace, into fractions individually smaller than those of a possible enemy." A. T. Mahan, "Retrospect upon the War between Russia and Japan, 1906," in *Naval Administration and Warfare* (Boston: Little, Brown & Company, 1908), p. 167.

[3]Hector C. Bywater, *Sea-Power in the Pacific: A Study of the American-Japanese Problem* (2d ed.; Boston and New York: Houghton Mifflin Company, 1934), pp. 244-45; Willis E. Snowbarger, "The Development of Pearl Harbor" (unpublished Ph.D. dissertation, University of California, 1950), pp. 165-67.

[4]U. S., Navy Department, General Board No. 425-3, Serial 614, dated January 15, 1917, Office of the Chief of Naval History. Hereafter, papers in the Office of the Chief of Naval History will be cited as OCNH.

Hugh L. Rodman, transited the Panama Canal in July and August, 1919, and proceeded northward to a series of reviews and demonstrations climaxed in a fleet review by President Wilson and Secretary of the Navy Josephus Daniels at Seattle on September 13, 1919.

The creation of two major fleets did not result in total independence for either of them. Theoretically, both the Pacific and Atlantic fleets were to have similar organization from the staff of the fleet commanders down to the organization of departments within the smallest units of each fleet. This arrangement would permit easy transfer of individuals or ships and would allow integration of the two fleets when combined maneuvers were held. The principle of competition would also be employed to stimulate top performance within the individual fleets. The command of all units in a combined fleet would go to the commander-in-chief of the Atlantic Fleet. However, the limited repair facilities on the Pacific Coast, especially for battleships, necessitated constant movement of ships back to the East Coast for annual major overhauls. Regardless of the international situation, the Pacific Coast was not physically equipped to maintain the fleet.[5]

Despite the problems involved in operating the Pacific Fleet on a station ill-equipped to service its vessels, the Navy Department proposed in the spring of 1921 an even heavier concentration of naval power in the Pacific. The presence of the Pacific Fleet and the existence of numerous unsolved diplomatic problems stimulated Japanese shipbuilding, and this in turn affected American naval planning. The consequent naval race between America and Japan showed possibilities of erupting into war. Secretary of the Navy Edwin Denby therefore asked Secretary of State Hughes for his opinion concerning a reorganization of the Navy and the stationing of a battle fleet in the Pacific which would comprise most of the Navy's battleships; the Pacific Fleet of 1919 had included only fourteen of the twenty-nine battleships then in commission.

---

[5]*Army and Naval Journal,* July 19, 1919, pp. 1599-1600; Harold and Margaret Sprout, *Toward a New Order of Sea Power: American Naval Policy and the World Scene* (Princeton: Princeton University Press, 1943), pp. 100-1; George T. Davis, *A Navy Second to None: The Development of American Naval Policy* (New York: Harcourt, Brace & Company, Inc., 1940), pp. 250-51.

The present arrangement violated all modern doctrine, wrote Denby; persons with only the most rudimentary military background should realize the need for one fleet commander over the two subordinate units (the Pacific and Atlantic fleets). He continued: "In fact so contrary to accepted practice does the present allocation of the vessels of our navy seem to be, that not we alone, but all the world must wonder at the policy which separates our major fighting ships in such a manner that in case of war with any first-rate power one-half of our ships may at the first blow fall a victim to superior enemy attack." Some foreign observers probably suspected that "we dare not make up our minds which ocean to leave unguarded or that we fear to arouse the suspicion which might result from properly organizing our fleet with the majority of our battleships concentrated in one ocean." Denby realized that the Pacific Coast was not well equipped to service a battle fleet; but, he concluded:

> It is time our keels become acquainted with the western ocean and our navy yards and bases on the west coast receive their crucial test. . . . We anticipate no enemy in either sea. None the less we must maintain the navy fit to fight and see well to it that from both coasts the navy can operate successfully and be adequately maintained.[6]

Within the State Department, and particularly in the Division of Far Eastern Affairs, there was considerable enthusiasm for Denby's project. Some felt, as did Under Secretary Henry F. Fletcher, that it might temporarily irritate the Japanese and the British, but in the long run the Powers would see the United States was merely "proceeding upon sound tactical and strategic lines, which needed no excuse or explanation." John Van Antwerp MacMurray, Chief of the Division of Far Eastern Affairs, was even more sanguine. The creation of such a "Grand Fleet," he predicted, would show Japan that the United States had power available to curb any aggressive intentions. Furthermore, Great Britain would see that the United States was not menacing her in the Atlantic, and through such a display of firmness in the Pacific the British would be disabused of any predilection to aid Japan against America. Finally, it would strengthen American relations with China by proving the United States' determination not

---

[6]Secretary of the Navy to the Secretary of State, Washington, April 15, 1921, U. S., Department of State, File 811.30/133, Archives.

74

to give Japan a free rein in the Far East, despite the Lansing-Ishii agreement.[7]

After nearly a month Hughes wrote Denby that he was "not disposed to interpose any objection upon diplomatic grounds to a step apparently so much needed to promote our security." He did include, however, a letter from President Harding suggesting that implementation of the plans be held in abeyance until a more propitious time, apparently after an arms limitation conference; fleet reorganization could endanger the possibilities of Japan's participation in such a conference.[8]

In the summer of 1921 the Navy Department quietly—and without publicity—reorganized the fleet. Vice Admiral Hilary P. Jones, who had been Commander-in-Chief of the Atlantic Fleet, was raised to the rank of admiral, and the Scouting Force of the Atlantic Fleet was given to Vice Admiral John D. McDonald. On the West Coast the Pacific Fleet became the Battle Fleet under the command of Admiral E. W. Eberle. Once the reorganization was publicly announced the following year, Admiral Jones merely changed his title to "Commander-in-Chief United States Fleet," and McDonald became Commander-in-Chief Scouting Fleet. During this period of change and "fleeting-up," Admiral Jones remained virtually hidden in the New York Navy Yard because he found it difficult to explain his four-star flag.[9]

With the Battle Fleet based on the West Coast, the Navy in the years after 1922 turned its attention increasingly toward acquiring adequate fleet base facilities. Between 1917 and 1923 four separate

---

[7]Memoranda by Henry P. Fletcher and J. V. A. MacMurray, April 21, 1921, D/S, Files 811.30/130, 131, Archives.

[8]The President to the Secretary of State, Washington, April 27, 1921, D/S, File 811.30/132; the Secretary of State to the Secretary of the Navy, Washington, May 31, 1921, File 811.30/129, Archives.

[9]"Fleeting-up" was a Navy term current for the 1920's meaning a temporary rise in rank for the period that an admiral commanded a fleet or major subdivision thereof. When a tour of duty in a fleet command ended, the admiral "hauled down his flag" and reverted to his two-star rank of rear admiral. Admiral Jones to Admiral E. W. Eberle, New York, August 4, 1921, Hilary P. Jones Papers, Box 1, LCMD.

studies made of West Coast facilities agreed on the need for fleet bases, at least one of which should be in San Francisco Bay.[10]

The most important study, directed by Rear Admiral Hugh Rodman in the fall of 1922, concluded, "The Nation should not be allowed to rest secure in the belief that an adequate naval defense is had in vessels only, even though it consist of a well-rounded navy, but it should know that without adequate bases the fleet cannot live." The West Coast and Pacific area were woefully weak in base strength; primary consideration should be given to developing a base at Oahu capable of handling the whole Navy. Once a Hawaiian base was developed, then the pressing need was for a fleet-sized naval base in San Francisco Bay and an enlarged base in Puget Sound. The Rodman board also recommended some East Coast developments, but the heart of its fairly objective report concerned the Pacific.[11] West Coast proponents of a San Francisco naval base were not so objective. Representative James A. MacLafferty of California raised the Japanese bogey at a Naval Affairs Committee hearing, declaring, "Most people believe the day is coming when the great trouble of this world will be in the Pacific Ocean. Some of us believe that plans are underway and have been for many years to force, at an opportune time, the issue upon us."[12] Lobbyists presented similar arguments, but Congress was interested in trimming expenditures, not creating more, and pre-

---

[10]U. S., Congress, House, Committee on Naval Affairs, *Hearings on Sundry Legislation, 1922-23,* 67th Cong., 2d, 3d, 4th Sess., January 30, 1923, pp. 1965-66; Earl S. Pomeroy, *Pacific Outpost: American Strategy in Guam and Micronesia* (Stanford: Stanford University Press, 1951), p. 60.

[11]"Report of the Special Board on Shore Establishments, January 12, 1923," in House, Committee on Naval Affairs, *Hearings on Sundry Legislation, 1922-23,* pp. 1577-96. In June, 1922, the Army planned to abandon or reduce its defenses of many naval bases, and the Navy listed its most important bases requiring Army defense in this order: Panama, Hawaii, Manila, and Narragansett Bay. On July 7, 1923, the Joint Board accepted the Navy's priority list for areas most important to it: 1. Hawaiian Islands, 2. Guam (maintenance only), 3. Manila Bay, 4. San Francisco Bay, 5. Puget Sound, 6. New York-Narragansett Bay region. Both lists may be found in: Joint Board to Secretary of War, Washington, October 11, 1923, J. B. 304 (Serial 218), RG 94, Adjutant General File 660.2 (10-11-23), Archives.

[12]U. S., Congress, House, Committee on Naval Affairs, *Hearings on Sundry Legislation, 1922-23,* January 26, 1923, p. 1945.

ferred to view anti-Japanese alarmists as self-seekers.

Naval operations and maneuvers after 1922 helped to emphasize the need for enlarged base facilities in the Pacific. The chiefs of naval operations repeatedly told the Congress that the fleet needed to exercise yearly as one unit, but the cost of oil and to some extent the wear on the ships caused congressmen to demur. The Navy was frank in admitting its wish to test the defenses and facilities of Hawaii;[13] possibly this frankness caused congressmen to realize the cost of remedying any weaknesses. This was not an uncommon attitude toward naval affairs during the 1920's. But by the fall of 1926 the Navy was grateful for enough oil to maneuver the Battle Fleet and Scouting Fleet annually and for tacit approval by Congress for biennial United States (combined) Fleet maneuvers. Occasionally the question was broached concerning the propriety of continuing the division of the Navy between the two oceans, but the viewpoint of the Navy was consistent, as indicated in Admiral Charles F. Hughes's reply to an Alabama representative: "It would be desirable, from my personal point of view, that it all operate together; but even as nearly self-sustaining as the fleet may be, it must have shore bases. We have not the facilities on the Pacific to base them all. . . ."[14]

By 1929 the Navy was authorized to construct two dirigibles to explore the possible use of lighter-than-air craft in fleet operations. Because of their gigantic size there was only one naval hangar available to them. The Congress therefore in March, 1929, authorized the Navy to search for another airship base site to supplement the Lakehurst, New Jersey, Naval Air Station. In April the General Board reported that any future airship base should be on the Pacific Coast and preferably in the Los Angeles-San Diego area. A special board appointed with Rear Admiral William A. Moffett, Chief of the Bureau

---

[13]U. S., Congress, House, Naval Subcommittee of Committee on Appropriations, *Hearings on Navy Department Appropriation Bill for 1925*, 68th Cong., 1st Sess., December 20, 1923, pp. 79-80, 92-93. For an insight into the problems involved in fuel costs see U. S., Congress, House, Naval Subcommittee of Committee on Appropriations, *Hearings on Navy Department Appropriation Bill for 1928*, 69th Cong., 1st Sess., December 4, 1926, H. R. 15641, pp. 336-49.

[14]U. S., Congress, House, Naval Subcommittee of Committee on Appropriations, *Hearings on Navy Department Appropriation Bill for 1929*, 70th Cong., 1st Sess., February 16, 1928, H. R. 12286, p. 144.

of Aeronautics, as chairman, reported almost unanimously in October, 1929, in favor of a site at the south end of San Francisco Bay near Sunnyvale, California.[15]

Location of the base site precipitated a bitter quarrel within the Navy, but it is most significant that the West Coast was selected. Congressional hearings developed, in the most guarded language, the desirability of a Pacific Coast site, because any future international problems were likely to arise in the West. The War Plans Division of the Navy, going even further than the General Board, suggested basing the two airships on the Hawaiian Islands where "Their usefulness will be principally in scouting areas of the sea where enemy fleets, or considerable detachments of enemy fleets, might be expected to appear. . . ."[16] Ultimately the Sunnyvale site was chosen, and Naval Air Station Moffett Field stands today as a monument to Admiral Moffett's interest in airships and to the Navy's consciousness of the strategic importance of the Pacific Ocean.

With the exception of the base at Pearl Harbor, very little had been done by 1931 to enlarge the shore facilities of the Battle Fleet. The fleet itself had been strengthened through progressive modernization of its principal units and by the addition of new construction such as the aircraft carrier *Saratoga* and the *Omaha* cruisers, but its existence was almost hand-to-mouth. Possibly the greatest enemy to base improvement was pork-barrel politics, increasingly evident once the nation was stricken with the depression in the fall of 1929. Though the Puget Sound Navy Yard direly needed to lengthen its drydock to accommodate the carriers *Lexington* and *Saratoga,* the money was redirected from the floor of the House to lengthen the drydock in

---

[15]General Board No. 449, Serial 1418, April 25, 1929, in U. S., Congress, House, Committee on Naval Affairs, *Hearings on Sundry Legislation, 1929-30,* 71st Cong., 2d Sess., 1930, pp. 2552-53; Report of Airship Base Site Board, October 31, 1929, *ibid.,* pp. 2533-43. See also Archibald D. Turnbull and Clifford L. Lord, *History of United States Naval Aviation* (New Haven: Yale University Press, 1949), pp. 262-63, 281-83. For a biography of Admiral Moffett with considerable detail on the use of airships in the Navy, see Edward Arpee, *From Frigates to Flat-Tops* (Chicago: Privately printed, 1953), 276 pp.

[16]Director of War Plans Division [Rear Admiral F. H. Schofield] to the General Board, Washington, April 13, 1929, in U. S., Congress, House, Committee on Naval Affairs, *Hearings on Sundry Legislation, 1929-30,* p. 3009.

78

Charleston, South Carolina. When the Navy attempted to economize, in order to spend the money more effectively in other areas, log-rolling interfered. The words of Rear Admiral Thomas P. Magruder have a familiar ring to them even now.

> Today there are seven navy-yards on the east coast of the United States. . . . There is not enough work to be done for the Navy to justify keeping all these yards in active operation. By disposing of superfluous yards and placing others on an inactive basis, the saving thus effected could be used to strengthen the naval base in the Hawaiian Islands. There is where our greatest navy-yard and naval base should be.[17]

The creation of a battle fleet for the Pacific Ocean and a continuing interest by the Navy in the development of West Coast and Hawaiian naval bases suggest that the Navy expected future trouble to originate west of Hawaii. Because of this viewpoint, the Navy gave a great deal of attention to its war plans during the 1920's. The Washington naval treaties scrapped not only more than 800,000 tons of American naval vessels built, building, or authorized, but also war plans which had been drafted in terms of the preconference Navy. Through cooperative efforts of the General Board, the War Plans Division, and the Naval War College, the Navy's plans were gradually reconstructed, but progress was slow.

Like any efficient organization of the business-conscious 1920's, the Navy wanted to complete its war plans as rapidly as possible; it was therefore fortunate in having Colonel Theodore Roosevelt, Jr., as assistant secretary of the Navy from 1921 to 1924. In a manner reminiscent of his father's tenure in the same position, Roosevelt enjoyed his job thoroughly. Appearances before the Senate and House Naval Affairs committees were generally marked by the Colonel's holding the center of the stage, answering questions briskly, and interrupting testimony of his bureau chiefs upon the slightest provocation. He pushed war planning heavy-handedly, and there is considerable evi-

---

[17]"Admiral Magruder's Hot Shot," *The Literary Digest,* October 8, 1927, p. 14; "The Fight Over the Navy Yards" (editorial), *Army and Navy Register,* February 25, 1922.

dence that the year 1926 became the target date for completion of all detailed plans.[18]

On June 13, 1922, the Assistant Secretary ordered the General Board of the Navy to study the grand strategy of the Pacific under peacetime and wartime conditions and to report what it considered would be the necessary organization to support its strategical analyses.[19] After almost a year of intensive study, hearings, and consultations with the War Plans Division and the Naval War College, the General Board reported. In the first section of its study, labeled "General Considerations," it oriented the report by commenting: "So far as can now be foreseen, any great war in the Pacific involving the United States will be with Japan." In the broadest terms (the War Plans Division would fill in the detail) the board sketched the necessary military activity to force a war with Japan to a successful conclusion: hold or retake Manila Bay, control or occupy all navigable harbors in the Philippines and the Japanese Mandated Islands, militarily and commercially blockade Japan, and pursue any other action [such as engaging the Japanese fleet or bombing Japan] that might cause Japan to sue for peace. As a peacetime strategy in preparation to meet the demands of such a wartime strategy the General Board recommended that the United States

1. Maintain 5-3 ratio with Japan in all classes of fighting ships and personnel.
2. Extend base facilities near Honolulu.
3. Build all vessels and ships to operate trans-Pacifically.
4. Take every legitimate measure to build up Guam and Manila so that they could hold out until reinforcements would arrive.
5. Prepare for: reinforcement of Manila Bay,
   recapture of Manila Bay,
   occupation or control of all naval positions in the Mandates and Philippines,
   close military and commercial blockade of Japan.
6. Shape Peace Strategy towards immediate naval action in the western Pacific on the outbreak of war.

---

[18]Captain W. T. Cluverius to the Chief of Naval Operations, Washington, October 2, 1925, Navy Department, Alphabetical File of Assistant Secretary: RG129, Box 2, Archives.

[19]Theodore Roosevelt, Jr., to the General Board, Washington, June 13, 1922, Navy Department, General Board, No. 425, Serial 1136, OCNH.

7. Provide mobile upkeep, docking and repair equipment for distant operations.
8. Keep an expeditionary force in readiness.
9. Foster good relations with possible benevolent neutrals such as Holland, Russia, or China.[20]

Fundamentally the General Board created its Orange War Plans on the premise of fighting Japan in the Far East. A great many people agreed with Commander [later Fleet Admiral] Chester W. Nimitz' view that American Far Eastern policy was hampering Japan, and therefore war "was certain to come the moment she found herself strong enough to stop by force our continual obstruction to her policies."[21] It was generally felt that the opening of war by Japan with the United States would be a surprise attack upon the Asiatic Fleet and an investing of the Philippines and Guam. Once the islands were taken and their limited objective attained, the Japanese could dig in and await what would necessarily be an unlimited war for the United States to recover her position. There would be no need for any Japanese action east of Guam, and the United States would be forced to operate from Hawaii, which is 5,000 miles east of the Philippines.

With a fleet twice the size of Japan's and with the Philippines and Guam strongly defended, the General Board had felt before the Washington Conference that the war could be reasonably won.[22] After the conference the board, in one brief statement, pessimistically summed up the future of American naval power in the Pacific:

---

[20]Navy Department, General Board, No. 425, Serial 1136, Washington, April 26, 1923, OCNH.

[21]"Class of 1923 Thesis: Policy, Its Relation to War" (manuscript, Naval War College, September, 1922), pp. 20-21.

[22]Class of 1927, "Class of 1927 Report of Committee on: A Logistic Study of the Pacific Area as a Theatre of Operations in an Orange-Blue War" (mimeographed, Naval War College, April, 1927), pp. 18-19. ("Blue" was the strategical name given the United States.) U. S., Navy Department, General Board, No. 425-3, Serial 614, January 15, 1917, OCNH. See also: Memorandum on Naval Matters Connected with the Washington Conference on the Limitation of Armament, 1921-22, compiled by William Howard Gardiner, New York, October 25, 1924, Hilary P. Jones Papers, Box 1, LCMD; Gardiner, "National Policy and Naval Power," *United States Naval Institute Proceedings* (February, 1926), pp. 229-48.

The General Board desires to record here its opinion that the naval situation of the United States in the Pacific, both as to ships and as to bases, resulting from the Treaty for the Limitation of Naval Armament agreed to by the Conference on Limitation of Armament will be such as greatly to lessen the power of the United States to prepare to defend its interests or unaided to enforce its policies in the western Pacific. . . .[23]

Once established in the Philippines, Guam, and in their own mandated islands, the Japanese would be in excellent position to harass an American advance into the Far East. American trade in the Orient could be driven from the seas, and any fleet sent to relieve the Philippines would be subject to constant submarine and air attack west of Hawaii. A resultant stalemate was considered likely until the American industrial potential would begin to build a navy of sufficient size. Some observers also felt that the American people would force the Navy to undertake early, and necessarily unwise, operations to relieve the situation and thus compound the problem.[24]

In operating against the Japanese in the Far East the Navy expected to be on the offensive, and the Japanese, once they had

---

[23]Navy Department, General Board, No. 420-2, Serial 1108, March 29, 1922, OCNH.

[24]Hector C. Bywater, "Japan: A Sequel to the Washington Conference," *United States Naval Institute Proceedings* (May, 1923), pp. 823-27. In a letter to the General Board, Assistant Secretary Roosevelt commented: "After the fall of the Philippines, there will unquestionably be an almost irresistible demand from the people of the United States to have our Fleet, numerically superior, proceed at once to Asiatic waters and force an engagement. It is more than probable that this demand will have to be acceded to. . . ." Memorandum to the General Board, July 24, 1924, Navy Department, Alphabetical File of Assistant Secretary 1921-40: RG130, Box 12, Archives.

By 1930 this belief was still current in the Navy Department. While discussing the strategy of the western Pacific at a meeting of the American delegation to the London Naval Conference, Rear Admiral A. J. Hepburn expressed an opinion to the group that the American public would probably force the Navy to rush to the Philippines though the situation was hopeless and defense impossible. Resumé of Opinions Expressed by Rear Admiral A. J. Hepburn in Answer to Questions by Delegates in Session, January 29, 1930, Harold C. Train Log, Vol. I. This volume of papers, in the possession of Rear Admiral (Ret.) H. C. Train of Annapolis, Maryland, deals with the London Naval Conference. Admiral Train was a technical adviser to the American delegation.

consolidated their gains, would be the defenders. By cleaving to this belief the Navy leaned heavily upon the teaching of Admiral Mahan, who rather dogmatically wrote that "War, once declared, must be waged offensively, aggressively. The enemy must not be fended off, but smitten down. . . ."[25] Assistant Secretary of the Navy Theodore Roosevelt, Jr., put it more colorfully when he said to the House Naval Affairs Committee, "One way of defending yourself is to hit the other fellow on the point of the jaw and knock him out." In less pugilistic tones Secretary of the Navy Curtis D. Wilbur testified before another committee: "The mission of a Navy in war is to defeat an enemy as near to its own home as possible. Only by this operation can our commerce be protected and the country defended in the fullest sense of the word."[26]

To carry the offensive to the Japanese in the Far East eventually required the War Plans Division to think in terms of island-seizing campaigns and forced a re-evaluation of the use of naval air power. Before the Washington Conference the General Board had realized that the "annexation [of the former German islands in the Pacific] by Japan would be an important move toward her naval domination of the Pacific."[27] After the conference Major General John A. Lejeune, Commandant of the Marine Corps, told the Naval War College of the magnificent role the Marines would play in any future Pacific war. In describing the role he commented: "The seizure and occupation or destruction of enemy bases is another important function of the expeditionary force of the Marine Corps. On both flanks of a fleet crossing the Pacific are numerous islands suitable for utilization by an enemy for radio stations, aviation, submarine, or destroyer bases. . . ."[28]

---

[25]A. T. Mahan, "Preparedness for Naval War, 1906," in *Naval Administration and Warfare,* p. 193.

[26]U. S., Congress, House, Committee on Naval Affairs, *Hearings on Sundry Legislation, 1922-23,* February 27, 1922, pp. 442-43; Naval Subcommittee of the Committee on Appropriations, *Hearings on Navy Department Appropriation Bill for 1926,* 68th Cong., 2d Sess., December 8, 1924, p. 619.

[27]Navy Department, *Report of the General Board on Limitation of Armaments* (Washington, 1921), p. 8.

[28]Quoted in Jeter A. Iseley and Philip A. Crowl, *The U. S. Marines and Amphibious Warfare* (Princeton: Princeton University Press, 1951), p. 28.

To be ready for any eventuality the Marine Corps by 1922 had created a West Coast expeditionary force and was in the process of building a base capable of handling an even larger number of troops. In its 1926 revision of the Orange Plan, the War Plans Division predicted the use of the expeditionary force to seize naval bases west of Hawaii. The Philippines would be relieved, but it would take time.[29]

In facing the problem of operating west of Hawaii against the Japanese from poorly developed naval bases, many men in the Navy turned with hope to naval aviation. The almost primitive level of carrier aviation development, in contrast to long years of battleship experience, made it difficult for the salesmen of air power to vend their wares.[30] But years of patient spadework by Rear Admiral William A. Moffett began to pay dividends by 1930, and in the following decade carrier-borne striking forces were recognized as units meriting further study and development. What the Navy learned in the 1920's was that naval aviation could be effective in protecting a fleet against land-based aircraft, and that carriers could take advantage of the principle of "concentration of force" by bringing superior numbers of planes to bear against shore installations when surprise was a factor. This latter value was proven most effectively in the fleet maneuvers of 1929 when *Saratoga's* squadrons successfully attacked the Panama Canal. For the War College and the War Plans Division the aviation developments provided an answer to the problem of defending the Philippines or of attacking them were it necessary to take steps for

---

[29]U. S., Congress, House, Committee on Naval Affairs, *Hearings on Sundry Legislation, 1922-23,* March 9, 1922, p. 647; Louis Morton, "War Plan ORANGE: Evolution of a Strategy," *World Politics,* XI (January, 1959), 232-34.

[30]The fight against naval conservatism has been presented in its clearest form by Elting E. Morison in his *Admiral Sims and the Modern American Navy* (Boston: Houghton Mifflin Company, 1942); for Admiral W. A. Moffett's role in naval aviation development see Arpee, *From Frigates to Flat-Tops;* for delightful reminiscences, though occasionally inaccurate, see Eugene E. Wilson, *Slipstream, The Autobiography of an Air Craftsman* (New York: McGraw-Hill Book Company, Inc., 1950); see also Turnbull and Lord, *History of United States Naval Aviation,* pp. 176-283; Ashbrook Lincoln, "The United States Navy and Air Power" (unpublished Ph.D. dissertation, University of California, 1946), and Gerald E. Wheeler, "Mitchell, Moffett, and Air Power," *The Airpower Historian,* VIII (April, 1961), 79-87.

their recovery. As a result, planning through the years found land-based bombers and carrier-borne aircraft assuming heavier roles in the protection of our Asiatic interest.[31]

The Navy felt hamstrung because of the Five-Power Treaty limitations on future naval base developments, and it therefore tried every possible means to increase fleet operating efficiency in the Far East. Improvement of the Pearl Harbor Naval Base was high on the list at all times, but this yard was 5,000 miles from the scene of expected naval operations. Guam could not be measurably developed, but there was some hope of making the Philippines, particularly Manila Bay, a better naval base within the limits of the Naval Treaty. Governor-General Leonard Wood suggested to the War Department that the Standard Oil Company be persuaded to build storage tanks in Manila rather than at Hong Kong, and that the drydock *Dewey,* then at Olongapo Navy Yard, be transferred to Manila. In these two projects Wood had the complete support of the Commander-in-Chief of the Asiatic Fleet, Admiral Joseph Strauss. To assist his plan further, the Governor-General assigned his naval aide to sit in with the City of Manila Port Authority Board in order to guide its deliberations on improvements along lines beneficial to commercial and especially naval interests.[32]

In his recommendations concerning the *Dewey* General Wood touched upon a subject increasingly important to the War Plans Division. The division recognized the unavailability of adequate docking west of Honolulu and therefore made plans to construct two mobile floating drydocks capable of accompanying the Battle Fleet, were it to move to the Far East. The department was unable to get funds for

---

[31]Rear Admiral Harris Laning to Fullam, Newport, September 18, 1923, William F. Fullam Papers, Box 262, LCMD. Laning was president of the Naval War College. See also memorandum—Why the United States Needs More Aircraft Carrier Tonnage Than Other Countries, undated, D/S, London Naval Conference File 252.26/13, Archives.

[32]Wood to Frank E. McIntyre, Manila, November 18, 1922, Leonard Wood Papers, Box 161, LCMD; McIntyre to Wood, Washington, December 30, 1922, *ibid.;* Admiral Joseph Strauss to Wood, Shanghai, June 14, 1922, *ibid.;* Secretary of the Navy to Secretary of State, Washington, March 2, 1923, D/S, File 500.A4b/129, Archives. This correspondence enclosed a letter from General Wood dealing with his recommendations concerning the Philippines.

new floating drydocks, but Congress in February, 1925, finally allowed the Navy $400,000 to move the *Dewey* to Cavite, in Manila Bay, and thus made it possible for the Navy to dock its cruisers and smaller vessels on the Asiatic station.[33] Though nothing came of the Navy's efforts in the 1920's to get mobile drydocks for its Battle Fleet, it is interesting that during World War II mobile floating drydocks and new developments in antifouling bottom paints made it possible to keep our ships in tropical waters long beyond the times normally expected in earlier years.

The plans for projecting a fleet into Far Eastern waters to uphold the national policies of the United States would have been fairly simple for the War Plans Division had the Japanese not possessed their mid-Pacific mandated islands. However, they did possess them, and war planning had to take them under consideration constantly. Under the terms of the mandate agreement with the League of Nations the Japanese could not fortify nor otherwise enhance the military value of the former German islands, but they were able to treat them as integral Japanese territory. The ports in the islands could be visited only with permission of the Japanese foreign office, whose policies in this matter were controlled completely by the naval ministry.[34] For the United States Navy the right of visit to all of the Japanese islands became a primary goal. Quite understandably the Navy wanted complete assurance that the islands were unfortified and not developed navally. Air bases or submarine facilities in the islands could make the

---

[33]Memorandum—Materiel Readiness Plan, January 3, 1924, Navy Department, Alphabetical File of Assistant Secretary: RG129, Box 3, Archives. In this memorandum it was recommended that the Navy prepare "Offensive Surprise" plans for an Orange War; but caution was urged in distant operations until mobile drydocks could be secured. Also: U. S., Congress, House, Naval Subcommittee of the Committee on Appropriations, *Hearings on Navy Department Appropriation Bill for 1926*, 68th Cong., 2d Sess., December 5, 1924, H. R. 10724, pp. 748-51.

[34]Green H. Hackworth, *Digest of International Law*, 8 vols. (Washington: Government Printing Office, 1940-44), I, 124-26; Tatsuji Takeuchi, *War and Diplomacy in the Japanese Empire* (Garden City, New York: Doubleday, Doran & Company, 1935), pp. 418-21; Acting Secretary of State to Secretary of the Navy, Washington, January 25, 1930, Navy Department, File EF37/7/A4-3 (300125), Archives.

passage from Pearl Harbor to Manila virtually impossible except by the most circuitous routes.

American naval vessels visited a few open ports in the Japanese islands during the decade after the Washington Conference, but on the whole such visiting was discouraged by the Japanese. Unannounced visits such as that of the cruiser *Milwaukee* to Truk in September, 1923, caused diplomatic repercussions, though the port was open for visiting if proper notification were given. Flights by Marine aviators over Rota, to the north of Guam, brought vigorous protests from the Japanese foreign office and caused Admiral Coontz, Chief of Naval Operations, to order the Governor of Guam to control the flights more carefully: ". . . every care should be exercised in the selection of carrier pigeons so that as far as possible they will return to Guam instead of landing on the Island of Rota," he concluded slyly. In 1929 the Navy Department on two occasions attempted to have vessels visit closed ports in the Mandates, and on both occasions was rebuffed by the Japanese; an invitation to visit such open ports as Saipan, Angaur, Truk, or Jaluit was substituted.[35]

By the summer of 1929 the Navy's patience had grown thin—or its curiosity unbearable—so it asked the State Department to force the issue with the Japanese.[36] The department's solicitor had made a careful study of the issue and decided the United States could claim nothing better than most-favored-nation treatment; if the Mandates were closed to all other Powers, the United States could expect nothing. The Navy rather reluctantly accepted the State Department's interpretations, but did concede the unwisdom of making an international

[35]Chief of Naval Operations to Governor of Guam, Washington, April 29, 1922, Navy Department, File 7266-300:1, Archives. For Japanese complaints see enclosed copy of letter from Minister of Foreign Affairs to United States Ambassador to Japan dated March 23, 1922. A full file of correspondence on this subject may be found in D/S, File 811.3394/23-101, Archives.

[36]Secretary of the Navy to Secretary of State, Washington, July 13, 1929, D/S, File 811.3394/104, Archives. Naval curiosity had undoubtedly been piqued since 1925 when it was learned that the Japanese were intending to build oil storage tanks throughout the Japanese home islands and possessions including three in the South Seas Islands at Ponape, Yabite (Jaluit), and Truk. Memorandum from Office of Naval Intelligence, April 10, 1925, D/S, File 894.3472/4, Archives.

issue of the matter, for the Japanese might thus be forced to take a public stand from which they could not later recede. It was agreed between the Navy and State departments that informal efforts should be made to change the views of the Japanese by working through the embassy staff and its naval attaché in Tokyo. At the end of 1929 the Navy was no better informed than before on the Japanese mandated islands; but there was a basic agreement that the Japanese should get no further concessions at the forthcoming London Conference in the matter of extending the nonfortification agreements.[37]

As for exchanging visits to areas held *in statu quo* under Article XIX of the Five-Power Treaty, the State and Navy departments came to reverse their earlier viewpoints. In January of 1923 Secretary of State Hughes had initiated an exchange of visits whereby a Japanese officer visited Guam and the American naval attaché at Tokyo visited the Japanese base at Bako in the Pescadores Islands. In a letter to the Secretary of the Navy and one to the Secretary of War, Hughes suggested that the British be allowed similarly to visit Guam, and that other closed areas coming under Article XIX be opened to mutual inspection. He justified his program by stating, "It seems desirable to this Department from the viewpoint of assuring a mutual confidence among the countries participating in the Naval Treaty of February 6, 1922." Secretary of the Navy Denby was hostile to the proposition and at first stated his objections in vague generalizations: "I think that there should be no question of the good faith of the signatory powers and that, in consequence, visits of inspection either to ships or to stations to verify the execution of the terms of a treaty are undesirable and may be provocative of friction." More to the point, Denby added that the United States had more to lose by inspection than Japan did. The proximity of the Philippines to Japan, and conversely, their distance from the United States, made it possible, in the event of war, for the installations at Corregidor to be overwhelmed long before they could be altered, strengthened, or modernized. On the other hand the Japanese could completely renovate any of their bases before the United States could bring military pressure to bear. In summation

---

[37]Memorandum—Office of Solicitor, August 21, 1929, D/S, File 811.3394/114; Memorandum—Division of Far Eastern Affairs, September 27, 1929, File 811.3394/120, Archives.

Denby recommended: no exchange of visits to fortifications; any visits to closed areas to be officially arranged; no written exchanges of information, "but rather that reliance be placed on the good faith of the powers concerned."

From the War Department Hughes received a response that showed that both letters must have been written after a meeting of the Joint Board, or at least after consultation between Denby and Secreary of War John W. Weeks. The War Department agreed with Hughes in principle, but feared the United States would gain nothing from inspections and would lose the slight potential advantage it had in the Philippines.[38] Reflecting a viewpoint common in the State Department, the chief of the Division of Far Eastern Affairs, John Van Antwerp MacMurray, wrote a bitter memorandum for Hughes: ". . . we will each of us cherish our own military and naval secrets and our suspicions as to the secrets of the other parties to the treaty. . . ."[39] Within the purview of the military departments of the United States this was an entirely reasonable attitude if the basic assumption was eventual war with Japan.

When one examines the work of the War Plans Division and the General Board in their preparation of the "Orange Plan," the defense of the Philippines stands out as of paramount interest. The whole concept of the ratio system embodied in the Five-Power Naval Treaty was predicated upon defending the Philippines, for if defense of the continental United States had been the only task of the American Navy,

---

[38]Secretary of State to Secretary of War, Washington, February 24, 1923, D/S, File 500.A4b/125a; Secretary of Navy to Secretary of State, Washington, February 28, 1923, D/S, File 500.A4b/127; Secretary of War to Secretary of State, Washington, March 5, 1923, D/S, File 500.A4b/128, Archives. The Office of Naval Intelligence had received several discouraging reports from the naval attaché in Tokyo, Captain Lyman A. Cotten. He had visited in September and October, 1922, several regular Japanese naval bases at Yokosuka, Kure, and Sasebo, had been shown very little, and in general was given the "brush-off." These bases were not so restricted as those covered by Article XIX. L. A. Cotten, Private Notes [Diary] 1922-23, Entries for September 27, 1922, and October 27, 1922, in the possession of Mrs. Cotten, Chapel Hill, North Carolina.

[39]Memorandum—Division of Far Eastern Affairs, March 7, 1923, D/S, File 500.A4b/127, Archives.

then it would have been possible to allow Japan naval equality. As matters stood, the inability of Japan to attack the Pacific Coast, except on what would amount to a suicide mission, was conceded; the only other problem was whether a tonnage of 60 per cent of American capital ship strength would leave Japan in a position to menace the Philippines. Upon these points there was virtual unanimity in the Navy after 1922: Japan could attack, and the Philippines would be extremely difficult to defend.[40]

It was widely believed in the American Navy of the 1920's that Japan was interested in acquiring the Philippines; therefore the Navy Department insisted on continuing American possession. If the islands were granted independence, the United States would be likely to lose its naval bases in Manila Bay and be forced to operate from Pearl Harbor, a logistic impossibility for that day. Were the Navy thrown back to the Hawaiian Islands, then there would be little likelihood of preventing Japanese aggression against a new Philippine nation. If Japan succeeded in overrunning the islands, there would be even less possibility of the Navy defending the Asiatic trade of the United States.[41]

This solicitude for American Far Eastern trade, characteristic of the Navy during the 1920's, was reflected in the official United States

[40]Navy Department, General Board, No. 420-2, Serial 1108, Washington, March 29, 1922, OCNH. Eight years later, Admiral H. E. Yarnell commented on the defensibility of the Philippines: "I think I can say this. . . . That at no time since we took the Philippines has the chance that we could go immediately to the Philippines with our fleet and conduct successful operations been anything more than a desperate gamble." U. S., Congress, Senate, Committee on Naval Affairs, *Hearings on Treaty on the Limitation of Naval Armaments,* 71st Cong., 2d Sess., May 17, 1930, p. 182.

[41]Joint Board, Serial 227, April 14, 1924, Mark L. Bristol Papers, Box 13, LCMD. Admiral H. P. Jones testified at length, as Senior Member of the General Board, before the Senate Committee on Territories and Insular Possessions on March 3, 1924. The burden of Jones's argument against Philippine independence was that the Navy would have to support the Open Door and therefore needed bases in the Far East. He noted quite strongly: "The Navy considers that we must possess bases in the Philippines. They are vital to our operations in the Western Pacific—so vital that I consider their abandonment tantamount to abandonment of our ability to protect our interests in the Far East." Typed transcript in Navy Department, General Board, No. 405, Serial 1202, March 3, 1924, OCNH.

Naval Policy. In terms of trade and commerce the Navy viewed its job as "exercising ocean-wide economic pressure," and supporting "in every possible way American interests, especially the expansion and development of American foreign commerce."[42] In language reminiscent of turn-of-the-century imperialists, naval officers spoke glowingly of "the undeveloped treasure-house of Asia [which] bids fair to make the Far East a future of great commercial activity." They deprecated talk of abandoning the Open Door policy, for "there [China] is a country of 400,000,000 peoples, the markets of which are opened to the world . . . as manufacturing increases as a means of supporting our people, we must go farther and farther afield to obtain markets for our goods. China, as a field for commercial enterprise is of great importance to this country, and this importance will continue to grow." The Five-Power Naval Treaty with its nonfortification clause visited irreparable damage upon the United States, because "a country's foreign trade must have the backing of its navy *on the spot*. A merchant ship arbitrarily detained by the order of some power *in the Far East* needs help in the Far East."[43] These were arguments couched in terms easily understood by the business-conscious Republican administrators. Yet there were movements afoot further to limit, not increase, the world's navies, and there was a strong sentiment, in Congress and throughout the nation (though resisted by the executive branches of these administrations) for cutting the Philippines adrift—to deny the Navy its base in the Far East.

When faced with the likelihood that the Philippines would be granted independence, the Navy Department worked assiduously to assure continued United States lease or ownership of some naval facilities in the islands. General Leonard Wood, Governor-General of the Philippines, felt the United States could get naval and military

[42]United States Naval Policy, March 29, 1922, Navy Department, General Board, No. 420-2, Serial 1108, OCNH.

[43]Commander C. C. Gill, "The New Far East Doctrine," *United States Naval Institute Proceedings* (September, 1922), pp. 1479-80; Captain J. K. Taussig, "A Balanced Fleet for the Navy," *United States Naval Institute Proceedings* (July, 1925), p. 1109; Captain Walter S. Anderson, "Limitation of Naval Armament," *United States Naval Institute Proceedings* (March, 1926), pp. 438-40.

bases from an independent Philippines upon request; five years later he was seconded in this view by Henry L. Stimson, who had succeeded him as governor.[44] Within the Navy Department the General Board went on record in March, 1924, when it stated, "In case independence is granted, the United States must retain a naval station in the Philippines." Were only partial independence granted or the United States agreed to some protectorate condition over the islands, then the Navy and the Joint Board believed the nation must maintain fortified naval bases in the Philippines.[45]

With Congress talking more seriously of Philippine independence in the spring of 1930, and with the London Naval Treaty before the Senate, the Navy still insisted upon the necessity of bases in the islands. Rear Admiral Mark L. Bristol, then senior member of the General Board, told a Senate committee, "If we gave the Philippines their freedom I am certain that if we wanted to protect our interests in the Far East—that is, I mean in every way, not necessarily in connection with war, but at all times—we would want to maintain a naval base in the Philippines. . . ." He felt this would be particularly true from a moral viewpoint were the Filipinos unable to defend themselves, for they would undoubtedly then turn to the United States. In this view he was supported by men like Rear Admiral H. P. Jones, who had helped to draft the naval treaty, and by Rear Admiral S. S. Robison, Superintendent of the Naval Academy.[46] However, the Navy did not speak with complete unanimity in this matter; the Joint Board in this very spring opposed the retention of any military or naval forces in the Philippines if complete independence were given. The Joint Board did agree that were a period of semi-independence initiated, similar

---

[44]Leonard Wood to Major General W. M. Wright, Manila, August 4, 1922, Interior Department, File 364-504B, Archives. H. L. Stimson to Wood, at sea, October 11, 1926, Leonard Wood Papers, Box 182, LCMD.

[45]Joint Board, No. 305, Serial 227, March 14, 1924, RG94, Archives.

[46]Foreign Relations, *London Treaty Hearings,* May 15, 1930, pp. 115-17. Admiral Jones pointed out that even if the United States gave up the Philippines it was still national policy to stand by the Open Door and the territorial integrity of China. Naval Affairs Committee, *London Treaty Hearings,* May 16, 1930, p. 133. For Admiral Robison's views see U. S., Congress, Senate, Committee on Foreign Relations, *Hearings on Treaty on the Limitation of Naval Armaments,* 71st Cong., 2d Sess., May 28, 1930, p. 348.

to a commonwealth status, then the Navy should remain in the Philippines at full strength.[47]

During 1930 and 1931 Congress studied further the question of Philippine independence; with the pressure of the depression, plus a resurgence of Democratic power in the House and Senate, it appeared in the fall of 1931 that Congress would set the islands adrift. During the summer of 1931 a team of legislators headed by independence-minded Senator Harry B. Hawes reinforced its preconceptions by visiting the islands. The Congressional junket was followed by a small party led by Secretary of War Patrick J. Hurley, who was making his own tour to find evidence against independence. Needless to say, Hawes and Hurley found just what they wanted. The "spontaneous" demonstrations wherever the Hawes party traveled were clear evidence to the legislators that the Filipinos wished to be free. In contrast, the confidential, off-the-record chats with Philippine politicos and business-men convinced the Secretary of War that the Filipinos neither expected nor desired independence, but that it was imperative for a politically ambitious Filipino to be pro-independence.[48]

Upon leaving the islands, Hurley cabled the War Department and ordered a study of the strategic value of the Philippines. He wanted the War Department, Navy Department, and the Joint Board to decide whether the islands were a military and naval liability or asset. He asked that the State Department look at the Philippines from the diplomatic point of view—asset or liability? Hurley expected the answers to be available when he met with President Hoover to report the findings from his excursion to the Far East.[49] Presumably the answers to the Secretary of War's questions, plus his personal observa-tions, would guide the President's actions were Congress to present him with a Philippine independence measure.

---

[47]Joint Board, No. 305, Serial 472, April 10, 1930, RG94, Archives.

[48]Garel A. Grunder and William E. Livezey, *The Philippines and the United States* (Norman: University of Oklahoma Press, 1951), pp. 189-94; Don Lohbeck, *Patrick J. Hurley* (Chicago: Henry Regnery Company, 1956), pp. 87-94; Gerald E. Wheeler, "Republican Philippine Policy, 1921-1933," *Pacific Historical Review,* XXVIII (November, 1959), pp. 380-85, 390.

[49]Joint Board, No. 305, Serial 499, October 23, 1931, RG94, Archives.

The replies of the War and Navy departments were incorporated, deliberately, into a single study by the Joint Board. In justifying this approach, the Board reported:

> All military operations in the Western Pacific must be *per se* joint Army and Navy operations, and, hence it is only from this standpoint that the war time value of the Philippines should be considered. A detached study of whether the Philippines are an asset to the Army alone or to the Navy alone serves no useful purpose. Neither service is capable of operating in this region independently of the other.

In the course of its lengthy reply the Joint Board left no doubt of its feeling when it posited: "The Philippine Islands are a military asset to the United States." "The Philippine Islands are a distinct naval asset to the United States." "The Philippine Islands are a positive asset to the United States from the standpoint of combined military and naval operations and strategy."[50]

Despite Hurley's relatively narrow precept, the Joint Board extended its investigations beyond strategical matters and directly into the field of foreign affairs. The board drew together the loose ends of American Far Eastern policy and restated what it believed were the foundations of that policy. In a section that could have been written by Mahan or by the late General Wood, the Joint Board securely tied the Philippines to America's economic future in Asia. "The Philippines constitute a potential commercial center upon which depend, to a large extent, the development and success of future American trade relations with the Asiatic continent and Australasia. . . . Far-seeing statesmen, economists and writers are agreed that there lie the future markets of the world." The board went further and opposed Philippine independence in terms of American national self-interest. "By withdrawal of sovereignty from the Philippines, we give up the opportunity to make them a commercial asset, and we surrender the potentialities of the Philippines as an *entrepôt* to the markets of the adjacent islands and the Asian mainland including the security afforded our commerce and investments in that part of the world by the presence there of our armed forces." Finally the Joint Board declared that "The United States has always supported the policy of the territorial integrity of China and the principle of equal

---

[50]Joint Board, No. 305, Serial 499, October 23, 1931, RG94, Archives.

94

trade opportunity for all countries as embodied in the Open Door Policy." Withdrawal from the Philippines would lessen American ability to support its Far Eastern policy.[51]

From the arguments of the admirals, the General Board, and Joint Board, it becomes obvious that American interest in retaining a Philippine naval base did not emphasize the importance of defending the Philippines as much as it did of keeping a fleet in Far Eastern waters. These groups appeared most interested in defending American trade and interests in the Far East, and felt a fleet in the area would do the job more effectively. It cannot be denied that a fleet in the Far East and a base that could service a larger naval concentration under emergency conditions might have had a deterrent effect on Japanese ambitions in eastern Asia.

In its exhortation to continue American sovereignty over the Philippines, and with it the Cavite naval base, the Navy Department seldom stated publicly that the Philippines were defensible. In the years before the Washington Naval Conference of 1921-22 the accepted view of the War and Navy departments was that Hawaii would first have to be built into a major naval base; then Guam would have to be strongly fortified and developed; then it would be reasonable to expect to defend the Philippines. And the United States Navy would have to be twice the size of Japan's if that country were the aggressor. These qualifications were not met, and by 1908 the United States had withdrawn its main line of defense to Hawaii.[52]

During 1920, when the momentum of war contracts and construction under the 1916 naval bill expanded the naval establishment, the General Board optimistically declared the Philippines defensible, though Guam was undeveloped. It qualified this viewpoint by adding that defense was possible "As long as the present comparative strength of the Navies of the United States and Japan are maintained and

---

[51]*Ibid.*

[52]Louis Morton, "Military and Naval Preparations for the Defense of the Philippines during the War Scare of 1907," *Military Affairs* (Spring, 1949), pp. 95-104; Pomeroy, *Pacific Outpost,* p. 32; Outten Jones Clinard, *Japan's Influence on American Naval Power 1897-1917,* University of California Publications in History, No. 36 (Berkeley and Los Angeles: University of California Press, 1947), pp. 63-64; Snowbarger, "The Development of Pearl Harbor," pp. 104-14.

Manila Bay remains in our possession. . . ." The Joint Board, War Plans Division, and Naval War College dissented; Philippine defenses were not modern, and 173 marines without modern artillery could hardly make Guam impregnable.[53] The Washington Five-Power Naval Treaty relegated all these propositions to an academic status when it limited the Navy to 40 per cent superiority over Japan and forbade any further development of Guam or modernizing of Philippine defenses.

Aviation became a more important weapon for western Pacific defenses as the impact of the treaty was felt in naval planning circles. Under the leadership of Rear Admiral W. S. Sims and later of Rear Admiral Harris Laning, the Naval War College devoted an increasing amount of time to studying the application of aviation to naval warfare. By the fall of 1923 Admiral Laning was cautiously admitting that land-based planes could be of great assistance in defending the Philippines, and that carrier-borne aircraft, owing to the mobility of their base, could probably aid in recovering the Philippines by giving temporary air superiority in areas where recovery attempts would begin.[54] In 1924 the Navy Department moved the patrol bombing squadrons and equipment ashore from their mobile seaplane tenders and steadily built up naval land-based aircraft strength in the islands. When the British announced their intention to build a new air base on Hong Kong, the Navy Department offered no comment, though it privately admitted to State Department officials that the base would violate the spirit of the Five-Power Treaty. The solicitor of the State Department merely commented, "We might desire to take similar ac-

---

[53]Memorandum for the Chief of Naval Operations by J. H. Oliver of War Plans Division, August 12, 1920, Navy Department, File 11158-83, RG80, Archives. For the views of the War Plans Division and Joint Board see *ibid.* For the views of the Naval War College expressed by Rear Admiral W. S. Sims see Rear Admiral W. S. Sims to the General Board, Newport, August 13, 1920, General Board, No. 404, Serial 1000, OCNH.

[54]The papers of Rear Admiral William F. Fullam, U.S.N., contain an interesting series of letters between Fullam and Sims, and Fullam and Laning written in 1922-23 and dealing with the projected use of naval aviation in the Far East. William F. Fullam Papers, Box 262, LCMD.

tion in the Philippines and it might, therefore, be useful to have this precedent."[55]

Between 1927 and 1930 naval strategists went all the way in planning an aerial defense for the Philippines. The Lampert Committee hearings of 1925, which dealt with the operations of Navy and Army aviation, had been educative to the Navy Department. The zealous followers of the Army's Colonel "Billy" Mitchell convinced many naval officers that land-based aviation alone could never defend the Philippine Islands. This would be so, not because aviation would be ineffective, but because the nation would never purchase sufficient aircraft for such work and place them in the islands. Thus the General Board in the spring of 1927 could insist that the Navy needed more planes and aircraft carriers. These would be used to establish local control of the air once the United States Fleet arrived in the Far East to defend the Philippines or to recover them had the Japanese already seized the islands.[56] By 1930 the position of the General Board was summed up in a memorandum written for the guidance of the London Naval Conference delegation: ". . . existing United States naval strength is insufficient if military force is ever to be employed in the defense of the Philippines or the Open Door. Recognizing this, present naval policy contemplates the use of 'overwhelming air strength' in serious operations in the Asiatic."[57] Quite obviously treaties, technology, and geography had forced a re-evaluation of the traditional methods of defending American Far Eastern interests, and air power and the aircraft carrier became accepted weapons in the naval arsenal.

Though the Navy was admittedly unable to defend the Philippines adequately after the Washington Conference, the resulting treaty system provided greater security for those islands than was originally

---

[55]General Board to Secretary of the Navy, Washington, November 21, 1924, Navy Department, File 27403-478:4; memorandum, Solicitor's Office, March 11, 1927, D/S, File 841.34593/2, Archives.

[56]U. S., Congress, House, Select Committee of Inquiry into Operations of the United States Air Services, *Hearings,* 68th Congress, February 16, 19, 1925, pp. 2261, 2763-64; Navy Department, General Board No. 438, Serial 1347-10(d), OCNH.

[57]Memorandum [for Admiral Moffett], undated, D/S, LNC 252.26/13, Archives.

anticipated. The Four-Power Treaty of December, 1921, effectively stabilized the western Pacific, and the Five-Power Treaty reduced the possibilities of naval armaments upsetting the stability accomplished. Japan was left in a position to dominate the western Pacific, but facing Japan were the United States in the Philippines, the Netherlands in the East Indies, Great Britain at Hong Kong and the Malay Peninsula, and the British Dominions of Australia and New Zealand. Cooperation among these Powers would have posed a formidable block to Japanese expansion toward the south and southwest, and the key to this cooperation was the British naval base at Singapore.

In June, 1921, after several years of agitation for action, the British began their first work on what was to become the great Singapore naval base. As a strategic necessity the project had been blessed by Admiral of the Fleet Lord Jellicoe in 1919, and from that time there had been a steadily mounting pressure from Australia and New Zealand for a great naval base in the Far East, though not necessarily at Singapore. Once begun, the work was halted twice—for six months in 1924 and temporarily in 1929 when the Labor Party under Ramsay MacDonald controlled the British government—but these interruptions were merely delays, and the base was slowly pushed ahead throughout the 1920's.[58] Ostensibly the base was to protect British interests in the Far East, but against whom was never clearly defined. The presumption throughout eastern Asia that the base was a backfire against Japanese expansionism was officially denied both in Britain and, interestingly enough, in Japan.[59]

---

[58]Great Britain, *Parliamentary Debates* (Commons), July 16, 1923, Columns 1870-71. See also C. Northcote Parkinson, "The Pre-1942 Singapore Naval Base," *United States Naval Institute Proceedings* (September, 1956), pp. 939-53; Admiral Sir R. H. Bacon, *The Life of John Rushworth Earl Jellicoe* (London: Cassell & Co., Ltd., 1936), pp. 426-48; Hector C. Bywater, *Navies and Nations: A Review of Naval Developments Since the Great War* (London: Constable and Company, Ltd., 1927), pp. 66-68; for a complete exposition on the strategic importance see Captain Russell Grenfell, *Main Fleet to Singapore* (London: Faber & Faber, Ltd., 1951).

[59]For British reasons on the necessity for the Singapore Base, see Great Britain, "Singapore Naval Base," *Correspondence with the Self-Governing Dominions & India Regarding the Development of the Singapore Naval Base: Command 2083, March 25, 1924* (London: HMSO, 1924), 15 pp.

The strategic effect of erecting a great naval bastion at Singapore was not lost on the Dutch. As a naval Power the Netherlands was decidedly second-class, but as a colonial Power it held one of the richest possessions in the world—the Netherlands East Indies. To protect those islands adequately would have required a first-class navy, and much to the disgust of many Hollanders resident in the islands, the mother country was not interested in providing it.[60] The result was a developing dependence upon Great Britain—without benefit of treaty—to act as a guardian for the Dutch islands, and a granting of economic concessions, particularly in oil field development, to the English as a payment for their protection. The situation at hand was perilous to British interests, particularly if the Japanese were to obtain lodgment in the Indies, and therefore a community of interests was strong enough to make treaties unnecessary.[61] After Nicholas Roosevelt, a

The Japanese official view on Singapore shifted constantly, depending on the party in power and the value of having the British as a whipping boy at the time. As Foreign Minister for Premier Kato, Baron Shidehara could see no danger in the Singapore Base. Tokyo *Asahi,* December 29, 1924, in D/S, File 711.94/533, Tokyo, January 5, 1925, Archives. As Premier, Baron Shidehara criticized the British heavily for building the base, D/S, File 711.945/1262, Tokyo, January 27, 1925, Archives.

[60]D/S, File 856E.00/1, Soerabaya, Java, July 23, 1923, Archives. On July 30, 1923, the *Soerabaiasch Handelblad* ran an article, "Big Brother," in which a reserve officers' magazine was quoted concerning the lack of naval appropriations for the Indies: "Economy maniacs [in Holland] will be glad to know that 'the big brother,' England, will defend Netherlands India for the Dutch so that large naval expenditures may be economized. National honor is too expensive, in these materialistic days no one is expected to trouble about unprofitable idealism. . . ." Enclosure in D/S, File 841.34546d/12, Soerabaya, Java, October 11, 1923, Archives. See also Nicholas Roosevelt, "The Strategy of Singapore," *Foreign Affairs* (January, 1929), p. 321.

[61]D/S, File 856E.00/2, Soerabaya, Java, January 17, 1924, Archives. Consul Rollin R. Winslow called the State Department's attention to British oil developments in Dutch Borneo and commented: ". . . The Dutch place great reliance upon the English to defend their precious and wealthy possessions and this may in some measure account for the fact that the British (Shell) have been given very large petroleum concessions to the exclusion of American firms." File 894.20256g/–, Soerabaya, Java, July 3, 1925; see also despatch 841.3356/1, The Hague, September 20, 1926, for Minister Tobin's views on British-Dutch naval collaboration in the Indies. For similar views in the British

special correspondent on Asiatic affairs for the *New York Times*, visited southeast Asia in 1925 and 1926, he wrote,

> Until I saw these Dutch-owned islands so close to Singapore I had not grasped how inevitable it would be that if the Japanese decide to take the Dutch East Indies, they would have to occupy Singapore, and if they wanted Singapore they would have to take the Indies. . . . In the Far East the Dutch and British are indissolubly linked together. . . . [62]

American interest in the British base at Singapore was also fairly strong. Roosevelt noted that the inhabitants of the Philippine archipelago recognized the lack of protection afforded by the American Navy and therefore looked "with just as friendly eye on the Singapore base as [did] the Dutch because they too, [cared] only about the preservation of the *status quo* in the Pacific. They realized that the provisions of the Washington Conference forbidding the strengthening of the existing island defenses, taken in connection with the distance of the islands from Hawaii, [made] difficult their defense by the American navy alone."[63] The General Board similarly recognized this weakness; in planning a "peace strategy" for the Pacific the board declared that the Navy should "foster such good relationships with other powers in the Far Eastern area, particularly with Holland, China and regenerated Russia, that in the event of war [with Japan] the United States may be assured at least of a benevolent neutrality on their part."[64] By 1927, in view of the Washington treaties and their

Straits Settlements see despatch 841.34546d/42, Singapore, May 2, 1927, Archives.

[62]Nicholas Roosevelt, *A Front Row Seat* (Norman: University of Oklahoma Press, 1953), pp. 143-44. With greater detail and accuracy the same story is presented in Roosevelt's earlier book, *The Restless Pacific* (New York: Charles Scribner's Sons, 1928), pp. 156-59.

[63]Roosevelt, "Strategy of Singapore," p. 321. See also, "A Timely Warning" (editorial), *The Manila Times,* May 26, 1929, enclosed in Interior Department, File 364-539D, Archives.

[64]Navy Department, General Board, No. 426, Serial 1136, April 26, 1923, OCNH. The General Board had recommended unity of action with the Canadians and Australians in matters concerning Japan and the racial question as early as August, 1920. Navy Department, *Report of the General Board on Limitation of Armament,* pp. 25-26.

effect on Philippine defenses, the General Board recommended resisting any attempts by Japan at the Geneva Naval Conference to bring Singapore under the nonfortification clause (Article XIX) of the Five-Power Naval Treaty of 1922. The result of these viewpoints was the gradual development over the years of a mutual concern between the British Pacific dominions and colonies, on the one hand, and the United States on the other, for matters of naval defense. It was nothing formal, but the interest was there and was recognized from time to time by other nations.[65]

Between the United States Navy and the Dutch in their East Indies there was an even closer linking of defense interests. To naval officers familiar with the Far East it was evident that the Dutch held their Indies only on the sufferance of Great Britain or Japan, and Japan appeared to them to be the nation most likely to trouble the Hollanders. The Asiatic Fleet Commander noted in 1923 that the more progressive elements in the Indies wanted to invite American capital on a par with the British so that there would be two parties interested in preserving the independence of the islands were the Japanese to apply pressure. Significantly enough Admiral E. A. Anderson felt this arrangement would be advantageous to the United

---

[65]The Embassy in Paris sent in an editorial, "Do Not Awaken the Sleeping Cat," *Le Figaro* of July 26, 1923. The article commented on how upset the Japanese were at the Singapore base, whereas the Americans paid very little attention to it. With close attention to American diplomatic history, the editorialist noted: "One would readily understand that, as an experiment, the same government which during a century found certain advantages in reconciling the Monroe Doctrine with the existence of an immense English fleet might find it profitable and perhaps convenient to tolerate temporarily at Singapore, opposite eternal Japan and the Philippines, which are little fortified, *a fleet in being,* capable of doing police duty in those distant waters." D/S, File 841.30/48, Paris, August 3, 1923, Archives. The *Montreal Star* for June 10, 1924, commented on the immigration bill, the dangerous trend in Japanese-American relations, and the mutual interests of the United States and the British Empire in the Pacific. It predicted that the Singapore base might be needed earlier than believed. D/S, File 711.945/1141, Montreal, June 16, 1924, Archives. For Japanese predictions of American-Australian cooperation see D/S, File 711.94/513, Tokyo, October 15, 1924, Archives.

States as well as to the Indies.[66] Throughout the 1920's American consuls in the Indies reported the pessimism of the Dutch concerning the intentions of Japan, and this pessimism was reflected from The Hague as well.[67] By 1925 Admiral Thomas Washington was reporting from the Asiatic station that a recent visit to the Indies "helped to cement the excellent relations existing between the two countries, and the Dutch Government . . . regards such visits as a material factor in off-setting the very great concern it feels because of the growing interest by Japan in their [Dutch] possessions."[68]

What became established in the 1920's was a definite community of interests in the Far East among the United States, Great Britain, and the Netherlands. All nations were concerned about possible Japanese pressure on their possessions, and the British and Dutch were particularly worried lest the United States open the road southward for Japan by freeing the Philippines. The Japanese, once in the Philippines, would soon engulf all of Southeast Asia including Australia and New Zealand. Hence, American naval officers felt, the Dutch and British bases would be available to them in the event of a Japanese-American war—a partial solution to Article XIX of the Five-Power Naval Treaty. It is in this light that one can explain, in part, the inconsistency of American naval insistence upon keeping the Philippines, or bases therein, though the possibility of defending those islands was rather remote.

The 1920's represented a period of organizing and planning for a future war which the General Board predicted would be fought in the Pacific Ocean against the Japanese. Within this decade the American Navy concentrated its most powerful units in the Pacific and forced the nation and Congress to give consideration to supplying

---

[66]Commander-in-Chief Asiatic Fleet to the Chief of Naval Operations, Manila, March 22, 1923, Navy Department, File 27403-437:2, Archives.

[67]Roosevelt in *A Front Row Seat,* pp. 152-53, noted: "Nearly all the Dutch with whom I spoke in the Indies echoed the fears expressed to me at the Hague by Prime Minister Colijn—that Japan would seize the Indies." Minister Richard M. Tobin reported similar views in D/S, File 711.94/545, The Hague, February 19, 1925, Archives.

[68]Commander-in-Chief Asiatic Fleet to the Chief of Naval Operations, Saigon, March 25, 1925, Navy Department, File 27403-500, Archives.

proper naval bases for handling the fleet. With the Washington treaties as a limiting framework, the War Plans Division, General Board, and War College rebuilt the "Orange Plan" and reconsidered America's Pacific Ocean strategy. Though somewhat weakened by the Washington agreements, the department did not ask for, or suggest, the abandonment of traditional American Far Eastern interests, but rather turned to other means of defending them. The gradual development of carrier aviation through the decade gave the Navy by 1930 a weapon that would materially aid in protecting the Philippines or in operating to recover them if the need arose. Though at first given little consideration by the General Board, carrier air power was to some extent a last hope by 1930. Even more significant for the protection of American Far Eastern interests was the gradual and subtle alignment of American, British, and Dutch naval policies in Southeast Asia. Through a developing community of interests, particularly in the face of an ever-pressing Japan, the United States found potential relief from the staggering burden of defending what the Washington Conference had made indefensible. Dependence upon the Four-Power and Nine-Power treaties to guarantee the Philippines and the Open Door was not a satisfactory solution for a "man-of-war's man," and the possibility of operating in the western Pacific, in the company of friends, made the Navy even more conscious of the need to round out its fleet and acquire the vessels needed for trans-Pacific operations.

5

The Fight for a Battle Fleet

THE MOST exasperating problem faced by the United States Navy in the years 1922 to 1931 was acquiring sufficient ships and personnel to meet fleet needs for an anticipated Pacific war against the Japanese Empire. Because of the vast distances between bases—and the dearth of them—the Navy would require twice the tonnage of the Japanese fleet. Every major unit must be constructed for extended operations in the area between Hawaii and the Philippines, using Pearl Harbor as the major naval operating base. But it was exceedingly difficult to convince the American taxpayer or his elected representatives of the Navy's needs. The man in the street was more interested in national than international affairs, in economies rather than military aggrandizement.[1]

---

[1]Frank H. Simonds, *American Foreign Policy in the Post-War Years* (Baltimore: The Johns Hopkins Press, 1935), pp. 49-55; George A. Grassmuck, *Sectional Biases in Congress on Foreign Policy,* The Johns Hopkins University Studies in Historical and Political Science, Series LXVIII, No. 3 (Baltimore: The Johns Hopkins Press, 1951), pp. 30-55; Thomas A. Bailey, *The Man in the Street: The Impact of American Public Opinion on Foreign Policy* (New York: The Macmillan Company, 1948), pp. 238-55; Dexter Perkins, "The Department of State and American Public Opinion," in Gordon A. Craig and Felix Gilbert, *The Diplomats, 1919-1939* (Princeton: Princeton University Press, 1953), pp. 284-85; John D. Hicks, *Republican Ascendancy, 1921-1933* (New York: Harper and Brothers, 1960), p. 49; John Chalmers Vinson, *The Parchment Peace: The United States Senate and the Washington Conference, 1921-1922* (Athens: The University of Georgia Press, 1955), pp. 4-5, 216-17.

President Warren G. Harding set the tone for the next ten years when his first message to Congress, in April, 1921, dealt almost entirely with domestic affairs. "I know of no more pressing problem at home than to restrict our national expenditures within the limits of our national income, and at the same time measurably lift the burdens of war taxation from the shoulders of the American people." A year and a half later the President said he brought "no apprehension of war. The world is abhorrent of it, and our relations are not only free from every threatening cloud, but we have contributed our larger influence toward making armed conflict less likely." President Harding's death brought another confirmed nationalist to the White House, who assured the public in December, 1923,

> For us peace reigns everywhere. We desire to perpetuate it always by granting full justice to others and requiring of others full justice to ourselves.
>
> Our country has one cardinal principle to maintain in its foreign policy. It is an American principle. It must be an American policy. We attend to our own affairs, conserve our own strength, and protect the interests of our citizens. . . .

Two years later President Calvin Coolidge was gratified to report that the country was enjoying "a general condition of progress and prosperity," and that it did not "appear to require radical departures from the policies already adopted." He concluded, "We are by far the most likely to accomplish permanent good if we proceed with moderation." These years of leadership by platitude convinced the taxpayer that there was no danger of war—that an economically strong America could easily cope with any challenge of the future without adequate preparation.[2] Unfortunately in the 1920's, when naval and military accretions were set aside in the name of tax reductions, the country was economically building itself toward the fateful "Black Friday" of October, 1929.

In its dealings with the Navy the Congress followed a bifurcated policy. There was a general eagerness to reassert Congressional leader-

---

[2]For a few generalizations on this viewpoint see Bailey, *The Man in the Street,* pp. 61-71, and Samuel Flagg Bemis, "The Shifting Strategy of American Defense and Diplomacy," in Dwight E. Lee and George E. McReynolds, *Essays in History and International Relations in Honor of George Hubbard Blakeslee* (Worcester, Mass.: Commonwealth Press, 1949), pp. 9-10.

106

ship in foreign affairs, a direct reaction to the heavy-handed guidance of President Wilson, and yet there was an obvious desire to fulfill the legislative programs of Presidents Harding, Coolidge, and Hoover. There was constant pressure by the Senate and House upon the Presidents to call another naval conference to finish the work left undone by the Washington Conference of 1921-22, and later the Geneva Conference of 1927. Further, naval authorization and appropriation acts were given the closest scrutiny to make sure that the country was getting the most for its tax dollar. Here Congress clashed as often as not with the Bureau of the Budget, which was an executive agency and therefore fair game for congressmen in both parties.

The creation of the bureau provided the President with a handy tool and Congress with a strong competitor, as time was to prove. The directors of the budget became presidential "no" men through the years, and served to restrain appropriation-hungry members of the official executive family. In the early 1920's the simple statement that an appropriation request was "in conflict with the President's financial program" usually ended the matter. By 1927, however, Congress began to realize that it had created a monster, at least in terms of Navy fiscal programs. Budget control could mean naval policy control, a prerogative jealously guarded by the House and Senate Naval Affairs committees. Committeemen began suggesting that the budget directors be summoned to defend their budgets and to explain why ships or personnel were eliminated by making funds unavailable. From the nature of the questions asked and the comments interjected into the hearings, it is quite obvious that Naval Committee members were not so interested in restoring funds to trimmed budgets as they were in returning responsibility for naval policy to Congress. In many ways these skirmishes, whether between Congress and Navy Department officials or Congress and Budget Bureau employees, were merely reflections of the traditional power struggle between the President and the legislative branch of the Government. Yet the total effect was to weaken naval effectiveness and obscure the relationship between foreign policy and its supporting agent. It became less and less clear whether the Department of the Navy, the Bureau of the Budget, or

107

the Naval Subcommittee of the House Appropriations Committee was charged with maintaining America's "first line of defense."[3]

The spring and fall of 1922 were hard for American naval officers. While the Washington Naval Conference was still in session, the Congress began its annual hearings on the naval appropriation bill for fiscal 1923. These hearings and those in the fall on the 1924 appropriation bill provided a gauge for measuring the attitude of Congress toward the postconference Navy. It was a year of worry for a Navy which left the conference table considerably less than satisfied. It entered the Washington Conference with the premise that Japan was a menace to American national interests, and it emerged with a few diplomatic guarantees for American Far Eastern interests and a naval establishment considered incapable of supporting them if challenged. The hearings of 1922 revealed that Congress was interested in reducing even further that Navy which the diplomats had not succeeded in scuttling.

First the House Naval Affairs Committee and the Naval Subcommittee of the House Appropriations Committee turned to an examination of naval personnel on the rolls in February and March, 1922. To the horror of the Navy, Secretary Edwin Denby's request for 96,000 enlisted men was brushed aside, and it was asked to base the distribution of personnel on 65,000 men—a reduction of approximately 54,000 seamen—yet to keep in service the ships allowed by the Five-Power Naval Treaty. In retaliation the Bureau of Navigation (later called the Bureau of Naval Personnel) sharply reported that

---

[3]In November, 1922, after just a year of operation, the Bureau of the Budget was submitted to heavy criticism in Congress. Generally on a partisan basis, the Democratic congressmen attacked the bureau's cuts of naval appropriations, and Republicans generally defended them. When the Secretary of the Navy was questioned about reductions he was usually torn between two loyalties: as a cabinet member he had to defend the President's budget, but as the Navy's head he found it difficult to refrain from urging that the cuts be restored. Democratic members of the House Appropriations Committee were able to use this confusion of loyalties to some advantage in their sniping at the Harding Administration. U. S., Congress, House, Naval Subcommittee of the Committee on Appropriations, *Hearings on Navy Department Appropriation Bill for 1924,* 67th Cong., 4th Sess., 1922, November 14, 1922, H. R. 13374.

such a reduction would mean discontinuing our Caribbean squadron, Yangtze River and South China patrols, and the Naval Forces Europe, retention of which was obviously desired by the State Department and commerce-conscious congressmen. Under further pressure the Navy Department admitted that the foreign squadrons could be kept and the problem of operating them with fewer men solved by putting six battleships and many submarines and destroyers on standby status. Secretary of the Navy Denby warned the Appropriations Subcommittee that the figure submitted (65,000 men) was "wholly inadequate in the estimation of the department to properly man the United States Navy. It will necessitate leaving ships of vital importance out of the battle line. The ratio established in the naval treaty . . . under the personnel allowance of 65,000 . . . will be reduced to 2½-5-3. . . . I need not comment on the extra-ordinary spectacle thus presented."[4]

The protests of the Navy Department did not go unheeded, and within two months Representatives Thomas Butler of the Naval Affairs Committee and Patrick H. Kelley of the Appropriations Subcommittee were forced to compromise at a level of 86,000 enlisted men.[5] Their aim in attempting heavy personnel reductions did not escape the Navy. In a letter to an old friend the president of the Naval War College, Rear Admiral William S. Sims, took stock of the situation:

I believe that the Congress understands exactly what they are doing. I believe they understand that cutting down the personnel will render the navy entirely insufficient as a fighting machine, in comparison with the other navies concerned, but I believe they think that in doing this they are carrying out the uninstructed will of the people . . . [who] do not understand the significance of the measures proposed. They do

---

[4]U. S., Congress, House, Naval Subcommittee of the Committee on Appropriations, *Hearings on Navy Department Appropriation Bill for 1923,* 67th Cong., 2d Sess., March 10, 13, 1922, H. R. 11228, pp. 347-54; Secretary of the Navy (Denby) to the Chairman of the House Appropriations Committee (M. B. Madden), Washington, March 18, 1922, *ibid.,* pp. 363-64.

[5]For reaction throughout the country against the heavy personnel cuts see "To Put Our Navy Into Third Place," *The Literary Digest,* April 8, 1922, pp. 17-18. The National Security League on April 12, and the United States Chamber of Commerce on April 14, 1922, both resolved against heavy naval personnel cuts. See letters in U. S., Department of State, Files 811.30/121, 122, Archives.

understand the pressure of taxation and they are strongly inclined to favor any measures which they think will materially decrease it.[6]

Fortunately for the Navy the drastic measures attempted in Congress were not repeated, though naval enlisted strength did not rise above 90,000 men until 1936. Obviously legislators were trying to encourage further international naval reductions by example rather than by treaty, a gesture that gained very little support from the naval establishment.

While examining the personnel needs of the Navy, the committees did not consider enlisted men alone. Ship and shore base complements were scrutinized minutely to determine whether they were overloaded with officers. The personnel of staffs, bureaus, and offices were culled to see whether reductions could not be effected, and even members of the 1922 Naval Academy graduating class were threatened with a return to civil life instead of billets in the Navy. However, Congressional probing generally showed the Navy to be actually underofficered, and the subject was dropped.[7] The ten years that followed saw the Navy constantly urging an increase in its regular line officer allowance, but no significant increase was permitted until the middle 1930's.

The 1922 investigations of naval personnel needs were symptomatic of Congressional committee sentiment toward other parts of the Navy. Every class of ship was examined to determine whether money should be appropriated for its operations, and a characteristic attitude was taken toward mine layers and mine sweepers. The Naval Affairs Committee wondered why such vessels were necessary in peacetime and showed general skepticism in regard to the value of training for their crews. The use of transport vessels as fleet flagships was attacked as an extravagance, though fleet commanders thought it desirable to remain free of the battle force itself when engaging in maneuvers, to permit thinking in terms of "forces" rather than individual units. The practical result of such Congressional pressure was to have the commanders and their staffs riding in obsolete coal-burning cruisers while

---

[6]William S. Sims to Fullam, Newport, March 23, 1922, William F. Fullam Papers, Box 262, LCMD.

[7]U. S., Congress, House, Naval Subcommittee of the Committee on Appropriations, *Hearings on Navy Department Appropriation Bill for 1924,* November 15, 1922, H. R. 13374, pp. 52-92.

maneuvering with oil-burning battleships. Eventually the fleet commanders returned to quarters aboard their battleships, but only after the old coal-burning cruisers were exhausted. Few admirals were sorry to see the Navy scrap such relics as *Huron, Birmingham,* and *Rochester.*[8]

The extensive hearings of 1922 were gale warnings for the Navy; it could expect very little in future appropriation bills under the subhead "Increase of the Navy." Yet, there was considerable work ahead if the Navy was to hold up its end of the 5-5-3 ratio system. Thirteen of the eighteen battleships needed considerable modernization. Except for the ten postwar *Omaha* class cruisers, the Navy had no modern vessels in this badly needed category. There was a superabundance of destroyers, but a slightly heavier type, the "destroyer leader," was considered imperative. Again, the Navy possessed a great many serviceable submarines, but it lacked high-speed, long-range vessels to cruise with the fleets. And, finally, there was a great deal of naval interest in acquiring modern aircraft carriers in order to test their value with the fleet. If all of these desires were satisfied, the naval establishment would be much larger, in view of the demand for crews to man the new construction and shore facilities to service them. Herein lay the roots of Congressional parsimony, and here one can find the answer, in part, for Congressional interest in naval limitation conferences.

From 1922 to 1931 both the Navy and Congress showed considerable interest in the American battleship fleet. To Congress the eighteen battleships allowed the United States by the Washington Five-Power Treaty were a drain on the taxpayer. To the Navy the battleships were the "backbone of the battle line"—the "heart of the fleet." It was these ships upon which the Navy depended to carry war to Japan's shores. Any tampering with the battleship fleet would make the successful prosecution of such a Pacific war infinitely more difficult, especially in view of inadequate bases in the Far East.

---

[8]U. S., Congress, House, Committee on Naval Affairs, *Hearings on Sundry Legislation, 1922-23,* February 17, 1922, pp. 322-27. In February, 1922, the transport *Columbia* was the flagship of the Commander-in-Chief United States Fleet, *Huron* was flagship of the Asiatic Fleet, *Birmingham* was the flagship of the Pacific destroyer squadron, and *Rochester* was the flagship of the destroyer squadrons in the Atlantic. *Ibid.,* February 14, 1922, pp. 256-69.

In dollars and cents the eighteen battleships represented a heavy annual expense. To be properly manned they required approximately 20 per cent of the enlisted strength of the Navy or an annual payroll of approximately $16,000,000. Over the years each vessel was charged, on the average, with $100,000 per year of repair and alterations, or an expenditure of $1,800,000 for all battleships.[9] Steaming an average of 20,000 miles per year required large supplies of oil, and annual gunnery practice was costly. Thirteen of the eighteen ships had undergone major modernization at approximately $6,000,000 per vessel, and by 1931 the most modern of the eighteen vessels, *Colorado* (1923), *West Virginia* (1923), *Maryland* (1921), *California* (1921), and *Tennessee* (1920), were requiring additional expenditures, averaging $1,000,-000 per vessel, for new antiaircraft batteries.[10] With battleship upkeep charges always before them, some congressmen sought a cheaper means of national protection.

Though put on the defensive from time to time by attacks from air power advocates, the Navy had a positive view which it consistently presented concerning the value and utility of battleships. Sea power, as any Naval War College graduate was quick to point out, consisted of three elements, all interrelated and none of which could be omitted, namely: the fleet, the merchant marine, and the naval bases.[11] Compared with Great Britain the United States was woefully weak in merchant marine and naval bases; therefore, the fleet was of vital importance if the United States was to maintain a ratio of equality with Great Britain. Were the battleships eliminated, the British would possess an overwhelming superiority in modern cruiser strength, and even Japan would be more powerful. The theoretical ability of the

---

[9]These figures represent a digest of information obtained from the published *Hearings* on each annual naval appropriations bill for the years 1922-31. An average of 86,000 enlisted men per year was used with an average pay of $890 per year.

[10]U. S., Congress, House, Naval Subcommittee of the Committee on Appropriations, *Hearings on Navy Department Appropriation Bill for 1928,* 69th Cong., 1st Sess., November 22, 1926, H. R. 15641, pp. 366-67.

[11]A full exposition on this can be found in a letter to Secretary of State Stimson from the president of the War College. Rear Admiral J. R. P. Pringle to Henry L. Stimson, Newport, November 29, 1929, D/S, File 500.A15A3/472, Archives.

British to convert some of their merchantmen to fast, armed raiders made their merchant marine superiority a marked menace to the United States and further emphasized the critical importance of the battleship fleet.[12]

From both a strategical and tactical viewpoint the battleships were highly valued in naval planning. The Navy was wedded to the gun as the final arbiter of all battles. The battleship was designed to carry the gun into fighting range, and to stay in battle, owing to defensive superiority, until the enemy was sunk or driven off. In the colorful phrases of Assistant Secretary of the Navy Theodore Roosevelt, Jr., the battleship's role was thus portrayed in 1922:

> The capital ship forms the body of the Navy in the same way that the Infantry forms the body of the Army. In order to function properly both capital ship and Infantry have to have vitally necessary auxiliary or complementary arms, but nevertheless, both remain the body of our respective services, and in final analysis, the old maxim about the Infantry that I think was put forward by Napoleon and other numerous gentlemen in the past, holds true of the capital ship . . . "The Infantry is the Army—when the Infantry is defeated the Army is defeated!" . . . That, in my opinion, holds good of the capital ship in the navy.[13]

The Navy was therefore convinced that the battleship with its large caliber gun was the most important class of vessel, and planned its future accordingly. Time after time naval representatives spoke of future sea battles as if Tsushima or Jutland were to be repeated. Secretary Wilbur in 1924 told a House committee, "It is believed that modern naval engagements between first class powers, except in sporadic instances, will be fleet engagements . . . in the ultimate struggle

---

[12]Elaborations of this theme were presented by the General Board in preparation for the 1927 Geneva Naval Conference and by Rear Admiral Joseph Mason Reeves when consulted before the London Naval Conference of 1930. U. S., Navy Department, General Board No. 438, Serial 1347-12(b), May 13, 1927, OCNH; Memorandum—Reduction and Limitation of Battleships, January 22, 1930, Mark L. Bristol Papers, Box 99, LCMD.

[13][Rear Admiral] Thomas P. Magruder, *United States Navy* (Philadelphia: Dorrance and Company, 1928), chap. i, *passim*; U. S., Congress, House, Committee on Naval Affairs, *Hearings on Sundry Legislation, 1922-23,* February 20, 1922, p. 329.

for supremacy between great naval powers the issue will be determined by a battle between the fleets of the combatant nations."[14]

With the passage of time, there was increasing domestic and foreign pressure for further reduction in United States battleship strength. From the British, suggestions were generally for a reduction in ship size to about 25,000 tons maximum, and in gun caliber from the current 16-inch maximums to 13.5 inches. In time Japan joined in such requests, though the Imperial Navy advocated delay pending careful study. In the United States legislators and statesmen toyed with the idea of reduction, which the Navy Department continually rebuffed.[15]

In its "Naval Policy" the General Board had decided that the "General Building and Maintenance Policy" of the Navy should be, in part,

To make superiority of armament in their class an end in view in the design of all fighting ships.

---

[14]U. S., Congress, House, Naval Subcommittee of the Committee on Appropriations, *Hearings on Navy Department Appropriation Bill for 1926,* 68th Cong., 2d Sess., December 8, 1924, H. R. 10724, p. 611. See also the testimony of Rear Admiral Thomas P. Magruder in U. S., Congress, House, Naval Subcommittee of the Committee on Appropriations, *Hearings on Navy Department Appropriation Bill for 1929,* 70th Cong., 1st Sess., February 13, 1928, H. R. 12286, pp. 1184-1201.

[15]An explanation of the British views on battleships can be found in the opening statements of their delegation at the Geneva Naval Conference, in League of Nations, *Records of the Conference for the Limitation of Naval Armament* (Genève, 1927), pp. 19-23. The American Embassy in Tokyo was quite aware of Japan's problem in meeting the financial demands of its naval program. The ambassador noted a trend, over a period of time, of public encouragement for further capital ship expense relief. D/S, Files 500.A4b/346, Tokyo, July 8, 1926; 500.A15A1/683, Tokyo, April 10, 1928; 500.A15A3/376, Tokyo, October 22, 1929; LNC 250 Japan/47, Washington, January 11, 1930, Archives. The United States Navy's case can be found in U. S., Congress, House, Committee on Naval Affairs, *Hearings on Sundry Legislation, 1922-23,* February 16, 1922, pp. 301-2; House, Naval Appropriation Subcommittee of the Committee on Appropriations, *Hearings on Navy Department Appropriation Bill for 1925,* 68th Cong., 1st Sess., November 18, 1924, pp. 80-82.

To provide for greater radius of action in all classes of fighting ships.[16]

As a corollary to these principles the General Board had further counseled as a part of its "Peace Strategy of the Pacific" that "all vessels should be built to operate trans-Pacifically." Any such vessel armed with 16-inch guns, able to stand in a battle line with sufficient armor, and having a speed of 21 knots, would require a displacement of at least 35,000 tons. Lower tonnage would require the sacrifice of some key feature.[17] In view of pessimistic prophecies concerning Japan and the necessity of defending the Philippines from Hawaii, cruising radius could not be sacrificed. The lessons of Jutland, especially the loss of the three British battle cruisers, showed dramatically that protection was essential. Reduction of gun caliber would help very little because guns accounted for a mere 8 per cent of battleship tonnage. And, finally, speed could not be further reduced because the American battleship fleet was relatively slow, and speed was considered vital for the selection of fighting ranges or for escape, as the situation required.[18]

When battleship reduction was finally forced upon the Navy at the London Naval Conference of 1930, it accepted a reduction in numbers only and a holiday in the battleship replacements that were to have commenced in 1931.[19] This approach had been urged by the British at the Geneva Conference in 1927 and was eagerly agreed to by the Japanese at London. For Great Britain, Japan, and the United

[16]"U. S. Naval Policy," in U. S., Congress, House, Naval Subcommittee of the Committee on Appropriations, *Hearings on Navy Department Appropriation Bill for 1930,* 70th Cong., 2d Sess., 1929, H. R. 16714, p. 40.

[17]Navy Department, General Board, Report No. 425, Serial 1136, April 26, 1923; Report No. 438, Serial 1385, August 11, 1928, OCNH.

[18]This information was drawn from a series of memoranda of conversations between State Department officials and General Board officers preparatory to the London Naval Conference of 1930. D/S, Files 500.A15A3/333, 334, 336, October 22-25, 1929, Archives.

[19]LNC 252.21/31; memorandum by Admiral W. V. Pratt, [1930]; see also File 500.15A3/582a, Washington, January 3, 1930, Archives. The very influential Rear Admiral (Ret.) H. P. Jones agreed with Pratt's view completely. See memorandum for the Secretary of the Navy, February 13, 1930, Harold C. Train Log, Volume I. In possession of Rear Admiral (Ret.) Harold C. Train, Annapolis, Maryland.

States, the holiday meant that money deferred from battleship replacements could be spent on auxiliary replacements for Japan and Britain, and for attaining auxiliary parity, particularly in cruisers, by the United States.[20]

The Navy Department eventually insisted on capital ship modernization in all respects, for Army-Navy bombing tests in 1921 proved that aircraft could sink naval vessels under certain conditions. The destruction of the old battleships *Virginia* and *New Jersey* in September, 1923, again by aircraft bombs, clearly pointed out that two direct hits, or even near misses with 2,000-pound bombs, could put battleships out of commission. Destruction of *Washington* in November, 1924, by naval gunfire, mining, and bombs proved that modern post-Jutland battleships exhibiting new construction principles could absorb a great deal of punishment.[21] With the results of these tests available to them, a board headed by Admiral E. W. Eberle investigated the future of sea power in the light of aviation developments and reported in January, 1925:

> The battleship of to-day, while not invulnerable to airplane attack, still possesses very efficient structural protection, as shown by the experiments on the *Washington*. The battleship of the future can be so designed as to distribution of her armor on decks and sides, and as to interior subdivision, that she will not be subject to fatal damage from the air. . . . It can not be said therefore that air attack has rendered the battleship obsolete.

The Eberle board recommended immediate modernization of the six coal-burning battleships, *New York, Texas, Wyoming, Arkansas, Utah,* and *Florida.* Another seven, *New Mexico, Mississippi, Idaho, Pennsyl-*

---

[20]The chargé in Japan noted that the Japanese were quite enthusiastic for a capital ship building holiday. The Japanese were planning on spending 88 millions Yen per year for auxiliary replacements during the five years after 1932, and were anxious to avoid having to spend an additional 80 millions Yen per year for capital ship replacements. D/S, File 500.A15A3/376, Tokyo, October 22, 1929, Archives.

[21]Archibald D. Turnbull and Clifford L. Lord, *History of United States Naval Aviation* (New Haven: Yale University Press, 1949), pp. 200-203.

vania, Arizona, Oklahoma, and *Nevada,* should be modernized "as soon as possible."[22]

The work progressed steadily. The first authorization for modernizing was made in December, 1924, and the last in February, 1931. The principal undertaking during these years was the conversion of the six oldest battleships from coal to oil burners, the strengthening of decks to resist bombing, the installation of aircraft handling apparatus, the improvement of turret guns elevating mechanisms on seven ships, and the addition of "blisters" to all thirteen.[23] After reconstruction—within the naval treaties—was completed, most of the Navy's admirals felt that the American battleship fleet was equal to or superior to Great Britain's. Ability to operate in the Pacific Ocean was assured by the change to oil-burning equipment. This major improvement added several thousand miles to the steaming radius of the Battle Fleet, made maneuvering easier, and rendered virtually obsolete the flag-hoist signal of "coal burners to the rear."

Possibly the greatest naval worry of all to the Coolidge administration, and even more so to Hoover's, was that the battleship fleet would require replacements in the not very distant future. By only the most arduous effort had the Navy Department been able to get eight new cruisers to supplement the ten modern cruisers in commission—twenty-five short of the number considered necessary.[24] In September, 1927, with the time for the first battleship replacement to be laid down less than four years away, Secretary of the Navy Wilbur asked the General Board to prepare a five-year building program for presentation

---

[22]"Report of Special Board (on) Results of Development of Aviation on the Development of the Navy, January 17, 1925," in Navy Department, *Information concerning the U. S. Navy and Other Navies* (Washington, 1925), pp. 153-54.

[23]"Blisters" or "bulges" were watertight compartments added below the waterline to the exterior of older vessels to provide additional protection against torpedo attack or near misses from aircraft bombs.

[24]Roger K. Heller, "Factors Influencing Naval Construction in the United States, 1922-1929" (unpublished Master's thesis, University of California, 1952), pp. 66-71. The estimated needs of the Navy in cruisers was a fairly fluid figure, but by December, 1929, Rear Admiral M. M. Taylor was asking for 43 cruisers in all. Director of War Plans Division to the Secretary of the Navy (Adams), December 21, 1931, Mark L. Bristol Papers, Box 116, LCMD.

to Congress. With the goal in mind of getting its auxiliaries laid down before heavy appropriations were necessary for capital ships, the General Board suggested the following schedule:[25]

	1929	1930	1931	1932	1933	Cost
Battleships	—	—	2	2	1	$ 185,000,000
Cruisers	5	5	5	5	5	425,000,000
Destroyers	—	—	5	13	13	105,400,000
Destroyer Leaders	4	4	1	—	—	45,000,000
Submarines	7	7	7	7	7	175,000,000
Carriers	1	1	1	1	1	95,000,000
Floating Drydock	1	—	—	—	—	350,000
						$ 1,030,750,000

After considerable consultation between the Secretary of the Navy, the Director of the Budget, and President Coolidge, a bill was drafted which met the auxiliary problems but completely evaded the question of battleship replacements. This measure would be the heart of a five-year building program, though no time limit was set upon it:[26]

Light Cruisers	25	$ 425,000,000
Destroyer Leaders	9	45,000,000
Submarines	32	160,000,000
Aircraft Carriers	5	95,000,000
	71	$ 725,000,000

Representative Thomas S. Butler introduced legislation (H. R. 7359) embodying this program, but the bill contained a clause allowing the President to suspend it in whole or part if a naval conference were called. Wilbur denied an allegation that the measure was designed to create a paper navy, and stated that it was the view of all concerned with the preparation that it was basically to be a five-year plan, although some units might not be constructed for as many as twenty

[25]Navy Department, General Board, No. 420, Serial 1358, the Secretary of the Navy (Wilbur) to the General Board, September 20, 1927; General Board, Report No. 420-2, Serial 1358, September 27, 1927, OCNH.

[26]U. S., Bureau of the Budget, File "Navy Department. Increase in Navy #1," Box 7; the Secretary of the Navy to the Director of the Budget, November 17, December 13, 1927; the Director of the Budget to the Secretary of the Navy, December 14, 1927, Archives.

years. Wilbur's testimony was readily seconded by his assistant secretary, T. Douglas Robinson, who reiterated the five-year idea. The President, he said, desired the following to be laid down the first year: one carrier, five cruisers, four destroyer leaders, and seven submarines.[27]

Public reaction to the 71-ship bill (H. R. 7359) was instantaneous and noisy. The cost of replacing the current navy outraged many newspapermen, and widespread comment favored considering another naval limitation conference. In view of these protests Chairman Butler of the House Naval Affairs Committee readily admitted,

> In all my experience in Congress . . . I have never known such widespread protest to be registered against any measure under consideration or about to be considered. These letters and telegrams, all voicing opposition to the bill we now have before us, come from all over the United States. They represent all classes. They are not confined to professional pacifists.[28]

A direct result of this outburst was the introduction of H. R. 11526 on February 28, 1928, authorizing the construction of fifteen cruisers and one aircraft carrier.[29] The voice of the people and the caution of the Director of the Budget had thus drastically modified the General Board's replacement program of September, 1927.

Once H. R. 11526, with its fifteen cruisers and one carrier, had passed the legislative hurdles, the Navy Department again reminded the President of the need for battleship replacements, due to begin in two years. A forecast in terms of authorizations and appropriations was sent to the Director of the Budget, and it was dutifully sent on to President Hoover. The figures showed in a rather shocking manner

---

[27]U. S., Congress, House, Committee on Naval Affairs, *Hearings on H. R. 7359,* 70th Cong., 1st Sess., January 12, 13, 1928, pp. 579-82, 677. The secretaries were supported by Admiral C. F. Hughes, Chief of Naval Operations, who was most interested in getting the ships in the water as soon as practicable. *Ibid.,* pp. 671-95.

[28]Quoted in "The 'Big-Navy' Congressman Hears from Home," *The Literary Digest,* March 3, 1928, pp. 10-11; see also "Billions Now Asked For A Huge Naval Program," *ibid.,* January 28, 1928, pp. 12-13; "Admiral Plunkett's War With England," *ibid.,* February 11, 1928; "Parlous State of Navy Increase" (editorial), *Army and Navy Register,* February 18, 1928.

[29]U. S., Congress, Senate, Committee on Naval Affairs, *Hearings on H. R. 11526,* 70th Cong., 1st Sess., p. 1.

what could happen when defense expenditures were deferred consistently as had been done in the years after 1922:[30]

NEEDED TO ROUND OUT THE FLEET		COST
Aircraft Carriers	4	$ 80,000,000
Destroyer Leaders	9	45,000,000
Submarines	32	160,000,000
Destroyers	19	58,600,000
Tenders, repair ships, drydocks, etc.		10,000,000
New authorizations needed		$ 353,600,000
Battleship replacements	15	555,000,000
Total new authorizations needed		$ 908,600,000
Balance due on 15 cruisers and 1 carrier authorized February 13, 1929		262,200,000
Cost of contemplated 12-year program		$1,170,800,000

To meet these requirements the Director of the Budget's annual appropriations estimate for "Increase of the Navy" called for between 100 and 150 millions of dollars yearly for ten years. Beginning in fiscal 1932 it was estimated that for ten years the Navy would require an annual appropriation of $450,000,000 to $500,000,000—over $100,-000,000 more than the average appropriations for the years 1922-29.[31]

The solution to this economic and political problem was to be a diplomatic one. The London Naval Treaty of 1930 delayed battleship replacements until 1937 and reduced the cruiser strength of other nations to a point where the United States could build to meet them without a tremendous strain on the American taxpayer. The *quid pro quo* for this solution was to be a new treaty navy that did not at first suit the Navy Department, and what appeared to be the virtual abandonment of naval support for American Far Eastern interests.

---

[30]This memorandum was found in D/S, File 811.34/391; memorandum from the Director of the Budget (Lord) to President Hoover, April, 1929, Archives.

[31]Memorandum from the Director of the Budget (Lord) to President Hoover, April, 1929, D/S, File 811.34/391, Archives. A listing of naval appropriations for the years 1921-31 may be found in U. S., Congress, House, Naval Subcommittee of the Committee on Appropriations, *Hearings on Navy Department Appropriation Bill for 1932,* 71st Cong., 3d Sess., January 14, 1931, H. R. 16969, p. 1.

Throughout this period the Navy never lost sight of the element indispensable to Pacific operations—large ships. Its battleships were modernized for increased capacity to absorb punishment under fire. Owing to structural changes which allowed higher elevation for turret guns, the American battleship fleet approached genuine parity with the British and a true superiority of 40 per cent over the Japanese. And the conversion of the six oldest battleships to oil burners almost doubled their cruising radii, thereby reducing the gap in naval bases between Honolulu and Manila. Hence, since it had become even more essential for those vessels operating in consort with the battleship fleet to be equally "long-legged," a demand arose within the Navy for the heavier 10,000-ton cruiser.

While battleships were the heart of the fleet, there were many other naval vessels in it of great significance, particularly cruisers. To the public, however, those magnificent mastodons were *the fleet,* and to the average naval officer the high point in his career was to hold a "battle wagon" command in the Battle Fleet.[32] Because of the new concentration of American naval power in the Pacific after 1919 the Navy Department became increasingly concerned with rounding out the fleet, that is, adding to the battleship divisions and squadrons the number of cruisers considered necessary to make the Battle Fleet effective. To the naval officer at sea the need for cruisers was immediately recognizable, but to the congressman and his constituency this need was not nearly so evident.

At the conclusion of the Washington Naval Conference the United States Navy had on its lists twenty-three cruisers built (all before 1912) and ten building. It also possessed some 302 destroyers and 113 submarines—with the allowed eighteen battleships, an impressive

---

[32]The service viewpoint on the importance of battleships was adequately stated by the Commander-in-Chief of the United States Fleet when he noted: "The battleship, or ship of the line, is the backbone of the fighting fleet. The fleet is built around this type." Admiral J. V. Chase, "Fleets: Their Composition and Uses," in U. S. Naval Institute, *The Navy and Its Relation to the Nation* (Annapolis, 1930), p. 13; see also Yates Stirling, *Sea Duty* (New York: G. P. Putnam's Sons, 1939), p. 196; Henry A. Wiley, *An Admiral From Texas* (Garden City: Doubleday, Doran & Company, 1934), pp. 194-95; Elting E. Morison, *Admiral Sims and the Modern American Navy* (Boston: Houghton Mifflin Company, 1942), p. 292.

array of naval power.[33] But unfortunately the twenty-three cruisers constructed before 1912 were superannuated. None was capable of cruising in formation with the ten *Omaha* class cruisers under construction. They were more than ten knots slower on the average, had a smaller volume of firepower, and could not compare with their more modern counterparts in cruising radius. Because they were coal-burning vessels, they were unable to work effectively with oil-burning battleships. By 1922 the Navy was using some of these older cruisers on foreign stations such as Manila, Constantinople, and London, and other cruisers were being used as flagships, but it was difficult to keep them in operating condition. They were constantly going into and out of commission as others of their class suffered casualties. Eventually, as in the case of *Pueblo,* the cost of reconditioning became so prohibitive that keeping them in commission was economically unfeasible.[34]

Congress, even with the repair bills before it, in the years after the Washington Conference was not sympathetic about the cruiser problem. In their desire to whittle naval appropriations, legislators looked suspiciously at the cruisers and even threatened to deprive the Navy of a few of its seagoing relics. They questioned the need for flagships or for more cruisers. The admirals, some said, ought to transfer their flags back to the battleships. Further complications arose as the *Omaha* cruisers neared completion in 1922, and the Navy Department found it needed more appropriations to finish the job, for labor and materials costs had risen considerably since the vessels were begun, and delay in itself was expensive. These requests did nothing to endear the

---

[33]Navy Department, *Ships' Data U. S. Naval Vessels: July 1, 1922* (Washington, 1922), 425 pp.

[34]U. S., Congress, House, Naval Subcommittee of the Committee on Appropriations, *Hearings on Navy Department Appropriation Bill for 1926,* 68th Cong., 2d Sess., November 17, 1924, p. 68; U. S., Congress, House, Naval Subcommittee of the Committee on Appropriations, *Hearings on Navy Department Appropriation Bill for 1927,* 69th Cong., 1st Sess., December 9, 1925, H. R. 7554, pp. 53-54; Hector C. Bywater, *Sea Power in the Pacific* (2d ed.; Boston and New York: Houghton Mifflin Company, 1934), pp. 121-25; Navy Department, *Annual Reports of the Navy Department for the Fiscal Year 1923* (Washington, 1924), p. 77.

Navy to the legislative branch and the watchdog Bureau of the Budget.[35]

Behind such Congressional opposition to the creation of a modern and balanced navy undoubtedly lay the Navy's failure to convince either Congress or the public that such a fleet was necessary. Blinded somewhat by the success of the Washington Conference, foreseeing no war in the near future (in fact the abolition of war "as an instrument of national policy" was just around the corner), and receiving few requests for more money from the executive branch outside of the Navy Department, Congress and its constituency rather justifiably dealt with the Navy in a most parsimonious manner. When there were threats to the international equilibrium, as existed in 1924, the reaction in Congress was not for more ships but for another naval conference.

In the post-World War period the Navy mission, in the event of war, was to secure command of the sea and then to exercise it— a traditional Mahan concept. If the expected war with Japan were to occur, a concentrated United States Fleet would bring the Japanese battle fleet to action or drive it into hiding. Once Japan's main fleet had been destroyed or neutralized, then its commerce would be driven from the sea. The key to accomplishing this feat was to assemble a more powerful force at a point where the enemy navy must engage or seek refuge. Until 1931, the heart of this striking force was conceded to be the battleship, but critical to the line of battleships were the combatant auxiliaries: cruisers and destroyers.[36]

How to use cruisers with fleet formations was the subject of constant development through the years after the Washington Conference. There had been enough battle action in the period since modern armored cruisers had taken to the sea that evaluation and careful consideration of a cruiser doctrine was possible. As a result of this constant

---

[35]U. S., Congress, House, Committee on Naval Affairs, *Hearings on Sundry Legislation, 1922-23,* 67th Cong., 2d, 3d, 4th Sess., 1923, pp. 73-74, 759, 1619-20; U. S., Congress, Senate, Committee on Naval Affairs, *Hearings on S. 1808,* 68th Cong., 1st Sess., January 16, 1924, pp. 48-50.

[36]In an essay that the Naval Institute's Board of Control considered significant and important for the times, these concepts were clearly presented; see Lt.(jg) William Webster, "The Cruiser," *United States Naval Institute Proceedings* (April, 1926), pp. 607-20; see also Samuel P. Huntington, "National Policy and the Transoceanic Navy," *ibid.* (May, 1954), p. 487.

study, practice, and "game-board" work at the Naval War College, it was concluded that cruisers, when operating with the fleet, played their most significant role as scouts and in working with the fleet destroyer flotillas.[37]

As a fleet scout the commanding officer of a cruiser sought out the enemy fleet, fought through the outer defense screen, ascertained the composition of the main body, and conveyed the information to his own fleet commander. During the 1920's this mission was made easier by scouting aircraft, and information was more easily relayed as radio communication equipment was improved. This work was best handled by cruisers because of their high speed in heavy seas and their fighting ability. Destroyers, however, were forced to share this burden in the American Navy because of the shortage of cruisers. Yet the cruisers were compelled to play another important role by defending the fleet against reconnoitering enemy cruisers. In this defensive function the destroyer was distinctly limited, for its primary weapon was the torpedo, not the gun.[38]

Of equal importance to the fleet was the work done by cruisers when working with destroyers. Because of their superior armament cruisers were used to protect destroyers when attacks were made against enemy capital ships. In this supporting role cruiser fire was directed against defensive cruisers, or if by chance these were engaged, then the cruisers maintained a harassing fire against the battleships' secondary batteries. Again, the cruiser had the opposite function of defending the battleships against destroyer attacks through gunfire against the attacking destroyers and their cruiser escorts. Here rapidity and volume of fire were all important if the destroyer attacks were to be broken up. Nevertheless battleships and their heavy-caliber rifles were

---

[37]Commander H. S. Howard, "Light Cruisers," *United States Naval Institute Proceedings* (September, 1926), p. 1735; also Webster, *op. cit.*, p. 616; Magruder, *United States Navy,* chap. ii, *passim.*

[38]Webster, *op. cit.*, pp. 607-20; Howard, *op. cit.*, pp. 1735-45. Fairly clear statements of the uses of cruisers were made by Secretaries T. Roosevelt, Jr., in May, and Curtis Wilbur in December, 1924. U. S., Congress, Senate, Committee on Naval Affairs, *Hearings on H. R. 8687,* 68th Cong., 1st Sess., May 31, 1924, pp. 14-17; House, Naval Subcommittee of the Committee on Appropriations, *Hearings on Navy Department Appropriation Bill for 1926,* 68th Cong., 2d Sess., December 8, 1924, pp. 615-16.

to be the ultimate determinants of success. The cruiser's mission was to contribute to victory in establishing the much-sought-after "command of the sea"; once this was attained the cruiser then assumed a role of primary importance, but not before.[39]

In "exercising command of the sea" the Navy visualized a dual role for its cruisers: attack upon enemy merchant shipping and defense of our own merchant marine. According to Navy Department representatives the United States needed cruisers of the maximum size allowable under the treaties in order to fulfill their mission of commerce protection. Admirals liked the 10,000-ton cruiser armed with 8-inch guns, and after 1922 the Navy Department and General Board gave very little consideration to any other type.[40] The 7,500-ton *Omaha* cruisers would be used for operation with the fleets when cruising in formation and to a limited extent for advanced scouting, but the bulk of the advanced scouting and all commerce work would fall to the heavier cruiser. The American public and Congress were told that British and Japanese merchantmen could be armed with 6-inch guns and become corsairs capable of challenging American convoys guarded only by the lighter cruisers,[41] and that since American foreign trade by

---

[39]Lieutenant H. J. Wright, "Discussion on 'The Cruiser,'" *United States Naval Institute Proceedings* (June, 1926), pp. 1175-76. An important study on cruisers and destroyers in action can be found in Holloway H. Frost, *The Battle of Jutland* (Annapolis: U. S. Naval Institute, 1936), pp. 208-45 and 367-77. A thorough discussion of using cruisers with the Battle Fleet to obtain command of the sea was made by the president of the Naval War College for the benefit of his associates at the London Naval Conference in January, 1930. Memorandum by Rear Admiral J. R. P. Pringle, January 28, 1930, [Commander] H. C. Train Log, Vol. I.

[40]In March, 1922, the Navy policy toward cruisers was: "To complete 10 light cruisers of the *Omaha* class now building. To replace all old cruisers by building 16 modern cruisers of 10,000 tons displacement carrying 8-inch guns. . . ." Navy Department, General Board, Report No. 420-2, Serial 1108, March 29, 1922, OCNH. In October, 1928, the policy was rewritten and stated *re* cruisers: "Cruisers—To support the Fleet and protect our commerce, replace all old cruisers with modern cruisers of 10,000 tons displacement carrying 8-inch guns. . . ." "U. S. Navy Policy, October 6, 1928," in U. S., Congress, House, Naval Subcommittee of Committee on Appropriations, *Hearings on Navy Department Appropriation Bill for 1930,* 70th Cong., 2d Sess., 1929, p. 40.

[41]Navy Department, General Board, Report No. 438, Serial 1347-7(c), April 25, 1927, OCNH; see also memorandum of a conversation with Rear

1929 was approximately equal to that of Great Britain, the United States deserved cruiser parity with Britain and 40 per cent superiority over Japan.[42]

When discussing cruiser needs, the representatives of the Navy placed heavy emphasis upon the desirability of having ships capable of cruising long distances because of the lack of adequate base facilities in the Pacific Ocean and other parts of the world. It was in view of this requirement that the long-ranging 10,000-ton cruiser was justified, yet the more important, though seldom emphasized, reason for the large cruiser was the desire for a ship capable of mounting the 8-inch gun.[43] When faced with the suggestion of building cruisers of 10,000 tons armed with 6-inch rifles, the Navy would have none of it. When naval constructors showed conclusively that the 8-inch-gun vessel was a poor fighting machine due to the lack of "corresponding protection," the Navy Department still stood by its 8-inch guns.[44] The argument of trade defense against heavier cruisers and armed

Admiral Andrew T. Long, October 22, 1929, D/S, File 500.A15A3/333, Archives. Admiral Long was a member of the General Board at the time, and a specialist in naval limitation problems.

[42]Navy Department, General Board, Report No. 438, Serial 1347-1(a), April 21, 1927, OCNH; "For a Huge Fleet—Steel or Paper?" *The Literary Digest,* January 7, 1928, pp. 12-14; see particularly Henry Cabot Lodge, "The Power of the U. S. Fleet," in U. S. Naval Institute, *The Navy and Its Relation to the Nation* (Annapolis, 1930), pp. 43-49.

[43]D/S, File 500.A15A3/333, memorandum of a conversation with Rear Admiral Andrew T. Long, October 22, 1929, Archives. Particularly illuminating is the reprint of a talk made by Captain Frank H. Schofield, a General Board member, given at the Naval Academy Post-Graduate School in October, 1922. Captain Schofield paid particular attention to the importance of having cruisers armed with 8-inch guns and capable of cruising in the far reaches of the Pacific. He noted that the decision to insist on the heavier cruiser was arrived at prior to the Washington Conference. Frank H. Schofield, "Lecture, The General Board and the Building Programs," October 14, 1922, Navy Department, Record Group 45, Box 580 UP, Archives.

[44]See the testimony of Rear Admiral Hilary P. Jones before the House Naval Affairs Committee, *Hearings on H. R. 7359,* 70th Cong., 1st Sess., February 2, 1928, pp. 1207-8. Full arguments against the 8-inch-gun cruiser were presented in 1930 by Captain H. A. Van Keuren; see memorandum by Captain H. A. Van Keuren, February 26, 1930, D/S, LNC 252/27; LNC 110.022/5, January 28, 1930, Archives.

merchantmen mounting 6-inch guns was used over and over again to justify what became derisively known as the "tin clad." Yet even the analyses based on trade defense were fairly hollow to the naval strategist of the day.

In his earliest writings Captain Mahan had theorized that a nation with a large merchant marine invariably possessed a strong navy establishment; yet he also knew that a nation which possessed a navy without merchantmen was "like a growth which having no root soon withers away." In the 1920's, when the American merchant marine was one-half that of Great Britain, and when the United States carried only one-third of its own foreign trade,[45] the Navy position seemed to contradict Mahan's; it was requesting a large number of cruisers to protect a somewhat insignificant merchant marine. Furthermore, even in American circles, commerce raiding was admitted to be more a nuisance than a positive threat to a nation which had gained control of the sea. And by the 1920's British experts were enunciating a related strategic principle: The threat of commerce raiding was in inverse ratio to the volume of trade—the heavier the volume, the less threatening the raider.[46] This maxim of Sir Julian Corbett was vividly substantiated when German surface raiders were eliminated during the first year of the World War and submarine raiders later neutralized, not by cruisers but by destroyers. Such lessons could not have been lost upon the American Navy. Why, then, did the Navy choose to dissemble in presenting its case for the 10,000-ton 8-inch cruiser?

One striking fact was evident to the Navy during the 1920's: The United States was falling behind the other major naval Powers in the

---

[45]Captain A. T. Mahan, *The Influence of Sea Power Upon History 1660-1783* (25th ed.; Boston: Little, Brown & Company, 1918), pp. 87-88; Lodge, "The Power of the U. S. Fleet," in U. S. Naval Institute, *The Navy and Its Relation to the Nation*, p. 47.

[46]Mahan never felt that commerce raiding was an important determinant in an international struggle. He noted that "The evidence seems to show that even for its own special ends such a mode of war is inconclusive, worrying but not deadly; it might almost be said that it causes needless suffering." Mahan, *Influence of Sea Power on History 1660-1783*, p. 136. Julian S. Corbett, *Some Principles of Maritime Strategy* (2d ed.; London: Longmans, Green & Company, 1919), pp. 249-55.

construction of cruisers, particularly the heavier 8-inch-gun type vessel. But publicity in this regard generally led to cries of concern over renewed "competitive" naval building; the Washington Conference theoretically had laid the specter of competitive armaments to rest.[47] The Navy, therefore, had to base its desire for more cruisers on some other form of need that would prove inoffensive both at home and abroad. Unfortunately the concomitant web of contradictions to some extent weakened its case.

At the very heart of the Navy's problem was its seldom voiced—and publicly unacceptable—premise that the next war would be fought on the Pacific between the United States and Japan. Instead of warmongering, the Navy chose to speak of its duty to defend the Philippines—even though it considered them indefensible—and to oppose Filipino independence. The department felt the Philippines were most important as a naval base for the defense of American Far Eastern trade and interests—somewhat evanescent future possibilities in Oriental markets. Fortunately for the Navy few congressmen questioned the real need for commerce defense against enemy raiders, although a few like Senator Hugo Black of Alabama did wonder whether the Philippines and American Far Eastern trade were really worth the cost of a Navy.[48] Finally, the Navy was never able to state its strongest case: American Far Eastern policy was evolved by the executive branch of the Government, to which the Navy also belonged. What became the less direct approach—but infinitely simpler in application—was to put all comparisons in terms of Great Britain and to base all needs for cruisers on grounds of trade defense.[49] To most Americans war with Great Britain was unthinkable, and thus Britain could be used as a

---

[47]"The Peril of Renewed Naval Rivalry," *The Literary Digest*, December 27, 1924, pp. 5-7; "The President's Naval Victory in Congress," *ibid.,* January 22, 1927, pp. 8-9; "For a Huge Fleet—Steel or Paper?" *ibid.,* January 7, 1928, pp. 12-14.

[48]U. S., Congress, Senate, Committee on Foreign Relations, *Hearings on Treaty on the Limitation of Naval Armaments,* 71st Cong., 2d Sess., May 16, 1930, pp. 115-17.

[49]This approach was advocated by Captain (Ret.) Dudley W. Knox in his 1929 "Honorable Mention" Naval Institute Prize Essay; see Captain Dudley W. Knox, "The Navy and Public Indoctrination," *United States Naval Institute Proceedings* (June, 1929), pp. 479-90.

handy whipping boy by the Navy. The immigration problems with Japan were too explosive to offer a similar arrangement. Furthermore, in returning to the concept of trade defense, the Navy could speak in terms of a tried and true *raison d'être* hallowed by Mahan: The merchant marine was a basic element of sea power, and the nation must have a navy to defend it.

But neither the nation nor its congress was dedicated to the proposition that navies were really necessary. During the years 1921-31 the American public looked hopefully to three naval conferences which it expected would reduce the world's navies—perhaps eventually to the millennial point of extinction. While America was by no stretch of imagination a nation of pacifists, there were plenty of taxpayers. Each could anticipate that naval reductions would mean tax decreases; each could also hope that every vessel scrapped or blueprint shelved would lessen the possibility of future wars. In many ways the Navy worried more about such a national outlook than it did about Congressional miserliness.

6

Diplomacy Through a Porthole:
The Geneva Naval Conference Failure

IN THE YEARS following the Washington Conference there was an increasing interest throughout the world in further meetings to finish the work left undone in 1922; nothing had been accomplished toward the limitation of naval combatant auxiliaries (cruisers, destroyers, submarines). In the absence of international restraint Japan began construction of five cruisers in 1922 and five more in 1924. Great Britain responded in 1924 by laying down five 10,000-ton cruisers carrying 8-inch guns. The Congress of the United States reacted similarly by authorizing the construction of eight cruisers in December, 1924, though the keel of the first vessel was not laid until October 27, 1926. By the end of 1928 the United States had laid down eight 10,000-ton 8-inch cruisers (later called heavy cruisers); Great Britain had laid the keels for fifteen cruisers, all carrying the 8-inch rifles; and Japan had begun fifteen cruisers, eleven of which carried 8-inch armament.[1] All three countries justified the construction in terms of replacements for older vessels, or need to "round out the fleet."

With the passage of time the American public brought considerable pressure to bear on Presidents Harding and Coolidge to call another conference to end the ruinous naval rivalry. Partisan political leaders like the perennial Democrat William Jennings Bryan and Republican Senator William E. Borah suggested that America might

---

[1]Benjamin H. Williams, *The United States and Disarmament* (New York and London: Whittlesey House, 1931), p. 162.

cancel the European war debts were the trans-Atlantic nations to disarm on land and sea. To Senator Borah, a leading figure on the Foreign Relations Committee, "the fight for disarmament [was] the fight for civilization."[2] Similar feelings were expressed through resolutions in the House of Representatives by Congressmen Hamilton Fish, Jr., and Frederick C. Hicks, but neither received encouragement from President Coolidge or Secretary of State Hughes.[3] In view of heavy demands for more cruisers in 1924, President Coolidge started a counteroffensive by declaring in his annual message to Congress that he believed "thoroughly in the Army and Navy, in adequate defense and preparation. But I am opposed to any policy of competition in building and maintaining land or sea armaments."[4] With the satisfactory negotiation of the Locarno treaties and the imminent establishment of the League of Nations Preparatory Commission for the Disarmament Conference, President Coolidge, in his December, 1925, message, admitted satisfaction with European efforts toward land disarmament, but suggested that the United States would be even more interested in matters of naval limitation.[5] The end product of this steady pressure was the issuing of invitations to the Geneva Naval Conference by the State Department on February 10, 1927.

Throughout Europe the State Department representatives reported considerable interest in the naval rivalry of the period. However, there was even greater concern in Europe over problems resulting from the Versailles settlements. The general attitude observed was that once the reparations and war debts were paid and boundary

---

[2]Bryan to W. E. Borah, August 5, 1922, William Jennings Bryan Papers, Box 45, LCMD. Bryan concluded: "I think the debt is worthless and will never be paid. If we can use a worthless debt to buy a priceless peace secured through disarmament . . . I think the offer is worth making." Borah to C. M. Lincoln, Washington, December 21, 1923, William E. Borah Papers, Box 237, LCMD.

[3]Representative F. C. Hicks to President Coolidge, Washington, May 28, 1924, U. S., Department of State, File 500.A12/9; Representative Hamilton Fish, Jr., to the Secretary of State, February 9, 1924, File 500.A12/-, Archives.

[4]U. S., The President, *Message of the President of the United States to Congress, December 3, 1924* (Washington, 1924), p. ii.

[5]"Message of the President of the United States to Congress, December 8, 1925," *Foreign Relations, 1925*, I, xii-xiii.

adjustments at such places as the Ruhr and Alsace were made, an international conference on naval problems would be possible. By the end of 1925 many in Europe felt the time was ripe for naval negotiations, though some nations agreed with the extreme French view that the Old World had done well without American assistance and could continue to do so.[6] More important, though, from the American position was the British interest in further naval limitation; this interest by the fall of 1926 had turned to a strong support for any naval conference that might be called by Coolidge.

In Japan the official attitude toward another naval conference varied, although in general there was widespread support for another one; as early as 1924 the naval ministry and foreign office were planning the Japanese position. Though the governments usually supported the idea of further limitation, the naval ministries from 1923 to 1930 presented serious obstacles to a satisfactory meeting. The naval ministers continually pressed for what was ultimately to be the Japanese position; and they insisted that Japan could never agree to any naval treaty that did not allow a ratio of 10-10-7 in auxiliaries and did not limit British construction at Singapore. The American embassy watched the determined effort to prepare Japanese public opinion to support these naval demands and to discredit the probable American position. Newspapers effectively played up naval statistics that were patent fabrications, to show the Japanese man in the street that Japan was greatly inferior to America in sea power, even in cruisers.[7] But despite the efforts exerted by the naval ministries, the

---

[6]Editorial response in Paris to the 1927 Geneva Conference invitations was generally unfriendly. Typical was the attitude in the *Leconte Matin*: "The League of Nations is studying the problem of disarmament in general and there would be serious objections to dividing this problem between two distinct conferences." D/S, File 500.A15A1/7, Paris, February 11, 1927, Archives. This view is amplified in F. P. Walters, *A History of the League of Nations* (2 vols.; London: Oxford University Press, 1952), I, 366-69.

[7]D/S, File 500.A12/30, Tokyo, November 28, 1924. A particularly gross example of using misleading statistics occurred in the *Japan Advertiser* for December 2, 1924. The Embassy sent in translations of the "Proceedings of the Lower House of the Diet" from the *Official Gazette* for February 10, 1925. A Mr. K. Michi spoke at length for an increase in the Navy's budget and noted in passing: "The United States at present has five aircraft carriers

Japanese Government entered the Geneva Naval Conference with a wholesome desire to end naval rivalries; money saved could be better spent to amortize the cost of reconstruction in Japan following the earthquake of 1923.[8]

The United States Navy took little comfort from the international movement for the further limitation of naval armaments, for war with Japan and preparations for that war remained foremost in the minds of the naval planners. Presidential economy and Congressional apathy had stalled efforts at rounding out the fleet, and by June, 1927, when the Geneva Naval Conference convened, the United States had begun but two cruisers (*Pensacola* and *Salt Lake City*) of the eight authorized in December, 1924. When the London Naval Conference of 1930 met, the Navy had the 1924 cruisers on the stocks, but no keels had been laid for the fifteen cruisers authorized in February, 1929.[9] In 1927 and 1929 there was undoubtedly fear in naval circles that those cruisers still on the drafting tables would be bargained away by the diplomats. The ghosts of the thirteen post-Jutland capital ships scrapped at the Washington Conference still haunted the Navy. New destroyers, submarines, and aircraft carriers were badly needed in the fleet; but the most pressing exigency was cruisers, the international competition in the building of which precipitated the naval limitation conferences.

The viewpoint of the Navy Department toward limiting naval armaments can be ascertained. Because the Navy is an executive agency, it is responsible to the President through his Secretary. However, the Navy as an institution does not suffer the Presidential liability of having a four-year term of office, and hence is theoretically above

---

[U. S. had three], while Japan has two under construction [Japan also had one carrier operating], the United States has fifteen airships [one blimp, one dirigible, four balloons], while we have but two. . . ." D/S, File 500.A12/47, Tokyo, March 4, 1925, Archives.

[8]D/S, File 500.A12/33, Tokyo, January 23, 1925; Secretary of State (Kellogg) to President Coolidge, Washington, December 16, 1926, File 500.A15A/258a, Archives; see also Hector C. Bywater, *Navies and Nations: A Review of Naval Developments Since the Great War* (London: Constable and Company, Ltd., 1927), pp. 273-74.

[9]U. S., Navy Department, *Ships' Data U. S. Naval Vessels: July 1, 1931* (Washington, 1931), pp. 22-23.

partisan politics. This freedom and its institutional structure make it possible for the Navy to have certain views, attitudes, and policies which can be continuous regardless of the party or President in office. For example, the likelihood of war with Japan profoundly affected naval thinking during both Wilson's administration and Harding's. Similarly, the views of the Navy toward limitation of armaments and disarmament had a certain continuity from the times of Mahan.

As the principal exponent of sea power in his day, Mahan had little use for the international attempts to limit naval armaments. Before the first Hague Conference of 1899, to which he was an American delegate, Mahan had written that national armaments do not necessarily beget international conflicts. "The immense armaments of Europe are onerous; but nevertheless, by the mutual respect and caution they enforce, they present a cheap alternative, certainly in misery, probably in money, to the frequent devastating wars which preceded the era of general military preparation." At the Hague Conference he refused to commit the United States to abstention from using certain weapons because he regarded all instruments of warfare as essentially barbarous—there was no reason to single out poisonous gases or submarine torpedoes.[10]

To Mahan wars were virtually a concomitant of civilization, and it would be folly for any nation to fall behind in the armaments race. His views had some impact on military thinking through the years.[11] Wars were seldom eagerly sought by naval officers, but they certainly expected conflict and prepared for it.

---

[10]A. T. Mahan, *The Interest of America in Seapower, Present and Future* (Boston: Little, Brown & Company, 1898), p. 104; Francis Duncan, "Mahan—Historian With A Purpose," *United States Naval Institute Proceedings* (May, 1957), pp. 499-501; Merze Tate, *The United States and Armaments* (Cambridge, Mass.: Harvard University Press, 1948), p. 44; see also Miss Tate's *The Disarmament Illusion: The Movement for a Limitation of Armaments to 1907* (New York: The Macmillan Company, 1942), pp. 285-86, 291-92.

[11]Robert E. Osgood, *Ideals and Self-Interest in America's Foreign Relations: The Great Transformation of the Twentieth Century* (Chicago: University of Chicago Press, 1953), p. 36; Charles Carlisle Taylor, *The Life of Admiral Mahan* (London: John Murray, 1920), p. 101; Captain W. D. Puleston, *Mahan* (New Haven: Yale University Press, 1939), p. 318.

By January, 1921, the General Board had been asked whether naval limitation without reduction of land armaments was practicable, and in replying the board expounded at length the value of armament limitation: Each nation had to decide for itself what its defensive needs were for "She cannot place unlimited trust in the perpetuity of common interests and mutual good will between her and her neighbors." Further, a nation which enters into limitation agreements places its security in the hands of others and to a great extent limits the growth of the nation's power. International ethical standards are no higher than those professed by individuals within nations, and there is no unlimited trust of one's fellow man at the personal or corporate level in this country. Therefore, the board could see no reason to trust other nations with American national interests:

> Each nation must decide for itself what proportion of its military establishment shall be assigned to the land and what to the sea. This proportion depends upon the relative importance which the nation attaches to threatened dangers by land or sea. It is certain that no nation will willingly surrender an existing military supremacy whether it be on the land, on the sea, or both. Putting it candidly, the nations are not willing to place implicit trust in each other and it must be acknowledged that a study of international history affords good reasons for that unwillingness.[12]

The accomplishments of the Washington Conference in the field of naval limitation and reduction vitiated the thesis of the General Board but did not alter the attitudes of those who felt limitation was dangerous. Year after year the *Proceedings* of the Naval Institute carried articles urging less thought on limitation and more on the creation of a stronger Navy. Most writers assumed the inevitability of war and the need for a substantial protective naval force. Many agreed with Admiral Edward W. Eberle, Chief of Naval Operations: "We are not a warlike nation. We do not want war and we seek in every honorable way to avoid it, but we must be prepared, for unpreparedness is a potent invitation to war."[13] Some returned to Mahan's views

---

[12]Navy Department, General Board No. 446, Serial 1052, Washington, January 19, 1921; original in Thomas J. Walsh Papers, Box 268, LCMD.

[13]Captain H. E. Yarnell, "The Peace Time Service and Costs of the Navy," *United States Naval Institute Proceedings* (September, 1924), pp. 1504-6; Rear Admiral (Ret.) W. L. Rodgers, "Military Preparedness Necessary to the

that it is the strong who determine the destinies of the world—the Big Four Powers drew up the Treaty of Versailles. They argued, "If America remains a first naval power she can call more [Washington] Conferences. Without a first Navy we cannot call another one, and even if invited to attend one called by a first naval power, she will wait outside until called in."[14]

The Navy was plagued by what Assistant Secretary Theodore Roosevelt, Jr., called "soft-headed pacifists" who urged that the United States set the world an example by disarming first. To the conservative and suspicious naval mind this was "Alice in Wonderland reasoning" that courted disaster at the hands of foreign aggressors or international revolutionists.[15] Navy men pointed to the travail of China as an example of what could befall a disarmed and impotent nation, and the Naval Institute advised its members to speak out on the importance of the Navy to America.[16] Admiral Hilary P. Jones, then Commander-in-Chief of the United States Fleet and later an American delegate to the Geneva and London conferences, summed up the Navy's sentiments in an address before the National Republican Club at New York City:

> All over the world today we are in contact with foreign peoples. We are seeking markets; our fellow citizens working abroad are in competition with citizens and subjects of foreign states. Large amounts of capital and the livelihood of a large number of people are involved.

Economic and Social Welfare of the United States," *ibid.* (October, 1925), p. 1850; Admiral Edward W. Eberle, "A Few Reflections on Our Navy and Some of Its Needs," *ibid.* (September, 1924), p. 1403.

[14]Captain L. M. Overstreet, "Danger of Disarming America," *ibid.* (September, 1924), p. 1497.

[15]U. S., Congress, House, Committee on Naval Affairs, *Hearings on Sundry Naval Legislation, 1922-23,* 67th Cong., 2d, 3d, 4th Sess., February 15, 1922, p. 282. Captain Luke McNamee, "Keep Our Navy Strong," *United States Naval Institute Proceedings* (May, 1923), pp. 801-10.

[16]The editor of the *Proceedings* wrote a "Foreword" to the May, 1923, issue and advised the membership that "Upon us, as naval officers, falls a part of the burden of keeping before the country at large the interests of the Navy, which are identical with the interests of the United States. Officers of the Navy are called upon to deliver addresses on the Navy, its position, its relation to the country's foreign and domestic policy, its mission in furthering that policy, and its needs." "Foreword," *ibid.* (May, 1923).

In the adjustment of the difficulties which are bound to arise from these conditions the United States should enter the discussion as an equal and not as an inferior. And we shall be inferior if we neglect our Navy. We must be strong enough to make arbitration more profitable to our competitor than fighting.

I beg of you not to be deceived by a dream of external peace. The same passions, prejudices and selfishness exist today as have always existed, and will have similar results. This nation of ours achieved its independence, preserved its integrity, and extended its borders by force. If we are to enjoy the fruits of the labors of our fathers, we must be prepared to use the same instrument.

"A Just Man Armed Keepeth His House in Order."[17]

After 1922 Navy spokesmen often advocated construction as a means of achieving naval limitation. A significant number of officers supported the ratio system established at Washington in the hope that Congress would build up to an established ratio in all categories of ships. When the Congress did nothing, important naval publicists like Captain (Ret.) Dudley W. Knox supported the move for another conference because he believed that once a ratio was established for auxiliaries, the people would support construction to meet the ratio. Secretary Curtis Wilbur amplified this viewpoint before the Senate Naval Affairs Committee and pointed out that the United States must build cruisers if it was to obtain limitation. According to Wilbur, Admiral Jones, and others, neither Great Britain nor Japan would reduce its fleet in order to create a ratio, and therefore the United States must build.[18] The logic was sound.

The strategy of the Navy in its program to round out the fleet took it down two divergent paths. On the one hand some officers bitterly resisted any further reduction of the Navy and emphasized in the most nationalistic tones the value of sea power to America; rather

---

[17]Admiral Hilary P. Jones, "A Just Man Armed Keepeth His House in Order," *ibid.* (May, 1923), pp. 764-65.

[18]"Professional Notes—'Second Naval Parley Needed, Says Expert,'" *ibid.* (February, 1925), pp. 339-40; U. S., Congress, Senate, Naval Subcommittee of the Committee on Appropriations, *Hearings on Navy Department Appropriation Bill for 1928,* 69th Cong., 2d Sess., January 12, 1927, H. R. 15641, p. 98. Admiral Hilary P. Jones concurred with the Secretary's views and told the committee that ships on paper, authorized but not appropriated for, would carry very little weight in a naval conference, *ibid.,* pp. 128-30.

than reduction or limitation, the country needed a stronger naval establishment. On the other hand those closer to the President and more responsible to public pressure could see the possibility of creating a balanced fleet were Congress merely to authorize and appropriate for auxiliaries in such numbers that the Navy would be at parity with Great Britain and five-thirds superior to Japan. By following either path the Navy would be in a position to defend the United States and its Far Eastern interests.

The Three-Power Naval Conference called for June, 1927, offered a serious challenge to the American Navy. This was the first attempt by conference to limit or reduce naval armaments since the Washington meeting five and a half years previously, and the United States Navy was in no condition, materially or psychologically, to be limited. Attempts to create a balanced fleet were progressing at a tortoise pace; in fact, 1926 had seen naval appropriations reach their lowest level in the postwar years. On the international scene, though Japanese-American relations had shown no marked deterioration since the Pacific maneuvers of 1925, the General Board had found nothing to change its pessimistic attitude toward the island empire.[19]

From the day the invitations to the Geneva Conference were issued an atmosphere of futility colored the proceedings. All invitees were careful in their replies, showing concern lest they accept and all others reject the bids. The conference was almost aborted in February, 1927, when France and Italy declined to attend, but State Department optimism carried arrangements forward for a meeting of Great Britain, Japan, and the United States as host. The absence of France and Italy caused the Japanese to question the value of a naval conference, but American and British assurances restored Japanese confidence. All three Powers agreed that an attempt at limitation was worth the effort.[20]

---

[19]The General Board's views on the national policies of Japan were presented in Navy Department, General Board, No. 438, Serial 1347-1(a), dated April 21, 1927, OCNH.

[20]The proceedings of the Geneva Conference with initiating correspondence can be found in U. S., Congress, Senate, *Document No. 55,* 70th Cong., 1st Sess., "Records of the Conference for the Limitation of Naval Armament" (Washington, 1928), 220 pp. Hereafter cited as *Geneva Conference.* The

However, the Geneva Conference had little chance of success from the day of conception. Of all the finally destructive difficulties, none was more significant than the lack of adequate advance consultation.[21] Between the United States and Great Britain there were a few brief meetings but no definite exploration of either's position. Rear Admiral Hilary P. Jones appears to have represented the United States twice on hurried visits to the Admiralty offices, but the firmest commitment he received was "Great Britain accepted unqualifiedly the Washington ratio [5-5-3] as extended to all categories of vessels [cruisers, submarines, destroyers, etc.] as far as the United States and Great Britain are concerned."[22] There were a few exchanges of views between the Ambassador in London and the British Foreign Minister, but these were generally on matters of procedure rather than of substance. With Japan there was even less attempt made to determine viewpoints before the conference. The Ambassador in Tokyo discussed the forthcoming meeting with the Japanese Foreign Minister, but as in the case of Ambassador Houghton in London, Ambassador Mac-Veagh was not empowered to do more than discuss procedure. The same situation apparently existed between Japan and Great Britain.

Precisely why the State Department did not make better preparations for the conference is conjectural, but two reasons can be deduced from the evidence at hand. Actually a great deal was known about the probable positions of Great Britain and Japan at the conference, and it is possible that the State Department believed this knowledge sufficient. It was surmised, for example, that the British would insist upon having a large number of cruisers, ostensibly to protect lengthy

uneasiness in Japan was carefully described by the Ambassador in Japan in his monthly surveys of political developments in Japan, D/S, Files, 894.00/240 of March 14, 1927, and 894.00/252 of April 11, 1927, Archives.

[21]Benjamin H. Williams, *The United States and Disarmament* (New York and London: Whittlesey House, 1931), pp. 167-68; Tate, *The United States and Armaments*, pp. 145-46; Arnold J. Toynbee, *Survey of International Affairs, 1927* (London: Oxford University Press and Humphrey Milford, 1929), pp. 39-41.

[22]Memoranda by Rear Admiral Hilary P. Jones, American Embassy, London, November 10, 1926, D/S, File 500.A15A/258a; Rear Admiral Hilary P. Jones to the Secretary of the Navy, London, March 9, 1927, File 500.A15A1, Archives.

trade routes. That they favored the abolition of submarines and desired a lower tonnage limitation for the size of capital ships than the current 35,000 tons was also understood.[23] As far as Japan was concerned it was predicted by the embassy in Tokyo that the Japanese delegation would press for an increase above 5-5-3 if ratios were to be applied to combat auxiliaries. Also the Japanese would probably seek further limitation of naval bases, particularly at Singapore.[24]

A second possible reason for limited advance consultation lies in the nature of the conference itself. When issuing invitations President Coolidge clearly stated that any agreements reached were designed to supplement the work of the League Preparatory Commission for the Disarmament Conference and intimated that the accomplishments would undoubtedly be dealt with by the General Disarmament Conference. With this in mind, the conference was limited to naval matters, and the personnel of the delegations were generally chosen from those at Geneva or those familiar with the work of the Preparatory Commission, naval specialists familiar with the issues. This approach obviated the need for prior technical conversations, since the five invitees had been participating in the Preparatory Commission discussions, but it also discouraged any political discussions that might have paved the way for naval agreements.[25]

---

[23]The naval policies of Great Britain were analyzed by the Navy in Navy Department, General Board, No. 438, Serial 1347-1(a), dated April 21, 1927, OCNH. The State Department's analyses can be found in Memorandum by the Chief of the Division of Western European Affairs (Marriner), June 1, 1927, *Foreign Relations, 1927,* I, 42-43; the Secretary of State to the Secretary of the Navy, Washington, March 23, 1927, D/S, File 500.A15A1/137a, Archives.

[24]Japanese interest in limiting Singapore was carefully covered by Ambassador MacVeagh in his despatch, D/S, File 500.A15A1/58, Tokyo, February 13, 1927, Archives. An analysis of the Japanese views on changing the naval ratios was sent in by the naval attaché in Tokyo; see Naval Attaché (Tokyo) to the Office of Naval Intelligence (copy), Tokyo, June 13, 1927, in D/S, File 500.A15A1/261, Archives.

[25]Tate, *The United States and Armaments,* pp. 141-43. Professor Williams commented that Admiral Jones: ". . . as a naval expert was thoroughly familiar with the technical aspects of the subject [of naval disarmament] and entirely honest in his approach but he viewed the world through a porthole." Williams, *The United States and Disarmament,* p. 166.

American inability to bargain was of great significance when one seeks general causes for the failure at Geneva. At the Washington Conference the United States possessed a large fleet in being and was building fifteen capital ships. Such a program presented an adequate reason for other nations to seek agreement. At the Geneva Conference, on the other hand, the United States, hoping to limit combat auxiliaries, could negotiate only from weakness. In destroyers, as well as in submarines, the American Navy led the world, but in cruisers, where naval competition had been the greatest, the United States was miserably weak. In postwar construction she possessed ten cruisers armed with 6-inch guns, was building two 8-inch-gun cruisers, and had six cruisers authorized for which the keels had not been laid. In terms of cruisers under twenty years of age the position of the United States was even worse:[26]

Great Britain	48 built	14 building	= 62
Japan	23 "	6 "	= 29
United States	16 "	2 "	= 18

Because of the weakness in cruisers the Navy warned Congress in January, 1927, not to expect too much at Geneva, but congressmen, like many Americans, believed that America's great potential for cruiser building would be as effective as ships in the water when it came to reaching an agreement.[27]

Underlying the failure of the whole conference and contributing materially to the inability of the United States and Great Britain to agree was the problem of Japan. The majority of the accounts written concerning the Geneva Conference have consistently pointed up the clash between the British and American delegations, and these studies have generally agreed that Japan was the most cooperative of those

---

[26]See the table in Toynbee, *Survey of International Affairs, 1927,* p. 32. The table is entirely accurate except for the entry "U. S. A., cruisers building." The entry should read "2" instead of "5."

[27]The Norfolk *Virginian Pilot* echoed this sentiment when it stated that the United States had unlimited financial power to throw in the naval balance when limitation was discussed at Geneva. "Mr. Coolidge's Fight for Disarmament," *The Literary Digest,* March 26, 1927, pp. 5-7.

present seeking naval limitation.[28] But a more careful study of the evidence indicates that the Japanese Navy and the ubiquitous pressure of the Japanese Empire in the Far East on British and American planning were the shoals upon which the conference grounded.

The preconference study for the American position at Geneva had developed certain points upon which there could be little or no bargaining. Because the American representation consisted principally of naval officers, there was little likelihood or reason for it to depart from the studied judgments of the General Board. As a codelegate, Ambassador Hugh Gibson was in general agreement with Rear Admiral Jones; both construed their instructions to mean that the United States sought a technical treaty designed to limit those vessels not covered by the Washington Five-Power Treaty. There was no particular need, as they saw it, for political clauses in the finished protocol, and the American group was not chosen to accomplish such an end.[29]

By 1927 the General Board had decided that the 10,000-ton cruiser armed with 8-inch guns best suited America's needs. The weight of the cruiser was necessary to allow machinery for speed, the mounting of 8-inch-gun turrets, armor, and the fuel capacity to operate independently or with the Battle Fleet in the vast reaches of the Pacific Ocean. At the conference the delegates never went on record to state which of these characteristics was most important, but privately they agreed it was the 8-inch gun. A naval adviser in the delegation and director of the War Plans Division, Rear Admiral Frank H. Schofield, summed up the Navy's position in his diary:

---

[28]Williams, *The United States and Disarmament*, p. 177; Tate, *The United States and Armaments*, pp. 151, 152. Toynbee described the Japanese as "the most reasonable and the most detached of the three parties. . . ." *Survey of International Affairs, 1927*, pp. 22-23.

[29]Rear Admiral Hilary P. Jones to the Secretary of the Navy, August 16, 1927, Navy Department, File A19 (Disarmament) /EM-Geneva (270816), Archives. Though Admiral Jones had deliberately commented on the fine cooperation between the State and Navy department representatives at Geneva, there were dissenting opinions. Rear Admiral Frank H. Schofield felt that the delegation's legal adviser, Allen W. Dulles, had tried to undermine the Navy's position through political agreements. Rear Admiral F. H. Schofield, Diary, August 1, 1927, quoted in (Captain) Ben Scott Custer, "The Geneva Conference for the Limitation of Naval Armament—1927" (unpublished Ph.D. dissertation, Georgetown University, 1948), pp. 180-81.

To build cruisers of less gunpower [less than 8 inches] for our purposes would be highly ineffective, as at the point of tactical contact such cruisers might be outclassed (out-gunned) by the 8-inch cruisers of other powers. Our lines of communication in the Pacific are so long and the necessity for protecting them so urgent that we could not afford to depend upon protection of those lines with a 6-inch gun cruiser or with two or three small cruisers, when the convoy they were protecting might be attacked by 8-inch gun cruisers. So long as the 8-inch gun cruiser exists, it is to our interest and practically our necessity to limit construction of cruisers to vessels of this class.[30]

When the American delegation assented to dividing the cruiser category into 10,000-ton cruisers armed with 8-inch guns and a second class of cruisers of less tonnage, it refused to accept equipping the lighter cruiser with anything but the 8-inch gun. When the British mentioned a 10,000-ton cruiser carrying 6-inch guns, the suggestion was completely ignored.[31] Constantly before the American naval delegation was the fact that Japan already had eight cruisers built or building that carried 8-inch guns.

With Congressional parsimony in mind, the General Board had also decided prior to the conference upon an acceptable maximum of 400,000 tons in cruisers for the United States and Great Britain, preferably closer to 300,000 tons. This maximum was adhered to throughout the conference despite British protests—Great Britain had approximately 388,000 tons of cruisers built or building, and there was little chance she would consider scrapping some of those. Further, the Board believed that to allow the Japanese to have cruiser tonnage above 240,000 tons (60 per cent of 400,000 tons) would give them too many vessels in excess of their battle fleet needs, ships which could wreak havoc as raiders on American lines of communication to the

---

[30]Rear Admiral F. H. Schofield, Diary, June 28, 1927, quoted in Custer, "Geneva Conference," pp. 84-85.

[31]At the eighth meeting of the Technical Committee the American delegation consented to dividing the cruiser category into two classes but commented: "We do not see any reason for limiting the caliber of gun in the smaller class of cruisers to anything different from that in the larger [10,000-ton 8-inch] class." Memorandum, H. P. Jones, July 5, 1927, Navy Department, File A19 (Disarmament) /EM-Geneva (270816), Archives.

Far East.[32] Hence, the intransigence of the Navy on the matters of total cruiser tonnage and of arming all vessels with 8-inch guns made agreement at Geneva virtually impossible.

The problem of ratios also had been considered carefully by the General Board before the conference. It had decided that the Japanese could not be allowed any increase over their 5-5-3 ratio under any circumstances. In the eyes of the board the United States had been too liberal at the Washington Conference and "Having in view the above . . . believe that the 5-3 ratio in the cruiser class with relation to Japan represents the maximum concession that can be made to Japan in cruisers."[33]

Closely related to ratios was the problem of further limiting naval bases in the Far East. The Navy from top to bottom had resented the nonfortification clause (Article XIX) of the Five-Power Treaty and was not kindly disposed toward further concessions. The Japanese newspapers had given considerable space to the danger of Singapore and Pearl Harbor to Japan.[34] In view of this propaganda the General Board decided that the United States would never allow any restrictions on the Hawaiian base and preferred that Singapore not be discussed. Theoretically, limitation of Hawaiian fortifications was possible, but only if the Japanese agreed to reduce their navy to a point where an attack on the Philippines was unfeasible.[35]

These factors—insistence on the 8-inch gun for cruisers, a maximum of 400,000 tons in the cruiser category, no increase above the 5-5-3 ratio for the Japanese, and no further limitation of Pacific fortifications—represented points that could not be yielded to Japan under any conditions. The mission of the Navy was the protection of American interests in the Far East; the national policy of Japan, as seen by the General Board in the spring of 1927, was the "Political, commer-

---

[32]Navy Department, General Board, No. 438, Serial 1347-7(c), April 25, 1927, OCNH.

[33]*Ibid.*; see also, General Board, No. 438, Serial 1347-1(a), April 21, 1927, OCNH.

[34]The analysis of the Embassy's views on Japan and Singapore was sent in a despatch, D/S, File 500.A15A1/58, Tokyo, February 13, 1927, Archives.

[35]Navy Department, General Board, No. 438, Serial 1347-3(h), April 22, 1927; No. 438, Serial 1347-11(j), May 7, 1927, OCNH.

cial, and military domination of the Western Pacific." In this light the Navy's opposition to compromise at Geneva is understandable.[36]

The importance of Japan at the Geneva Conference is further demonstrated by examining the problems confronting the British Empire. As a Far Eastern Power Great Britian confronted strategic problems similar to those of the United States. British trade with China was greater than America's, and there were colonies, protectorates, and dominions requiring defense by the Royal Navy. Because of its world-girdling chain of naval bases, the British navy had found that small cruisers, averaging in the neighborhood of 5,500 tons and armed with the 6-inch gun, suited its needs admirably. Long cruising radius was not necessary, for it was never distant to the next naval base. British trade routes covered some 80,000 miles, and the Royal Navy, therefore, felt that a large number of small cruisers were necessary to protect those routes. From the viewpoint of the British it was highly desirable to eliminate or sharply restrict any vessels carrying guns in excess of six inches, otherwise they would have to match the construction of such cruisers with ships for which they had no genuine use.[37]

By January, 1927, the British were faced in the Far East with eight Japanese cruisers carrying 8-inch guns built or building. To meet this challenge the British laid down fourteen 8-inch-gun cruisers between 1924 and the opening of the Geneva Conference, and had in service four *Hawkins* class cruisers armed with 7.5-inch guns. However, the British were building cruisers carrying 8-inch guns, with one eye on the French and Italian navies, which had begun construction of six 8-inch type cruisers. In view of this competition the British delegation at Geneva set twelve cruisers of the 8-inch type as the maximum allowable for Japan. Beyond this, they believed, their Pacific dominions, Australia and New Zealand, would be imperiled. Furthermore, the stronger the Japanese Navy became, the more vessels the Royal

---

[36]Navy Department, General Board, No. 438, Serial 1347-1(a), April 21, 1927, OCNH.

[37]A full statement of the British position can be found in the minutes of the second plenary session held on July 14th at Geneva. See *Geneva Conference,* pp. 37-45. This was given earlier amplification at the third session of the Technical Committee on June 28, 1927; *ibid.,* pp. 120-31.

Navy would have to station in the Far East at the expense of protection of home waters.[38]

Another point upon which the British delegation was forced to stand firm was the Singapore naval base. Construction had been halted in 1924 during the MacDonald tenure, but with the return of the second Baldwin government, work was again continued. Britain considered the base to be of highest importance for British interests in the Far East and refused to entertain the idea of limiting its effectiveness. In this matter no voices concurred more loudly than those of the Antipodean delegates.[39] Fortunately for all concerned the Japanese never raised the issue at the conference, though both the American and British groups were expecting it.

The British came to Geneva prepared to discuss one other point on which they felt quite strongly. They wanted to reduce the size of battleship replacements and eventually hoped to reduce the number of battleships in commission.[40] The closer the nations came to abolishing the battleships, they felt, the more powerful Britain's large cruiser

[38]This maximum was inferred at the Jones-Beatty meeting of November 10, 1926, and was never departed from. D/S, File 500.A15A/258a, London, November 10, 1926, Archives. The same problem was discussed in private by the British and American delegations on July 6, 1927; see the Chairman of the American Delegation (Gibson) to the Secretary of State, Geneva, July 6, 1927, *Foreign Relations, 1927,* I, 74.

[39]An extremely valuable survey of empire-wide opinion concerning the Singapore Base can be found in Great Britain, "Singapore Naval Base," *Correspondence with the Self-Governing Dominions and India Regarding the Development of Singapore Naval Base: Command 2083, March 25, 1924* (London: HMSO, 1924), 15 pp. The defeat of MacDonald's government caused rejoicing in Australia and New Zealand because they realized that construction at Singapore would be resumed. "Australia and New Zealand Hail the British Elections," *The Literary Digest,* December 20, 1924, p. 19. An analysis of the Singapore problem was sent in from Singapore by the Consul General. He emphasized the size of the British stake in the Far East as a factor influencing the construction of Singapore. D/S, File 841.34546d/42, Singapore, May 2, 1927, Archives.

[40]*Geneva Conference,* p. 30. The Navy and State departments were against any reopening of the battleship question without France and Italy being present. *Foreign Relations, 1927,* I, 54-55, 97. Naval opposition to tampering with the Washington agreement on battleships is fully presented in Navy Department, General Board, No. 438, Serial 1347-12(b), May 13, 1927, OCNH.

fleet would become. Were all battleships abolished, then British cruiser preponderance in numbers, plus the large tonnage of merchant ships that could be armed with 6-inch guns, would give the British Empire absolute mastery of the seas and would certainly ease the problem of matching the Japanese fleet in the Far East.

Evidently the two English-speaking delegations were working basically toward the same objective. Both were anxious for the same reasons to reduce or limit Japanese power in eastern Asia. Maintaining the Open Door would benefit the United States and Great Britain, and both had dependencies in the Far East to protect. With battleship strength already closely limited, the British and American naval delegations were determined to allow no relative increase in Japanese cruiser power, particularly in 8-inch-gun vessels. Thus Japanese cruiser strength could not exceed 60 per cent of America's, nor could the total tonnage be more than 240,000. For the British a maximum of twelve 8-inch-gun cruisers was the most permissible for Japan. Neither the United States nor Great Britain would permit any tampering with the nonfortification agreement embodied in the Five-Power Naval Treaty, and the American delegation was prepared to back Great Britain if Japan broached the subject. Finally, at the conference the British and American naval delegations forced the Japanese to agree to the limitation of all submarines when the Japanese suggested that those less than 700 tons be unlimited. It was pointed out that such vessels were not designed merely for coastal defense; they could operate effectively against the American Philippines or the British trade routes to Southeast Asia.[41] In view of such unanimity between the naval advisers of Great Britain and the United States, it is surprising that they permitted the conference to fail.

Most obviously the Geneva Conference came to nothing because the United States and Great Britain could not agree on cruiser limita-

---

[41]The General Board had concluded before the conference that the submarine category should not be split, and therefore all submarines, regardless of tonnage, should be limited. The board felt that submarines could be used more effectively by Japan than by the United States, and therefore Japan should be closely limited to the 5-5-3 ratio. Navy Department, General Board, No. 438, Serial 1347-9(3), May 20, 1927, OCNH. The American delegation presented its view to the British privately. Memorandum, June 23, 1927, D/S, File 500.A15A1/315½, Archives.

tion. The American naval advisers insisted on having cruisers, with the exception of the ten *Omahas* in commission, capable of carrying 8-inch guns. They desired somewhere between fifteen and twenty-five cruisers of the 10,000-ton class, depending on whether the cruiser category was to have 300,000 or 400,000 tons allotted to it. They agreed to accept a small number of vessels, in addition to the *Omahas,* which would displace less than 10,000 tons, but the delegation was adamant on the right to arm them with 8-inch guns.[42] In submarines and destroyers they readily came to agreement with Japan and Great Britain.

The British position, developed by Admiral of the Fleet Earl Jellicoe, Delegate for New Zealand, consisted of the demand for approximately seventy cruisers and the right to parity with the United States in the 8-inch type vessel. During the second plenary session of July 14, Jellicoe proposed Empire requirements as a minimum of seventy cruisers, of which twenty-five would operate with the battle fleet and forty-five would be stationed at strategic points for trade protection. He told of his experiences as commander-in-chief of the Grand Fleet and the problems he had had with German raiders. "Once again I would reiterate that, if we found 114 cruisers insufficient during the Great War, are we not putting our requirements at the lowest possible figure when reducing this number to seventy?" At no time during the conference did the British recede far from this figure of seventy cruisers.

The American naval delegation's tonnage maximum of 400,000 made compromise impossible between the United States and Great Britain. The British felt they could meet this figure by having a cruiser fleet of seventy ships averaging slightly less than 6,000 tons per vessel, and these would necessarily be armed with 6-inch guns, owing to their size. When the American advisers demanded at least twenty-five 10,-000-ton 8-inch-gun cruisers, were the 400,000-ton limit used, there could be no meeting of the minds. If the British were to match the United States, they would require twenty-five large cruisers at a total of 250,000 tons; only 150,000 tons would be left for the other forty-five cruisers they needed. The British were further embarrassed because they could not allow the Japanese, within the 5-5-3 ratio, to have

---

[42]D/S, File 500.A15A1/442, Washington, July 19, 1927, Archives.

more than twelve 10,000-ton 8-inch-gun cruisers. This imposed a limit of twenty on the United States (200,000 tons), and would make it necessary for the British to squeeze fifty cruisers out of the remaining American maximum of 200,000 tons—again an impossibility. The conference therefore was adjourned with no agreement reached.

The Japanese, although failing to push their own desires vigorously at the conference, acted as a catalytic agent in their effect on the British and American viewpoints. The propaganda build-up before the meeting, demanding an improvement in the 60 per cent ratio and limitation at Singapore, had caused the American and British naval policy-makers to move to extreme positions and adhere to them. The United States required 8-inch-gun cruisers capable of operating across the 5,000 miles of water between the Philippines and Hawaii. This was a strictly naval viewpoint, formulated by men who believed war with Japan would eventually come to America and who had no faith in political arrangements to preserve the peace. The British had determined as early as November, 1926, that the Japanese could not increase their 8-inch-gun cruiser fleet beyond twelve ships. If the Americans insisted on more 8-inch-gun cruisers than the British considered safe, then the Japanese ratio had to be reduced, a patent impossibility in view of the Japanese demands for a higher ratio. Thus the Geneva Conference failed. Any future meeting would require a thorough exploration of each nation's problems before the opening of the first plenary session, but at least the civilian chiefs of the department, and the nation to some extent, had been alerted to the limitations of naval officers in diplomacy.[43] For the United States Navy the conference deadlock had gratifying results. Congress soon passed another cruiser authorization act giving the Navy fifteen more of its highly valued 10,000-ton cruisers and a new aircraft carrier.

The abortive Geneva Naval Conference resulted in two years of tense relations between the United States and Great Britain, but even within the charged atmosphere of those years, the goal of naval limitation never dropped from sight on either side of the Atlantic. For the

---

[43]This point was emphasized by Allen W. Dulles in a memorandum prepared for the State Department evaluating the causes for failure at Geneva. Memorandum by Allen W. Dulles, September 7, 1927, D/S, File 500.-A15A1/612½, Archives.

American Navy the conference failure had particularly beneficent results, a new naval authorization bill. In the longer run, however, the resulting naval act "for the increase of the Navy" also increased the desire in both countries for another try at limitation, which resulted in the London Naval Conference of 1930.

The refusal of the British delegation at Geneva to accept a maximum tonnage of 400,000 tons in cruisers apparently convinced President Coolidge of the need for more cruisers. In his annual message to Congress on December 6, 1927, Coolidge wrote:

> While the results of the Conference were of considerable value, they were mostly of a negative character. We know now that no agreement can be reached which will be inconsistent with a considerable building program on our part. . . .
>
> We have a considerable cruiser tonnage, but a part of it is obsolete. Everyone knew that had a three-power agreement been reached it would have left us with the necessity of continuing our building program.[44]

The General Board had already been at work preparing a study of the Navy's needs, and this was introduced by Representative Thomas S. Butler on December 14, 1927, as H. R. 7359. The immensity of the "71 Ship Bill" appalled economy-minded legislators and fulfilled the worst fears of some newspapers that the United States was about to begin vigorously competing in naval armaments.[45]

On the international scene the reaction to the "71 Ship Bill" was equally vociferous. In Amsterdam *De Telegraaf*, struck by the enormous cost of the proposed program, commented:

> A million guilders a day, Sundays included and that for five successive years—that is what the Government of the United States proposed to expend for expansion of its fleet. The first reaction of every peace-loving European is: "What a wealthy land, and how badly they spend their money."

In England there was concern but no rush to increase a British building program. According to the London *Times* the American program

---

[44]"Message of the President of the United States to Congress, December 6, 1927," *Foreign Relations, 1927,* I, vii-viii.

[45]"What the Failure of the Naval Conference Means," *The Literary Digest,* August 20, 1927, pp. 8-9; "How the Geneva Conference Hits Our Taxpayers," *ibid.,* August 27, 1927, p. 5.

should be taken seriously, though there was a tendency in some quarters to consider the bill as pure Yankee bluff. In many corners of the world there was a scoring of the United States on its inconsistency in attempting to outlaw war by agreement and launching a huge naval program.[46]

The substitution of the less costly "15 Cruiser Bill" (H. R. 11526) for the "71 Ship Bill" on February 28, 1928, cooled down many of the irate editorialists and caused the subject to drop almost from sight on the international scene, but in Congress the bill ran into innumerable delays and a barrage of opposition from sundry sources, pacifistic and political. Navy Representatives, who had tried to present the earlier bill as merely an attempt to lay out a sound replacement program, were somewhat astounded over the opposition to the more modest plan.[47] The cruiser bill was not voted in the spring of 1928, and succeeded in passing the following February only after Anglo-French negotiations in Europe increased sentiment for a stronger Navy as a wise investment.

During the spring of 1928 the French and British exchanged views on the method of limiting land and naval armaments, to make it possible for each nation to accept certain features of a draft plan for general disarmament being considered by the League Preparatory Commission. As matters stood before the initiation of the Anglo-French conversations, the British believed in limiting ships by closely described categories (cruisers, submarines, destroyers), whereas the French merely wanted each country limited by a total tonnage figure. The two nations also disagreed on how to limit land forces. The British wanted to limit soldiers on active duty and trained reserves as well,

---

[46]Translation from *De Telegraaf*, January 12, 1928, in D/S, File 811.-34/332, The Hague, January 14, 1928; clipping from the London *Times*, December 17, 1927, in D/S, File 811.34/316, London, December 20, 1927, Archives; "As the British View our Big-Navy Program," *The Literary Digest*, January 14, 1928, pp. 16-17.

[47]"Parlous State of Navy Increase" (editorial), *Army and Navy Register*, February 18, 1928, p. 150; "The Big-Navy Congressman Hears from Home," *The Literary Digest*, March 3, 1928, pp. 10-11; "Billions Now Asked for a Huge Naval Program," *ibid.*, January 28, 1928, pp. 12-13; "The 1928 Naval Building Program" (editorial), *Army and Navy Register*, March 3, 1928, p. 196; "Pacifist Enmity of Naval Defense" (editorial), *ibid.*, March 17, 1928, p. 244.

but the French insisted that only those soldiers "with the colors" should be restricted. By July 28 they reached agreement whereby the French position on nonlimitation of army-trained reserves and the British views on naval limitation were to be mutually supported. On July 30 the British Foreign Office sent out the text of the "Accord" to Washington, Tokyo, and Rome. The principal feature of the naval agreement was that ships should be limited in the following categories:[48]

1. Capital ships
2. Aircraft carriers
3. Surface vessels less than 10,000 tons and armed with guns greater than six inches
4. Ocean-going submarines over 600 tons

The American answer was a sharp refusal to enter into any negotiations based upon the Anglo-French agreement. The State Department called attention to the fact that the 10,000-ton 8-inch-gun cruiser was restricted while the smaller cruiser was wholly unlimited. The State Department also disliked the restriction of the larger submarine when the smaller vessel was unlimited. On the whole the State Department believed this Anglo-French accord would result in "the imposition of restrictions only on types peculiarly suited to the needs of the United States." In conclusion, the State Department maintained that "If there is to be further limitation upon the construction of war vessels so that competition in this regard between nations may be stopped, it is the belief of the United States that it should include all classes of combatant vessels, submarines as well as surface vessels."[49]

Possibly disturbing the United States Navy was Japan's satisfaction with the Anglo-French arrangement. Japanese newspaper opinion had not greeted the agreement with particular enthusiasm, though

[48]John W. Wheeler-Bennett, *Disarmament and Security Since Locarno 1925-1931* (London: George Allen & Unwin, Ltd., 1932), pp. 127-31; Walters, *A History of the League of Nations,* I, 371-72; Williams, *United States and Disarmament,* p. 179; Tate, *The United States and Armaments,* pp. 162-64; Great Britain, "Papers Regarding the Limitation of Naval Armament," *Miscellaneous No. 6 (1928): Command 3211* (London: HMSO, 1928), pp. 27-28.

[49]Mr. Houghton to Lord Cushenden, London, September 28, 1928, *ibid.,* pp. 34-38.

many recognized with the Osaka *Mainichi*: "The agreement may have prepared a way for Great Britain and France to resist America in matters of naval disarmament." The Government, however, replied to the British on September 29, 1928, and "expressed its concurrence to the purport of the present agreement." Baron Giichi Tanaka's answer did say that attention must be paid to the needs of other countries where the 8-inch-gun cruiser and submarines over 600 tons were concerned.[50] Japan's acceptance was natural in terms of its national defense needs. Japanese naval officers at the Geneva Conference had requested that the smaller submarines be unlimited, and furthermore, they had supported attempts to limit the numbers of the heavier cruisers to be allowed each country. For the United States Navy it was an uncomfortable situation—three countries agreed to limit the ships best suited to American needs.

Public concern in America at the "Accord" was based generally on two points. The French and the British had attempted to limit the heavier cruisers, even though the United States favored the 10,000-ton 8-inch-gun cruiser and none other. The lighter cruisers, with which the British navy abounded, were to be unlimited, and Great Britain, free to arm its horde of merchantmen with 6-inch guns, would thereafter be untouchable as a naval power. Even worse, in the minds of those unacquainted with naval affairs, evidence indicated that these negotiations had been consummated in secret—in an age of "open covenants, openly arrived at." Had it not been for William Randolph Hearst's *New York American* the world might never have known the whole story.[51]

The "15 Cruiser Bill" pending in Congress received a healthy push from President Coolidge on Armistice Day, 1928. He told an assembly of American Legionnaires that the United States had long coastlines, lengthy trade routes, and a large population to be protected, and therefore needed the large ocean-spanning 10,000-ton cruisers. "Having few fueling stations, we require ships of large tonnage, and

---

[50]Translation from Osaka *Mainichi Shimbun* (August, 1928), in D/S, File 894.00P.R./9, Tokyo, September 6, 1928, Archives; Mr. Dormer (Tokyo) to Lord Cushenden, September 29, 1928, Great Britain, *Command 3211,* 1928, pp. 38-39.

[51]Wheeler-Bennett, *Disarmament and Security Since Locarno,* pp. 136-37.

having scarcely any merchant vessels capable of mounting five or six-inch guns, it is obvious that, based on needs, we are entitled to a larger number of warships than a nation having these advantages." With obvious reference to the Anglo-French agreement he concluded, "It no doubt has some significance that foreign governments made agreements limiting that class of combat vessels in which we were superior, but refused limitation in the class in which they were superior. . . ."[52]

With this ringing reintroduction of the "15 Cruiser Bill" Congress buckled down to bringing the United States Navy up to date, and on February 13, 1929, passed H. R. 11526. The legislators, however, were unwilling to abandon all hope of naval limitation and inserted a provision in the Act which permitted the President to suspend construction of the fifteen cruisers and one carrier if an international conference for naval limitation were called. Though the Navy League of the United States had assured the legislators that the American press was 7.8 to 1 for the cruiser bill, and President-elect Herbert Hoover had given his approval to the measure, the public by February, 1929, was undoubtedly tired of the whole matter of cruisers and naval competition and looked forward to an end to the current naval race.[53]

The first four months of President Hoover's administration provided the world with the hope for an end to competition in naval

---

[52]"Coolidge's 'Call Down' to Europe," *The Literary Digest,* December 1, 1928, pp. 8-10. It is interesting to note that Coolidge's address was delivered just after the Navy Department released its newly revised "U. S. Navy Policy" in which it stated that the Navy would "replace all old cruisers with modern cruisers of 10,000 standard tons displacement carrying 8″ guns. . . ." The speech itself was carefully read for content by the Chief of Naval Operations, Admiral C. F. Hughes, Rear Admiral A. T. Long, then a member of the General Board and later a naval adviser at the London Conference of 1930, and by Rear Admiral H. P. Jones. All agreed that Coolidge should put in a "plug" for the 15-Cruiser Bill pending in Congress. "Around the World in 60 Years," unpublished manuscript in the Andrew T. Long Papers, p. 272, Southern Historical Collection, University of North Carolina.

[53]William Howard Gardiner to the Secretary of State, January 7, 1929, D/S, File 811.34/364, Archives. Herbert Hoover to Coolidge, Belle Isle, Florida, January 28, 1929 (telegram), Calvin Coolidge Papers, Box 375, File 4450, LCMD.

armaments. In his inaugural address the new President set a primary goal for his quadrennium by declaring, "Peace can be promoted by the limitation of arms, and by the creation of the instrumentalities for the peaceful settlements of controversies. I covet for this administration a record of having further contributed to advance the causes of peace."[54] How this record was to be achieved was not clearly indicated, although on April 22, 1929, Hugh Gibson gave evidence at Geneva that the work might be done through the General Disarmament Conference which was being carefully planned at that time. Gibson told the Sixth Session of the Preparatory Commission that the United States was willing to discuss naval limitation along category lines earlier proposed by the French. More importantly, the United States would not insist upon mathematical parity in all classes, cruisers included. A formula could be derived that would make it possible for some nations to have more tonnage than others, yet there would be equality of power.[55] This *démarche* by the United States provided many with the hope for a solution to the problem that had stalemated discussion at the Geneva Conference: Britain's insistence on a large number of small cruisers and America's demand for the 10,000-ton 8-inch-gun vessels.

Interest in Hoover's plans continued at a high pitch through the spring of 1929. In April Charles Gates Dawes's appointment as Ambassador to the Court of Saint James's received considerable notice in the newspapers at home and abroad. At Geneva Ambassador Hugh Gibson had quietly made plans for Dawes and the new British prime minister, J. Ramsay MacDonald, to discuss naval limitation, and in England Edward Price Bell, a prominent foreign correspondent highly trusted by the Administration at Washington, was doing his best to create a favorable press reception for the projected Dawes-MacDonald conversations.[56] On Memorial Day, 1929, President Hoover added a

[54]*New York Times*, March 5, 1929, p. 6.

[55]*New York Times*, April 23, 1929, p. 22; Wheeler-Bennett, *Disarmament and Security Since Locarno*, pp. 69, 143; Walters, *A History of the League of Nations*, I, p. 375.

[56]Drew Pearson and Constantine Brown, *The American Diplomatic Game* (Garden City, N. Y.: Doubleday Doran & Company, 1935), pp. 72-75. The work of Bell is given extended treatment in George V. Fagan, "Anglo-American

fillip to the mounting interest in disarmament by referring directly
to the new naval "yardstick":

> . . . to arrive at any agreement through which we can, marching
> in company with our brother nations, secure a reduction of armament
> but at the same time maintain a just preparedness for the protection
> of our peoples we must find a rational yardstick with which to make
> reasonable comparisons for their naval units and ours and thus main-
> tain an agreed relativity.
>
> So far the world has failed to find such a yardstick. To say that
> such a measure cannot be found is the counsel of despair; it is a
> challenge to the naval authorities of the world; it is the condemnation
> of the world to the Sisyphean toil of competitive armaments.[57]

These phrases, and the colorful picture of General "Hell-and-Maria"
Dawes with his underslung pipe, "talking turkey" with the new Prime
Minister, were heartening to many Americans and gave promise that
the two new administrations might save the world, given time.

Naval Relations, 1927-1937" (unpublished Ph.D. dissertation, University of
Pennsylvania, 1954), chap. ii. Dr. Fagan used the Edward Price Bell Papers
at the Newberry Library in Chicago, and obtained Hoover-Bell correspondence
from former President Hoover. See also Robert H. Ferrell, *American Diplomacy
in the Great Depression: Hoover-Stimson Foreign Policy, 1929-1933* (New
Haven: Yale University Press, 1957), pp. 73-75, and Elting E. Morison, *Turmoil
and Tradition: A Study of the Life and Times of Henry L. Stimson* (Boston:
Houghton Mifflin Company, 1960), pp. 319-20.

[57]"Address by President Hoover at the Memorial Exercises at Arlington
Cemetery," *Foreign Relations, 1929,* I, 113-16.

7

The State Department Takes the Helm:
The London Naval Conference

THE LACK of preparation that characterized the Geneva Conference was not duplicated in the months before the London meeting. On June 18, 1929, Ambassador Dawes delivered a speech before the Pilgrims Society in London which was taken to be the beginning of his by then highly publicized conversations with MacDonald. The speech itself contained little more than platitudes and generalizations, but two points of significance did emerge: The United States and Great Britain would not allow the issue of neutral rights to bog down the greater problem of eliminating competition in armaments, and statesmen, not naval officers, should guide the destinies of the nations when naval armaments were discussed. In keeping with the stated desire of both countries, even this introductory speech was discussed with the Japanese ambassador, Tsuneo Matsudaira, the French ambassador, and the Italian chargé. There was to be no *fait accompli* handed Japan or the other naval powers for their acceptance or refusal. Both MacDonald and Dawes insisted at all times that their conversations were exploratory, that a method of meeting the cruiser problem was being studied, and that quantities of tons, guns, or ships would not be absolutely decided on. This was to be the work of a later conference.[1]

---

[1]Charles G. Dawes, *Journal as Ambassador to Great Britain* (New York: The Macmillan Company, 1939), pp. 17-21. The Japanese were particularly touchy on the subject of being handed a *fait accompli*. See U. S., Department of State, File 500.A15A3/47, Tokyo, June 17, 1929, Archives. In Great Britain similar pressure was being exerted by Ambassador Matsudaira; Mr. A. Hen-

Upon the problem of whether naval officers or civilians should dominate in any future conference there was unanimity of thought. The narrow, technical line of reasoning that made agreement in Geneva impossible was not to be allowed. Secretary of State Stimson felt strongly on this subject; he and the British ambassador concurred, "In general the service man was bound to look at these questions from the standpoint of possible war . . . while the civilian statesman representing the people of the country might be able and willing to take chances which the professional service man could not take." Dawes reiterated this view in his Pilgrims Society address when he commented that a naval officer could hardly favor "a partial destruction of his own navy. The proper pride of a naval officer's life is his navy." The Japanese ambassador in Washington was similarly in agreement with Sir Esme and Stimson: "There would be small hope of agreement if the work was left to the naval representatives. . . ."[2] Hence the Admiralty and the Navy Department were consulted on technical matters, but queries addressed to them were generally for information to buttress a prior political decision.

The diplomats took one other lesson of Geneva to heart, the problem of the publicists and press relations in general. Once the decision for a conference was made in July, 1929, MacDonald and Stimson generally gave the press very little into which it could sink its teeth. Carefully worded written statements to the newspapermen were the general rule. Later, at the London Conference, the dearth of solid information caused the newspapermen to react as bitterly toward Stimson as they had toward the Geneva delegation. In August, 1929, the story of William Baldwin Shearer's public relations work during the Geneva Conference came to light when he sued his retainers for expenses. Shearer had been hired as an agent of Bethlehem Shipbuilding Corporation, Newport News Shipbuilding Corporation, and American Brown Boveri Corporation, to work against naval limita-

---

derson to Sir J. Tilley (Tokyo), London, July 9, 1929, in E. L. Woodward and Rohan Butler (eds.), *Documents on British Foreign Policy 1919-1939,* Second Series (2 vols.; London: HMSO, 1946), I, 7-8, 20-21. Hereafter cited as *DBFP,* 2:I; see also *Foreign Relations, 1929,* I, 130-31.

[2]*Foreign Relations, 1929,* I, 112, 125-27.

tion during the Geneva meeting.[3] For Hoover and Stimson this information that publicity devices had been employed against naval limitation came as a windfall, and the President noted this when he wrote his Secretary of State: "I think it would be desirable if some inquiry could be made as to the character of this lawsuit. . . . It may be a useful public example and one that we will need before we are finished." This revelation and the Senate investigation that followed undoubtedly weakened the efficiency of big-Navy pressure groups during the sessions of the London Conference.[4]

The most significant result of the preconference discussions between Prime Minister MacDonald and Ambassador Dawes was their arrival at a settlement on the allotment of cruiser tonnage between the United States and Great Britain. Though the agreement was not final in details, the premises involved were of vast importance in determining the naval relationships among the United States, Japan, and Great Britain.

As at Geneva, the controlling factor in the British-American discussions was Japan. Britain again insisted upon its basic position: that the Japanese could never possess more than twelve 8-inch-gun cruisers. The Admiralty had decided that empire needs could be satisfied with fifteen of the 8-inch-gun cruisers, and therefore hoped that the United States would be satisfied with eighteen. MacDonald candidly wrote in a personal letter to Ambassador Dawes that were the problem confined to their two countries alone the matter of cruisers could be quickly settled "because my country had not been assuming that yours was a potential enemy." But complicating the ability to agree was the fact that "There are three other naval powers armed very effectively and in a position to damage my country and the people for whose existence I am responsible." And finally, he pointed out, "There are our dominions with their needs and their fears. . . ." The American desire for

---

[3]"Betrayed by Mr. Shearer" (editorial), *The Journal,* Milwaukee, Wisconsin, August 26, 1929; clipping in D/S, File 500.A15A1 Shearer/44, Archives. This particular file is rather rich in information on William Baldwin Shearer for the period August-December, 1929.

[4]The President to Stimson, Washington, August 30, 1929, D/S, File 500.A15A1 Shearer/44; memorandum from the Division of Western European Affairs, October 3, 1929, File 500.A15A3/250, Archives.

twenty-three of the 10,000-ton cruisers would give Japan sixteen, at a 70 per cent ratio—which would be one more than the British—and at 60 per cent would allow Japan fourteen—which was two more than the dominions could allow.[5]

The Japanese left no one in doubt on how they felt about the ratio question. The Imperial Navy wanted 70 per cent of the cruiser strength of the United States Navy, not of Great Britain's. In fact, the Japanese ambassadors in Washington and London and the minister at Geneva, all had pressed the Japanese case. Even before the Dawes conversations began, Ambassador Debuchi had warned Secretary Stimson that his country was "quite sensitive" on applying the 5-5-3 ratio to combatant auxiliaries for Japan. From London Dawes cabled in August that Ambassador Matsudaira had called on him and mentioned that at any future naval conference Japan would ask for 10-10-7 in heavy cruisers. A few weeks later a letter to the department from Consul General Hugh Wilson at Geneva stated that Minister Naotake Sato had told him that Japan was planning on 70 per cent of American strength in 8-inch-gun cruisers. And the British felt the pressure also. Dawes reported in September that he had talked with MacDonald, who had just returned from Geneva. The Prime Minister told Dawes that he had spoken with Matsudaira, and "the latter notified him [MacDonald] that Japan desired to apply its ratio to the number of United States large cruisers."[6]

The United States position during the Anglo-American exploratory conversations was consistent with its stand taken at Geneva in 1927. Stimson and Hoover hoped for a cruiser agreement permitting the United States to reduce its authorized cruiser program, arriving finally at a cruiser category tonnage "somewhere from 200 to 250 thousand tons." This hope conflicted with the British insistence that they needed fifteen large cruisers and forty-five of the smaller vessels,

---

[5]This point was very bluntly spelled out in a personal letter from MacDonald to Dawes which was forwarded to the State Department by cable. D/S, File 500.A15A3/146, London, August 31, 1929; State Department acceptance of the British view is given in memorandum from the Chief of the Division of Western European Affairs (Marriner), November 2, 1929, File 500.A15A3/409½, Archives.

[6]D/S Files 500.A15A3/8, 115, 158, 242, Archives.

with a total tonnage approximating 376,000 tons.[7] The old problem was still present: The United States wanted parity with Great Britain at the lowest possible tonnage level, and the British wanted sixty cruisers (a reduction of ten since the Geneva Conference), with no more than fifteen in the 8-inch-gun class. The Prime Minister summarized the American position on August 1 when he cut to the core of the problem: "I see your President's difficulty. At the moment the bulk of your cruiser strength is in a program; ours is on the water. If you have parity you have to build a part of your program. This is an increase . . . [not naval limitation and reduction]."[8]

On August 9, 1929, the British broke the deadlock over cruisers by modifying their position. They conceded that fifty cruisers would satisfy their needs; fifteen of the ships would be in the 8-inch-gun cruiser class and the other thirty-five would carry 6-inch guns. For another month the United States refused to withdraw from its stand—twenty-three cruisers in the 10,000-ton class—but on September 24 Secretary Stimson showed the Japanese ambassador statistics in which the United States had lowered its requirements to twenty-one, a figure considered by the General Board to be the maximum concession that the United States could make to the British. As matters stood, the cruiser tonnage allowed Great Britain exceeded that of the United States by 24,000 tons (339,000 to 315,000), and a further reduction in 8-inch-gun cruisers for America was out of the question.[9] The visit of Prime Minister MacDonald to the United States in October, 1929, was good publicity for the forthcoming naval conference, but during

[7]*Foreign Relations, 1929,* I, 163; Merze Tate, *The United States and Armaments* (Cambridge, Mass.: Harvard University Press, 1948), p. 172.

[8]Ambassador in Great Britain (Dawes) to the Secretary of State, London, August 1, 1929, *Foreign Relations, 1929,* I, 171-74.

[9]*Ibid.,* 186-87; memorandum by the Secretary of State, September 24, 1929, D/S, File 500.A15A3/215, Archives. The General Board had originally demanded absolute tonnage parity with Great Britain at 339,000 tons. With considerable pressure from Stimson and Hoover the General Board decided to apply the much-talked-about but little used yardstick, and found in September, 1929, that the United States could manage with just 315,000 tons of cruisers. U. S., Congress, Senate, Committee on Foreign Relations, *Hearings on Treaty on the Limitation of Naval Armaments,* 71st Cong., 2d Sess., May 16, 1930, pp. 128-33.

his stay the United States refused to budge from its demand for twenty-one cruisers when the subject was broached. President Hoover and Prime Minister MacDonald therefore agreed that three cruisers should not delay the London Conference, and the British extended invitations on October 7, 1929.[10]

The preconference conversations and Prime Minister Mac-Donald's visit to the United States resulted in a firm Anglo-American resolve to deny Japan's demand for a 10-10-7 ratio in the 8-inch-gun cruiser category. Great Britain had agreed that it would be satisfied with fifteen of the heavier cruisers. The United States still insisted on twenty-one cruisers in the 10,000-ton 8-inch class, but it was already evident that this position would require modification if there was to be a final agreement at the conference. Unless the British were to be allowed an increase in total tonnage, which would undoubtedly cause the General Board to demand a similar rise for the United States, the American position would have to be altered at the London meeting.

In regard to other ship categories the United States and Great Britain reached agreement during the preconference negotiations. Submarines and destroyers posed no problem to speak of. In July Stimson had assured MacDonald that the United States would be willing to scrap down to the level of Britain in destroyers and submarines. During the October visit of the Prime Minister the subject was discussed in detail, and both nations agreed that 150,000 tons of destroyers would meet their needs. Hoover agreed that the United States could meet the British at 50,000 tons in submarines, and surprisingly enough it was agreed that Japan could retain up to 70,000 tons. Now, possibly,

---

[10]A summation of the discussion on cruisers at Hoover's Rapidan Camp on September 6, 1929, is given in *DBFP*, 2:I, 107. A full discussion of the MacDonald visit can be found in Robert H. Ferrell, *American Diplomacy in the Great Depression: Hoover-Stimson Foreign Policy, 1929-1933* (New Haven: Yale University Press, 1957), pp. 79-86; Elting E. Morison, *Turmoil and Tradition: A Study of the Life and Times of Henry L. Stimson* (Boston: Houghton Mifflin Company, 1960), pp. 320-24. Chapters on the Dawes-MacDonald conversations and the MacDonald visit can be found in George V. Fagan, "Anglo-American Naval Relations 1927-1937" (unpublished Ph.D. dissertation, University of Pennsylvania, 1954), and in Raymond G. O'Connor, *Perilous Equilibrium: The United States and the London Naval Conference of 1930* (Lawrence: University of Kansas Press, 1962), chaps. iv, v.

Japan could accept the 60 per cent ratio in 8-inch-gun cruisers.[11] The British still hoped to have the treaty tonnage and gun-caliber limits on battleships reduced further, but Stimson and Hoover preferred to delay replacements for five years. They told the British that the United States could not consider using 12-inch or 14-inch guns on future battleship construction because the 16-inch gun gave the United States a slight advantage over the Japanese fleet. The battleship question was therefore set aside for discussion at the conference, but with the tacit agreement that replacements would begin in 1936 rather than in 1931.[12]

Of even greater significance than the various agreements reached between Great Britain and the United States was the fact that both were actively collaborating and planning together. The worried interest of the Japanese ambassadors in London and Washington (despite attempts to show indifference) was sufficient evidence that Anglo-American cooperation was noticeable. An honest effort had been made to keep Japan, Italy, and France apprised of the progress in the naval discussions, but it would have been unrealistic to expect the State Department or the Foreign Office to tell the Japanese and the world that Japan was the focal point of Anglo-American planning. As evidence accumulated that the British and Americans were doing more than talking in terms of generalities, the Japanese showed their uneasiness by requests at London and Tokyo for Japanese bilateral conversations with the English and the Americans. In accepting the British invitation to the London Conference the Japanese suggested that they hold some preliminary negotiations at London of the same character that had been so successfully concluded between MacDonald and the Americans. In America Secretary Stimson possibly

[11]The Secretary of State to the Ambassador in Great Britain (Dawes), Washington, July 21, 1929, *Foreign Relations, 1929*, I, 149-50; *DBFP*, 2:I, 108.

[12]*DBFP*, 2:I, 106-7; State Department interest in a battleship replacement holiday was expressed in a letter of instructions to Ambassador Dawes in July, 1929, *Foreign Relations, 1929*, I, 162; Navy Department views were expressed in interviews between State Department officers and individual members of the General Board; see the following memoranda of conversations: (Admiral Pringle), 500.A15A3/415, October 28, 1929; (Admiral Hughes and Admiral Long), 500.A15A3/334, October 22, 1929; (Admiral Chase), 500.A15A3/336, October 25, 1929; (Admiral Day), 500.A15A3/392, November 6, 1929, Archives.

set the Japanese at ease by inviting them to stop at Washington while en route to London. He refused to commit the United States to any position on ratios but welcomed a frank discussion.[13]

Any hope that the Japanese might have entertained of a pre-conference commitment to raise their ratio to 70 per cent of American tonnage in 8-inch-gun cruisers was blasted during the month of November. Ambassador Matsudaira raised the issue in talking with Prime Minister MacDonald and was politely told that the British were not sympathetic. In Washington the next day (November 12) Ambassador Debuchi was handed a carefully worded *aide-mémoire* rejecting the Japanese request for a 10-10-7 ratio. Secretary Stimson's memorandum noted, quoting Baron Kato's speech at the Washington Conference, that the Japanese had "gladly" accepted the 10-10-6 ratio, and therefore could see no reason to reopen the subject. If the Japanese insisted on pressing for a 10-10-7 ratio, then the United States would have to re-examine its position on limiting fortifications at Guam and Manila.[14] A copy of the *aide-mémoire* was sent to the British Foreign Office, and on November 14 the embassy in London cabled an observation on the British reception of the *aide-mémoire*:

> Foreign Office informally advises me Japanese memorandum has been read with great satisfaction and that Great Britain, although not taking any action that might give rise to suspicion of Anglo-American agreement versus Japan, will follow the same line in regard to Japan's desire for ten-seven cruiser ratio.[15]

Ambassador Matsudaira visited MacDonald again on November 18 to inquire whether he had altered his views since the conversations of a week before, and was assured in the Prime Minister's most temperate tones that the British still adhered to their earlier statement. When Matsudaira pressed the matter of Japanese security being bound up in a ratio increase, MacDonald had two observations to make:

---

[13]Memorandum of a conversation between the Secretary of State and the Japanese Ambassador, Washington, October 16, 1929, D/S, File 500.A15A3/278, Archives.

[14]*Aide-mémoire* from the British Embassy, Washington, November 11, 1929, *Foreign Relations, 1929*, I, 284-86; *aide-mémoire* from H. L. Stimson, Washington, November 12, 1929, D/S, File 500.A15A3/387, Archives.

[15]D/S, File 500.A15A3/393, London, November 14, 1929, Archives.

. . . firstly, that in these modern days security was being sought for more in the effective creation of a peace organization than in competitive and comparative building; and secondly, that Japan would have to be very careful that in seeking her own security she did not upset the sense of security of other nations. Nobody wanted Japan to be insecure, nor did any other nation wish to feel insecure herself.[16]

After this interview the Japanese press, which until mid-November had remained optimistic, began to face realities. At the end of the month the Tokyo *Chugai,* which on November 9 had predicted the higher ratio, suggested on November 30 that the delegation not be afraid to return home without a treaty.[17]

The six months of Anglo-American negotiations, seen in review, had resulted in the virtual isolation of Japan. In naval matters Great Britain and the United States had reduced their differences to a matter of three cruisers and had reached solid agreement that Japan's ratio in the 8-inch-gun 10,000-ton cruisers was not to be increased above 60 per cent. This agreement had been tested in London and Washington by the Japanese ambassadors, and both parties had held firm. It is little wonder, then, that the American chargé in Tokyo could close his monthly political summary of conditions in Japan:

> December was a month of anticipation. The events awaited were . . . the impending reduction of naval armaments. . . . This prospective attitude was perhaps enhanced by a wave of freak weather which brought the plum trees unseasonably into bloom and made the people feel that the unusual precedence of winter and spring had been reversed.

The London Naval Conference, opened by King George V on January 21, 1930, presented a problem of major proportions to the

---

[16]Mr. A. Henderson to Sir J. Tilley (Tokyo), London, November 20, 1929, *DBFP,* 2:I, 144. An *aide-mémoire* of this conversation was given to the American Embassy in London and was forwarded to the State Department, D/S, File 500.A15A3/411, London, November 20, 1929, Archives.

[17]Tokyo *Chugai,* November 9, 1929; translation in D/S, File 500.- A15A3/470, Tokyo, November 18, 1929; Tokyo *Chugai,* November 30, 1929, File 500.A15A3/531, Tokyo, December 4, 1929, Archives.

American delegates and their naval advisers.[18] President Hoover and the country wanted a treaty limiting or possibly reducing naval armaments, and to the civilian mind the way had been cleared. The United States and Great Britain were in basic agreement on almost all points, and the principal problem ahead was to convince Japan that the British-American position was sound and equitable. This in itself would be a formidable task, but it was complicated by the lack of Navy conviction that the arrangements arrived at with England would serve the best interests of the United States. It was only with extreme reluctance that the General Board scaled down its requirements in 10,000-ton 8-inch-gun cruisers from twenty-five to twenty-three and finally to twenty-one vessels. Yet those cruisers were not considered sacred by the delegates. The Japanese demand for 70 per cent of this tonnage could not be granted, from the viewpoint of the General Board, and the current 60 per cent ratio would give Japan too many cruisers according to British Admiralty estimates. If a treaty was to emerge from the conference, someone would have to give ground.

The Japanese Government continued its preparation of public opinion to back its demand for a new ratio of 10-10-7. In Tokyo the American embassy kept the State Department informed and pointed up the month-by-month developments with an abundance of newspaper clippings, translations, and analyses. By the middle of October the chargé in Tokyo, commenting on the propaganda for a 70 per cent ratio, warned the department, "not only has [the Japanese Government] so definitely committed itself to this position, but it has inculcated so firmly in the minds of the people the idea that anything less [than 70 per cent] would imperil Japan's safety, that it is difficult to see how it could accept anything less at the Conference and avoid serious reverberation at home."[19] The principal argument used by the Japanese to describe their need for a higher ratio was that times had

---

[18]The American delegates to the London Conference were: Henry L. Stimson, Secretary of State; Charles G. Dawes, Ambassador to the Court of St. James's; Charles Francis Adams, Secretary of the Navy; Joseph T. Robinson, Senator (Democrat) from Arkansas; David A. Reed, Senator (Republican) from Pennsylvania; Hugh Gibson, Ambassador to Belgium, and Dwight W. Morrow, Ambassador to Mexico.

[19]D/S, File 500.A15A3/376, Tokyo, October 22, 1929, Archives.

changed since 1922. The Anglo-Japanese Alliance was long a thing of the past, and Japan had shown its good faith by withdrawing from Shantung and Port Arthur. The Japanese were worried about the state of affairs in China and needed more cruisers to supplement their fleet in Chinese waters. A few forthright souls were willing to admit that if war were to occur between Japan and America a 70 per cent ratio in cruisers would be more comforting than 60 per cent, but generally the appeals were based on the China operations or on Japan's emergence as a major Power.[20] By the time the conference met, the Japanese demand for a ratio revision had become one of the delegation's "Three Fundamental Claims": 70 per cent ratio with the United States in 10,000-ton 8-inch-gun cruisers, 70 per cent of the total combatant auxiliary tonnage allowed the United States, and no reduction in Japan's current submarine tonnage of approximately 78,000 tons.[21]

Even behind their wall of solid popular support for a new ratio, the Japanese were not invulnerable to pressure from the United States and Great Britain. The Japanese were hard pressed financially and would have liked to delay the replacement program for battleships due to begin in 1931. The Anglo-American strategy was obvious: With no agreement on cruisers there could be no treaty, and with no treaty new and modern battleships would be laid down by the two English-speaking nations.[22] An even more powerful weapon was available and was

[20]Memorandum of a conversation between the Secretary of State and the Japanese Ambassador (Debuchi), June 11, 1929, D/S, File 500.A15A3/8; memorandum of a conversation between the Assistant Secretary of State and the Japanese Ambassador (Debuchi), August 27, 1929, File 500.A15A3/142, Archives; *Foreign Relations, 1929*, I, 9-10.

[21]D/S, File 500.A15A3/1174, Tokyo, October 2, 1930, Archives. This opinion was also presented in Kikujiro Ishii, *Diplomatic Commentaries*, William R. Langdon, ed. (Baltimore: The Johns Hopkins Press, 1936), p. 322; Tatsuji Takeuchi, *War and Diplomacy in the Japanese Empire* (Garden City: Doubleday, Doran & Company, 1935), pp. 288-89.

[22]Naval Attaché report (copy) to the Office of Naval Intelligence, Tokyo, April 10, 1928, D/S, Files 500.A15A1/683; 500.A15A3/376, Tokyo, October 22, 1929. The economic problems of the Japanese were carefully analyzed by the chargé in File 894.51/285, Tokyo, July 17, 1929, Archives. The Chairman of the American Delegation to the Ambassador in Tokyo (Castle), London, January 21, 1930, D/S, LNC 110.001/24, Archives.

used by the British and American delegations—the threat of an Anglo-American bilateral naval treaty. There had been close cooperation between the two delegations from the day the conference began, and with some justification Secretary Stimson was able to tell Prime Minister MacDonald that the Japanese would never dare leave the conference without a treaty:

> I knew from my first visit to Japan [1928] they must have financial relief on replacement of battleships; second, that if they went home we might make a treaty without them and they would know that in that case they ran a great danger of having two cruisers laid down to their one by both the United States and Great Britain and if it was done under those circumstances those four cruisers would be more likely than not used against their one in case of trouble. . . .[23]

On two critical occasions MacDonald agreed that a treaty between the two Powers should be made if necessary. This knowledge strengthened the American demand that Japan agree to a cruiser compromise in early March, and later made it possible to force acceptance of the compromise on the first of April.[24] The months of Anglo-American negotiations paid off handsomely in bringing Japan to terms, but there were significant concessions by the United States written into the agreement achieved.

The principal burden upon American diplomacy at the London Conference consisted of persuading the Japanese to accept less than a 70 per cent ratio with the United States in 8-inch-gun cruisers. To a great extent the success of the conference hinged on this point. Actually, however, a sharp engagement had to be fought between the American delegates and their naval advisers before a compromise with Japan could be suggested.

---

[23]Memorandum of a conversation between the Secretary of State and MacDonald, London, January 17, 1930, D/S, LNC 110.001/19, Archives.

[24]*Foreign Relations, 1930*, I, 47, 58-59. When it appeared that the Japanese might reject the Reed-Matsudaira agreement, Stimson wired the State Department, repeat to Tokyo, that "if this agreement is repudiated by Tokyo we would have difficulty in continuing to negotiate with a Delegation which is without power and without support of its Government. If Tokyo repudiates or sends a so-called counter proposal, we will immediately commence preparation of a two power agreement with Great Britain. . . ." D/S, LNC 250 Japan/111, London, March 21, 1930, Archives.

When the American delegation arrived at London, the question of whether the United States should have twenty-one or eighteen heavy cruisers had not been settled.[25] The British had pressed the United States to accept eighteen, but the delegation had left the question open until the conference began. On January 25 the American naval advisers were called to Admiral W. V. Pratt's office to discuss a rough "tentative plan" of tonnages desired by the United States in all categories. Given to Pratt by Senator David A. Reed for consideration by the naval group, the plan immediately created a storm of dissension because it proposed eighteen heavy cruisers for the United States rather than the General Board's twenty-one. The next day, after several hours of discussion, Admiral Pratt cut the meeting short with the word that "the paper [tentative plan] had to go in as Senator Reed wanted, and we are just asked to put his words into proper language."[26] This blunt statement by Admiral Pratt aptly describes the work to which the naval advisers were put during the balance of the conference.

On January 28 the delegates listened to the views of the various naval advisers concerning the value of adhering to the General Board's plan or to Senator Reed's. Rear Admiral H. P. Jones and several others stood by the General Board's reasoning that the 8-inch-gun cruiser could hit harder, could shoot farther and more accurately, and was the best cruiser for trade route protection. He much preferred having fewer 6-inch-gun (light) cruisers if the treaty had to be written in such a manner. Opposing Rear Admiral Jones were Admiral Pratt and others, but most importantly the only naval constructor in the delegation, Captain A. H. Van Keuren, sided with Admiral Pratt. He preferred eighteen heavy cruisers or even fewer if there were to be more light cruisers for the United States. Captain Van Keuren believed

---

[25]After the London Treaty the Navy began to call all cruisers armed with 8-inch guns "Heavy Cruisers" and designated them "CA," and all cruisers armed with 6-inch guns, regardless of tonnage, were designated "Light Cruisers—CL." In naval literature the term "Treaty Cruiser" generally refers to the 10,000-ton 8-inch-gun cruiser that was a product of the Washington Conference. The "London Treaty Cruiser" generally refers to the 10,000-ton cruiser armed with 6-inch guns that became somewhat popular after the London Conference.

[26]Rear Admiral (then Commander) Harold C. Train, Daily Log: I, entries for January 25 and 26, 1930. (In possession of Rear Admiral (Ret.) Harold C. Train, Annapolis, Maryland.)

that the 10,000-ton 8-inch-gun cruiser was a monstrosity of naval architecture and a bad risk in combat. The heavy cruiser was too lightly armored for engagements at close ranges, and even worse, its volume of fire was 30 per cent that of the 6-inch-gun vessel. He felt the delegation would do well to ask for fifteen heavy cruisers and take the "bonus" 18,000 tons in two more light cruisers. To strengthen his point he produced statistics showing the type of 6-inch-gun vessel that could be built on 9,000-ton displacement.[27] The testimony of Captain Van Keuren, with its wealth of authoritative detail and undoubtedly its agreement with the preconceptions of the delegates, led the delegation to accept as the American position Senator Reed's "tentative plan," calling for the following distribution of cruiser tonnage for the United States:[28]

UNITED STATES			UNITED STATES (OPTION "A")		
18 10,000 ton	8″ guns	180,000 tons	15 10,000 ton	8″ guns	150,000 tons
10 *Omahas*	6″ guns	70,500 tons	10 *Omahas*	6″ guns	70,500 tons
— New	6″ guns	70,500 tons	— New	6″ guns	118,500 tons
		321,000 tons			339,000 tons

Senator Reed's proposals were not finally agreed upon by the American delegation, but in debate it was made clear that the American group no longer seriously considered asking for twenty-one heavy cruisers. On February 3 Stimson, Secretary of the Navy Adams, Senator Reed, and Ambassador Morrow met MacDonald in the Prime Minister's quarters at the House of Commons and hammered out what became the basic British-American proposals. The United States was to be allowed 327,000 tons of cruisers—eighteen 10,000-ton 8-inch-gun cruisers, the ten *Omahas,* and 76,500 tons of new construction. The battleship fleets of the United States and Great Britain would be reduced to fifteen vessels apiece, and Japan would scrap one, leaving her nine. In submarines and destroyers there was to be parity between Great Britain and the United States.[29] This agreement

---

[27]Memorandum by H. P. J[ones], January 28, 1930; Memorandum of Talk Before Our Delegation by AHVK, January 28, 1930, Train, Log: I.

[28]D/S, LNC 252 U. S./31, undated, Archives.

[29]Memorandum by the Chairman of the American Delegation (Stimson), London, February 3, 1930, D/S, LNC 250.11 GB-US/8, Archives.

was reached, it should be emphasized, without naval advisers and without the Japanese. After this meeting Secretary Stimson sent a cable to the State Department informing Acting Secretary Joseph Cotton of the decisions made:

> . . . While Admiral Jones approves the balance of the program, he still is convinced that 21 cruisers are essential. The entire plan is cordially endorsed by Admiral Pratt, and all seven American delegates are now united in believing that the 21 cruiser program could be insisted upon only with great danger to the Conference's success.[30]

The wisdom of appointing senators to the delegation was manifested on February 5 when Senators Robinson and Reed sent cables to Senators Claude Swanson (Democrat) and Frederick Hale (Republican) urging them to prepare their Senate colleagues for acceptance of eighteen instead of twenty-one heavy cruisers.[31]

Once the American delegation had decided upon eighteen heavy cruisers, it was still faced with the Herculean chore of reducing the Japanese demand for 70 per cent of the 180,000 tons allotted the United States in 8-inch-gun vessels. The Japanese were expected to stand by their "three fundamental claims" and to propose suspension of capital ship replacements for at least five years. However firmly the Japanese delegation was wedded to these convictions, the British would never accept a settlement were the Japanese allowed 70 per cent of the American tonnage of 8-inch-gun cruisers. The civilian delegates were aware of the lack of enthusiasm in the naval staff for the acceptance of eighteen heavy cruisers. They realized that if any further concessions were given the Japanese, heavy resistance would develop not only within their own delegation but probably from the Senate as well.[32]

American negotiations with the Japanese fell principally to Senator David Reed, and after nearly two months of patient exploration he and Ambassador Tsuneo Matsudaira arrived at a settlement—the "Reed-Matsudaira Compromise"—which was sent to Japan for ap-

---

[30]Stimson to the Acting Secretary of State (Cotton), London, February 4, 1930, *Foreign Relations, 1930,* I, 13.

[31]*Ibid.,* I, 18.

[32]In talking with MacDonald, Secretary Stimson agreed Japan's ratio could not be increased because the Senate would reject it. *Ibid.,* I, 2.

proval. Because it departed from the written instructions of the Japanese delegation, another two weeks passed before word came from Tokyo, but on April 1 the Japanese Government accepted the agreement. From this date onward the conference consisted of finishing up details and working out a final draft of the treaty, which involved several significant changes in the American naval strategy in the Pacific. These changes, it must again be stressed, were generally the result of State Department—not Navy or General Board—advice.

The principal understanding in the Reed-Matsudaira Compromise concerned cruisers. Japan was to have a ratio of 10-10-7 ratio in all combatant auxiliaries and 70 per cent of American heavy cruiser tonnage during the life of the treaty. The United States would be allowed eighteen heavy cruisers (180,000 tons) but would not begin construction on its sixteenth cruiser until 1933, on its seventeenth until 1934, and on its eighteenth until January 1, 1935, at the earliest. Japan would build no heavy cruisers during the life of the treaty, but would keep twelve 8-inch-gun vessels. In light cruisers the United States agreed to a 10-10-7 ratio.

This agreement directly contravened the studied judgment of the General Board and ignored the advice of Admirals H. P. Jones, J. M. Reeves, and A. T. Long, naval advisers to the delegation. The General Board, since its naval policy statement of October, 1928, had stood firmly against building any more 6-inch-gun cruisers, yet the Reed-Matsudaira arrangement called for the construction of 76,500 tons of new cruisers in this 6-inch-gun class. For the General Board, Jones, Reeves, and Long, twenty-one heavy cruisers were a rock-bottom minimum for the United States. Their strongest arguments dealt with the trans-Pacific operations of the Navy which were predicated upon 10,000-ton cruisers armed with 8-inch guns for defense of the Philippines, trade route protection, and carrying a war into the western Pacific.[33]

---

[33]Memorandum of a conversation with Rear Admiral A. T. Long, Washington, October 22, 1929, D/S, File 500.A15A3/333, Archives. During this conversation Long emphasized that he would prefer four heavy cruisers to five of the light cruisers. He stated that he wanted cruisers capable of operating in the western Pacific and of holding their own against any vessels encountered. See also U. S., Navy Department, General Board, No. 438, Serial 1347-7(c), April 25, 1927, OCNH.

Senator Reed and the State Department, with some support from a few of the naval advisers, rejected this Navy view, particularly where it concerned the Philippines. As it turned out, the State Department had taken care to become well-informed on Pacific Ocean matters. As early as July 3, 1929, Under Secretary Joseph Cotton had recognized that "American naval strategy and the plans of the General Board which have led to the insistence on the larger type of cruisers, is generally based on naval maneuvers in the Pacific in defense of the Philippine Islands. It is obvious that for such maneuvers the United States would need the larger type of cruiser and big battleships." But he considered the big-Navy concept to be out of step with the isolationist sentiment in the United States and concluded:

> If we can approach naval reduction on the theory that the navies which we can justifiably maintain should be capable of maintaining the defense of the home area but not necessarily powerful enough to keep open all of the sea lanes or to defend island possessions, thousands of miles from the home area, against aggression by any combination of powers, then there will be a reasonable basis for reaching an agreement.[34]

In arriving at this conclusion Cotton had decided that the United States could not and really should not plan to defend the Philippines:

1. A navy large enough to defend the Philippines would alarm Japan.
2. Defense of the Islands depends on the Filipinos, ultimately, and a navy would not be able to do an adequate job if the airfields were held by an enemy.
3. There is no real pressure from Japan against the Philippines.
4. "The attitude of Australia and the British at Singapore is an additional safeguard against Japan."[35]

There is no direct evidence that Cotton's reasoning was pressed upon Senator Reed, but it is known that Secretary Stimson agreed with Cotton and trusted his judgment completely. During the search for concessions to make to Japan, it was Cotton's suggestion from Washington that led to the American proposal to delay construction

---

[34]Memorandum by the Under Secretary of State, Washington, July 3, 1929, D/S, File 500.A15A3/49½, Archives.

[35]Memoranda by [Cotton], July, 1929, D/S, LNC Box 48, Archives.

of the last three heavy cruisers during the life of the treaty.[36] It was Cotton also who assured Stimson that as a result of the tonnage offered Japan by Senator Reed "The Japanese fleet . . . would still be greatly inferior to the American fleet and no national anxiety as to our dominance in the Pacific in case of controversy need be caused by it."[37]

Being a senator and possessing the politician's sensitivity to public opinion, Senator Reed undoubtedly was prejudiced toward agreement at any price he considered reasonable. The arguments of Admirals W. V. Pratt, H. E. Yarnell, A. J. Hepburn, and Captain Van Keuren apparently convinced the Senator and the rest of the delegates, with the possible exception of Secretary Adams, that the 6-inch-gun cruiser would be a valuable addition to the American Navy and certainly should not stand in the way of a final treaty.

A concession more apparent than real was made to Japan in submarines. During the Hoover-MacDonald talks it had been decided that Japan could be allowed parity in submarines, and when hard pressed for an agreement during the first week in March, President Hoover authorized the delegation to offer parity in submarines to all nations, provided the tonnage allowed was held to a reasonably low limit. The naval advisers agreed with this reasoning, though they were more cautious in offering complete parity. At the agreed figure of 52,700 tons and with no exempt group of submarines, the Japanese would barely have enough vessels for defensive requirements.[38] In regard to destroyers the same reasoning held true. American naval planners did not consider a figure of 105,500 tons for Japan high

---

[36]The Acting Secretary of State to the Chairman of the American Delegation, Washington, February 18, 1930, *Foreign Relations, 1930*, I, 27. For estimates of Joseph Cotton see Henry L. Stimson and McGeorge Bundy, *On Active Service in Peace and War* (New York: Harper and Brothers, 1947), pp. 161, 191-92, and Elting E. Morison, *Turmoil and Tradition: A Study of the Life and Times of Henry L. Stimson* (Boston: Houghton Mifflin Company, 1960), pp. 308-9.

[37]The Acting Secretary of State to the Chairman of the American Delegation, Washington, March 5, 1930, *Foreign Relations, 1930*, I, 46.

[38]Minutes of a meeting of the American Naval Technical Staff, February 12, 1930; memorandum of a Special Meeting at St. James's Palace, April 4, 1930, Train, Log: I.

enough to worry about, even though it was 70 per cent of the American tonnage.[39]

The results of the London Naval Conference left the United States Navy with mixed feelings. From the viewpoint of the General Board the delegation had acted most unwisely in abandoning the right to build twenty-one heavy cruisers. To accept a treaty creating a new category of cruisers, possibly suited only to the needs of the other Powers, would be to abandon the ability to defend American Far Eastern interests. Yet many within the Navy could find much that was good in the treaty. Japanese and British attempts to reduce aircraft carrier tonnage from 135,000 to 100,000 had been resisted. Because 66,000 tons were tied up in *Lexington* and *Saratoga,* a further reduction would have prohibited the building of sufficient carriers for American needs. The new provision allowing 25 per cent of the total cruiser tonnage to be built in cruisers with a "landing on deck or platform" opened the door for further experimentation in aircraft carriers and was heartily endorsed by the Navy's Bureau of Aeronautics and its chief, Rear Admiral William A. Moffett.[40] The agreement on battleships was not welcomed by the older officers in the Navy, yet all saw that Japan was weakened by the treaty. The loss of one battleship of nine in combat would mean a heavy percentage loss to the island empire. And after modernization the American battleship fleet would probably be slightly superior to that of Great

---

[39]The Acting Secretary of State to the Chairman of the American Delegation, Washington, February 10, 1930, D/S, LNC 250 U. S./23, Archives.

[40]The "flying-off and landing-on platform" cruisers aroused considerable interest among members of the Naval Affairs Committees of Congress, but outside of the Bureau of Aeronautics there was little interest shown by the Navy Department. The General Board would have been interested in experimenting with the hybrid cruiser if Congress wanted to appropriate the money, but in the confidential opinion of the board it considered the new vessel to be useless. Ashbrook Lincoln, "The United States Navy and Air Power, A History of Naval Aviation, 1920-1934" (unpublished Ph.D. dissertation, University of California, 1946), pp. 190-200. The public opinion of the General Board was given by the president of the Executive Committee, Rear Admiral M. L. Bristol, in U. S., Congress, House, Committee on Naval Affairs, *Hearings on Sundry Legislation, 1930-31,* 71st Cong., 3d Sess., December 17, 1930, pp. 3346-57. The private views of the General Board can be found in the memorandum, "Cruiser Types" [1931], Mark L. Bristol Papers, Box 13, LCMD.

Britain.[41] Finally, the negotiation of the London treaty revealed that the Navy Department was not solidly behind the General Board and its judgments. A significant number of naval advisers, among them Admirals Pratt, Yarnell, and Hepburn, strongly supported the treaty and were to give it further backing when it was under consideration in the Senate.

As we have seen, many senior officers in the United States Navy were clearly disturbed at the thought of the London treaty becoming the law of the land. After a decade of study the Navy's leadership expected the next war to be in the Pacific against the Japanese Empire; yet Secretary of State Stimson had helped to close the London Conference with the roseate prediction that the treaty established America's naval relationship with "our good neighbor across the Pacific and insures the continuous growth of our friendship with that great nation towards whom we have grown to look for stability and progress in the Far East."[42] Despite these encomiums the Navy believed the London agreement to be a danger to the best interests of the United States, and its actions until the Senate consented to the treaty were designed to defeat it. The clearest expositions of the Navy's attitude toward the treaty were delivered before the Senate Foreign Relations and Naval Affairs committees. Here the solons provided a podium from which the proponents and opponents of the agreement could present their views, and here the Navy fired its heaviest—and most fruitless—salvos in one last effort to defeat the treaty. The President and public opinion, and the Senate which was responsive to both, were decidedly in favor of the agreement.

At the close of the London meeting the *Literary Digest,* surveying American newspaper opinion concerning the conference and treaty, concluded that some large metropolitan newspapers, exemplified by the big-Navy and Republican *Chicago Tribune,* believed that the London Conference was a total failure—acceptance of the treaty

---

[41]D/S, LNC U. S./27, London, February 23, 1930; memorandum by Admiral Pratt [1930], D/S, LNC 252.21/31, Archives. Brief statement made to delegates by Rear Admiral Yarnell, January 29, 1930, Train, Log:I.

[42]U. S., State Department, "Proceedings of the London Naval Conference of 1930 and Supplementary Documents," *Conference Series, No. 6* (Washington, 1931), p. 106.

would be a positive evil for America. But on the whole the *Digest* found "the most popular editorial view of the treaty, the most widely prevalent, considers the conference moderately successful and quite worth while because of certain definite achievements and appreciable progress toward the goal of disarmament and peace."[43] A similar attitude was reflected by the chairman of the Senate Foreign Relations Committee, Senator William E. Borah of Idaho, when he wrote to a constituent: "I have been unable to see any real merit to the Naval Treaty, I have no enthusiasm for it and *yet I doubt if it would be helpful to defeat it.*"[44] From the Democratic side of the Senate Thomas J. Walsh expressed the belief "that [treaty] before us is by no means satisfactory but we must confront the alternative if it was rejected, namely, to build to catch up with Great Britain and Japan, now far ahead of us in cruisers, with full opportunity on their part to continue expansion. As it is, we must spend over a billion to catch up with them."[45] There were others, of course, who were more pessimistic about the benefits of the treaty, but they were balanced by the more sanguine senators who saw, as did Senator Arthur Capper of Kansas, that the conference could ultimately result in "peace, parity, and profit." Finally, far in the van, leading the support for the treaty was President Hoover. He wanted quick action by the Senate but was denied it.[46]

---

[43]"Success or Failure at London?" *The Literary Digest,* April 26, 1930, p. 9. Some of the papers supporting the treaty were: *New York Herald Tribune,* New York *World, Wall Street Journal, Boston Transcript, Indianapolis Star, Chicago Daily News,* Norfolk *Ledger-Dispatch, Nashville Tennessean,* New Orleans *Times-Picayune, St. Louis Star, St. Louis Globe-Democrat, Philadelphia Record, Atlanta Journal,* Baltimore *Sun,* and *Detroit Free Press.*

[44]Borah to John Maher, Washington, May 19, 1930, William E. Borah Papers, Box 310, LCMD (my italics).

[45]Walsh to J. N. Newlin, June 6, 1930, Thomas J. Walsh Papers, Box 295, LCMD.

[46]The London treaty was submitted to the Senate, May 1, 1930, and most of the month was absorbed in hearings by the Senate Foreign Relations and Naval Affairs committees. When the Senate failed to act on the treaty during the second session of the 71st Congress, President Hoover called it back into special session on July 7, 1930. U. S., *Congressional Record,* 71st Congress, Special Session, July 7, 1930, p. 4 *et seq.*

In the closing days of the conference, Secretary Stimson and the State Department attempted to gather advance support for the treaty. On April 13 Secretary Stimson spoke to the American public via short-wave transmission of the benefits to be derived from the London treaty, then in final drafting stage. The next day, following a good reception by the press, Acting Secretary Cotton cabled that Secretary of the Navy Adams should make a similar broadcast. Cotton optimistically believed that the Secretary's message should include a statement that

> . . . the treaty will have the result of real betterment of the Navy because it will modernize the fleet; allow the Navy to make plans sufficiently far ahead and will take the naval appropriations out of the sphere of politics. We hope he can add that he has had the co-operation and approval of Admiral Pratt and his naval advisers. . . .[47]

At Washington the State Department busied itself lining up support from such prominent men as Ambassador Charles G. Dawes, Dwight Morrow, Charles A. Lindbergh (" a few whispered words from Papa Morrow would probably do the trick"), Senator Arthur H. Vandenberg, Owen D. Young, Rear Admiral Richard E. Byrd, General John J. Pershing, and Rear Admiral Andrew T. Long ("the Department has expended much effort and no little expense to bring about his election to the International Hydrographic Bureau").[48] In a somewhat presumptive mood Cotton suggested to Stimson that the General Board should make a statement supporting the treaty; Secretary Adams might have them issue something similar to the following:

> The General Board, after examination of the terms of the Treaty agreed on at the London Conference, is of the opinion that it is the wise course for the United States to accept that treaty. The treaty does not in all respects fulfill the desires of individual members of the Board but the Board is of the opinion that as a whole it has great advantages and that under it the United States will have the right to build and maintain during the treaty period a balanced and effective navy.[49]

---

[47]D/S, LNC 319 U. S./201, Washington, April 14, 1930, Archives.

[48]Memorandum from Division of Western European Affairs, April 15, 1930, D/S, File 500.A15A3/891, Archives.

[49]Memorandum from the Under Secretary, Washington, April 30, 1930, D/S, File 500.A15A3/891½, Archives.

But once the Senate hearings on the treaty began, the State Department was rapidly disabused of its optimism.

The principal Navy Department objection to the London treaty was that it did not give the United States a navy with which it could keep its house in order. Acceptance of the treaty would leave American commerce undefended, would force the abandonment of Far Eastern interests, and would leave Japan unnecessarily stronger in the Pacific Basin. To support these views some twenty-two naval officers, on active duty and retired, men who held or had held the major administrative posts and commands in the Navy, gave testimony critical of the conference delegation's work. Against this impressive array of naval experience stood the testimony of four witnesses: Secretary of State Stimson, Secretary of the Navy Adams, the Chief of Naval Operations, Admiral William V. Pratt, and Rear Admiral Harry E. Yarnell.[50]

With its insistence that American commerce would be deprived of national protection were the treaty accepted, the Navy returned to a theme considered sound for explaining naval needs.[51] The president of the Executive Committee of the General Board, Rear Admiral Mark L. Bristol, read to the Foreign Relations Committee a statement issued in 1923 by the General Board concerning the importance of foreign trade.

> . . . the General Board has repeated for many years, the United States Navy in peace and war protects United States commerce, and in so doing it raises the standard of living of the American citizen. It gives not only military protection in war but economic protection in peace and war. America is passing by rapid stages to an industrial status that requires for the prosperity of our people an assurance of the maximum stability in the foreign demands for our products. *Our great merchant marine, supported by a Navy at least as great as that of any other power, is the surest guarantee we can have that foreign markets*

---

[50]U. S., Congress, Senate, Committee on Foreign Relations, *Limitation and Reduction of Naval Armament*, 71st Cong., 2d Sess., *Report No. 1080: Part 2*, cited in *Congressional Record*, 71st Cong., 2d Sess., June 30, 1930, p. 12026.

[51]Captain Dudley W. Knox, "The Navy and Public Indoctrination," *United States Naval Institute Proceedings* (June, 1929), pp. 488-89.

181

will remain open to us. When foreign markets close to us American prosperity ends. . . .[52]

From this premise the Navy opposed consenting to an eighteen-ship heavy cruiser limit. The United States needed powerful ships, capable of steaming alone or with convoys over vast distances and possessing armament enough to meet the commerce raiders of an enemy. Because long-ranging 10,000-ton 6-inch-gun vessels were allowed by the treaty, the Navy maintained that arming the ships with the 8-inch gun was the most important factor, to prevent attack by enemy cruisers and fast merchantmen carrying 6-inch guns. To emphasize this point Rear Admiral Hilary P. Jones commented, "I believe, sir, that you will find that the vast preponderance of opinion in the Navy, of those who have studied these things in the War College and elsewhere, is that the 8-inch gun unit is the best unit for us."[53] When Admiral Pratt commented that the light cruisers, with their rapid-firing 6-inch guns would make the Battle Fleet stronger, he was answered by Captain (Ret.) Dudley W. Knox and Commander Harold C. Train. Captain Knox said acceptance of Pratt's analysis would place improper emphasis upon the Battle Fleet rather than on the commerce-protecting role of the Navy. Knox was earlier supported by Commander Train, who told the committee, "I think most of the engagements that you might have in a war would be distant engagements, separate engagements, and not an engagement of the battle fleet, where of course the 6-inch gun ship could be used to advantage."[54] Captain Knox's assumptions differed greatly from those of Secretary of the Navy Curtis Wilbur, who told a naval committee in

---

[52]U. S., Congress, Senate, Committee on Foreign Relations, *Hearings on Treaty on the Limitation of Naval Armaments,* May 15, 1930, pp. 106-7 (my italics).

[53]*Ibid.,* May 15, 1930, pp. 98-99. Rear Admiral Frank H. Schofield believed that "fully seven or eight out of ten officers would subscribe to the 8-inch idea as against the 6-inch." *Ibid.,* May 22, 1930, p. 241.

[54]*Ibid.,* May 23, 1930, p. 259. Commander Train was the most junior officer to testify at the hearings. He had been an adviser at the Geneva Naval Conference and had worked with Hugh Gibson and Admiral Jones during the Fifth and Sixth sessions of the League Preparatory Commission at Geneva. He was later to attend the General Disarmament Conference and the London Naval Conference of 1935.

1924, "It is believed that modern naval engagements between first class powers, except in sporadic instances, will be fleet engagements. . . ." But in fairness to Train it must be noted that by 1930 the use of task forces instead of major fleet movements was being explored. Fast carrier task forces, using *Saratoga* and *Lexington,* had proved surprisingly effective in maneuvers.

In their criticisms of the treaty many naval officers belabored Japan's increased ratio in combatant auxiliaries from 60 per cent to 70 per cent; the 5-5-3 ratio of the Washington treaty, coupled with the provision of maintaining the *status quo* in island fortifications, was a considerable concession to the Japanese. Further, they said, the non-fortification provision should have been changed or the increased ratio denied. This viewpoint was elaborated by Captain J. K. Taussig:

> I feel—and I wish to say this from experience in dealing with this Far Eastern question—that the 5-3 ratio combined with our agreement to limit fortifications in the Far East gave us only a sporting chance for victory. Any advance in the Japanese ratio beyond the 60 per cent I feel quite sure would prove a very decided embarrassment to the Commander in Chief of our fleet should there happen to be action, and I feel that our chances of victory would be very slim.[55]

At later sessions naval representatives argued that an increase in the Japanese ratio made the Philippines indefensible. In a particularly heated session Rear Admiral S. S. Robison, a former Battle Fleet commander, described his job as "to either retain or help regain the Philippines in case we had a war." An increased Japanese ratio would make the work of defense even more difficult. When asked whether granting the Philippines their independence would change matters, the Admiral pointed out that the United States still had its Far Eastern trade to defend, and besides, the country would never permit the Philippines to be seized by another Power. In a sweeping answer to these arguments, Rear Admiral H. E. Yarnell presented considerable evidence that the Philippines were impossible to defend at the time, then concluded,

> . . . this Nation never provided the essentials necessary to a naval defense of the Philippines even when no treaties existed, and most probably never would have provided them even if no treaties were

---

[55]*Ibid.,* May 27, 1930, p. 320.

signed, it appears that the defense of the islands is in the hands of the statesmen to bring about by the cultivation of friendly relations and understandings with the possible enemy.[56]

The professional arguments presented during the hearings were later used extensively during Senate debate on the treaty. The effectiveness of the Navy's position can only be measured in terms of results, and the final vote of 58 to 9 for the treaty ended the matter. The testimony of the treaty proponents in the Senate was neither extensive nor particularly cogent, but it did not have to be. The President and the people wanted the London agreement accepted, and an executive agency, whose very existence depends upon the will of the people, was in no position to thwart it.[57]

In the first year following ratification of the London Naval Treaty the worst fears of the Navy began to be realized. The optimistic assurances of Secretary of State Stimson and Admiral William V. Pratt that the treaty would now provide the Navy and the nation with a blueprint for future naval construction were rapidly forgotten. Admiral Pratt had predicted, "Now for the first time in our history we can lay down a definite program extending over a period of time and visualize a Navy which is not a creature of great ups and downs in the matter of a naval building program." Not only would this treaty give a goal for building, Stimson averred, but it would provide at long last a "balanced navy,"[58] for which, of course, the General Board had striven during the past eight years. But already there were signs

---

[56]*Ibid.*, May 28, 1930, pp. 330-32, 344-45 and 348 for Robison, pp. 358-59 for Yarnell.

[57]In a study of the Navy League of the United States Dr. Armin Rappaport of the University of California described the fight made by the League and the Navy against the London treaty. In evaluating the failure to prevent ratification of the treaty Dr. Rappaport concluded that the Navy League directors should have known better than to fight such a prevailing sentiment as existed at the time. Armin Rappaport, *The Navy League of the United States* (Detroit: Wayne State University Press, 1962), pp. 130-33; see also Dr. Rappaport's "The Navy League of the United States," *South Atlantic Quarterly* (April, 1954), p. 212.

[58]U. S., Congress, Senate, Committee on Foreign Relations, *Hearings on Treaty on the Limitation of Naval Armaments*, May 14, 1930, pp. 66, 38.

that Stimson and Pratt had not correctly gauged the temper of Congress or public opinion.

During debate on the London treaty Senator David I. Walsh of Massachusetts introduced Senate Resolution 328, calling for the country to build all tonnage allowed by the treaty, and to do so by December 31, 1936. This resolution was defeated partly on parliamentary grounds and partly by lack of interest. When reintroduced as a reservation to the treaty it failed of passage, 54 to 11. Obviously the Senate did not want to pledge itself to build the navy allowed by the treaty.[59]

In the House, Representative Burton L. French of Idaho, Chairman of the Appropriations Committee and of its Naval Subcommittee, had been concerned about the rising naval appropriations requests in January, 1930, and was openly hostile toward increased appropriations a year later. In view of the depression and the need to take care of more pressing relief matters, French expressed displeasure at the desire of the Navy Department to construct 240,200 tons of new vessels at a cost of nearly a half-billion dollars.[60] He commented to the Naval Appropriations Subcommittee,

> I have in mind that the Congress, this committee, and the country have all hoped that in the several naval conferences we have had there would be reduction instead of expansion; and I question very much whether we ought to look forward to an expansion program up to the bounds of the treaty. For myself I rather hold to the thought that the bounds of the treaty are intended to be guides beyond which no nation may go, but not intended to be mandates upon the several nations to build their navies up to a certain required strength.[61]

Though this statement may have worried naval officials, the actions of Congress in succeeding years should not have been particularly discouraging. In February, 1931, money was appropriated, after sharp debate, for the modernization of the last three battleships needing

---

[59]*Congressional Record,* 71st Cong., Special Session, July 14, 1930, pp. 319-20; July 21, 1930, pp. 370-71.

[60]"Naval Parity to Cost a Billion," *The Literary Digest,* May 24, 1930, p. 14.

[61]U. S., Congress, House, Naval Subcommittee of the Committee on Appropriations, *Hearings on Navy Department Appropriation Bill for 1932,* 71st Cong., 2d Sess., January 14, 1931, H. R. 16969, p. 123.

it, *New Mexico, Idaho,* and *Mississippi.*[62] The fifteen cruisers of the 1929 bill were not laid down at the rate the Navy desired, but progress was evident. The keels for *Astoria, Portland,* and *Indianapolis*—all heavy cruisers—were laid in 1930, and heavy cruisers *New Orleans, Minneapolis, Tuscaloosa,* and *San Francisco* were commenced in 1931. The aircraft carrier *Ranger,* authorized in 1929, was also laid down in 1931. However, owing to the critical financial situation in the country, only three destroyers were begun in 1932, and a heavy cruiser (*Quincy*) and eight destroyers were laid down in 1933. At this point naval construction received a decided stimulus when four new light cruisers of the 10,000-ton 6-inch-gun class (*Brooklyn, Philadelphia, Savannah,* and *Nashville*) were ordered in pursuance with the National Industrial Recovery Act of 1933.[63] If the Navy was growing more slowly than was thought wise by the General Board, a little comfort could be derived from the world-wide economic distress causing a similar reaction in Great Britain and Japan. The change in heart among congressmen during 1931 can be attributed to two factors: Japanese aggressiveness in the Far East, which certainly forced attention to a larger navy; the realization that 90 per cent of a ship's cost goes into labor, a point which encouraged spending in the depression-ridden shipyard cities.

---

[62]U. S., *Congressional Record,* 71st Cong., 3d Sess., January 16, 1931, pp. 2351-58. Public Law 746 (S. 4750) 71st Cong., approved February 28, 1931, U. S., *Statutes at Large,* Volume XXXXVI, p. 1453.

[63]Oscar Parkes (ed.), *Jane's Fighting Ships, 1934* (London: Sampson Low, Marston & Co., Ltd., 1934), pp. 524-25.

Conclusions

From 1921 to 1931 Japan exerted its principal influence upon American naval policies by filling the role of the hypothetical enemy. The General Board of the Navy in 1922 set down in writing the fundamental naval policy of the United States:

> The Navy of the United States should be maintained in sufficient strength to support its policies and its commerce, and to guard its continental and overseas possessions.

In the Far East this policy required the Navy to support the Open Door and guard the Philippine Islands. The nation most likely to challenge the American Navy was Japan, and over the years this premise became the most important factor in American naval planning.

To safeguard effectively the nation's Far Eastern interests, the Navy after the World War concentrated its power in the Pacific. A reorganization of the Navy in 1922 resulted in the creation of the United States Fleet with its most powerful subdivision, the Battle Fleet, based on the Pacific Coast. Naval planners took an increased interest in constructing an adequate shore establishment to service the Battle Fleet and anxiously sought to make Hawaii a focus of American naval power in the Pacific. Once the Washington Five-Power Naval Treaty became effective, Guam and Manila had to be kept *in statu quo,* and the Pearl Harbor naval base therefore grew in importance. Oahu, however, was 5,000 miles from Manila.

Operations in the Pacific west of Hawaii in the event of a Japanese-American war required a navy of great steaming endurance. Hence the United States Navy turned increasingly toward larger naval units. Once converted to oil burners, the American battleships were able to operate in Philippine waters, with Pearl Harbor as a base. Cruisers accompanying the Battle Fleet needed range, and the natural result was insistence by the General Board upon building cruisers of the maximum size allowed by the Washington treaty— 10,000 tons. To patrol effectively and to convoy shipping in the

187

western Pacific, the Navy armed its cruisers with 8-inch guns and insisted upon at least 32 knots speed. To meet the demands of endurance, speed, and 8-inch armament, the General Board could see no possibilities in a cruiser displacing less than 10,000 tons.

Japan's influence on the Navy's war planning was obvious. All efforts were bent to create a workable "Orange War" plan, and it was given the highest priority. In its progression from premise to war plans the Navy encountered the problem of legislative-executive relationships in government. As a component of the executive branch the Navy was responsible to the President and at times worked closely with the State Department. In common with all government agencies the Navy Department depended on Congress for its funds, and an abundance or scarcity of money was an important determinant in the Navy's planning. Congress also affected the Navy indirectly when it legislated on matters relating to foreign affairs.

The administrations of Harding, Coolidge, and Hoover functioned within the framework of a Far Eastern policy inherited from the McKinley-Roosevelt period. They wanted to preserve the Open Door in China, and Filipino independence requests were rejected until the end of Hoover's administration. The secretaries of state through these years attempted to maintain good relations with Japan; at the same time the Navy was indoctrinated with the idea of supporting Far Eastern policy. As a result the proper executive relationships existed. There was unity of action from the time of policy creation to its implementation. From the Navy's viewpoint there was weakness in the fact that the President and his budget director did not believe there was any urgency in creating a stronger fleet in the minimum amount of time. However, every business-minded Chief Executive undoubtedly regarded America as Japan's best customer and assumed the Japanese to believe, along with Al Smith, that "you don't shoot Santa Claus."

The three Republican administrations inherited a capricious Congress as well as a traditional Far Eastern policy. The years of heavy-handed direction by President Wilson had resulted in the resurgence of a demand for Congressional leadership in all areas of government. The Presidents, particularly Harding and Coolidge, were

188

satisfied with the new relationship, but the situation was pregnant with danger in foreign affairs.

The Washington Naval Conference was called as a result of unremitting pressure from Congress, particularly in the Senate, and the results showed the mark of the legislator as well as the diplomat. The reductions in capital ships and the agreement to keep the Pacific island fortifications *in statu quo* were made with the thought in mind that Congress would never appropriate for the completion of either. That the treaty provisions vitally impaired the Navy's support of American Far Eastern policy made no impression on the legislators. The General Board knew who was responsible for the emasculation of the Navy and in private blamed Senators Henry Cabot Lodge and Oscar W. Underwood and particularly the elder statesman Elihu Root.

After the Washington Conference, when Japanese-American relations were excellent, Congress created a new atmosphere of hostility through passage of the Immigration Act of 1924 with its Japanese exclusion provision. This was clearly a show of Congressional strength in a sensitive area of foreign affairs. Regardless of the motivation involved, the results were destructive of Japanese amity. For a group of legislators who considered Japan's protest a veiled threat, their later miserly naval authorizations showed unmistakable inconsistency.

Naval appropriations and construction bills in the 1920's reveal Congressional unwillingness to legislate with support of an active foreign policy in mind. The money appropriated for the construction of six gunboats to be used in Chinese waters is the only evident exception. That naval appropriations declined steadily until 1926, though 1924 and 1925 were critical years in Japanese-American relations, suggests again that Congress did not consider the times to be as unpropitious as the Navy believed. Later rises in naval appropriations after 1926 were not the result of a renewed concern for foreign affairs but merely represented the cost of equipping the fleet with aircraft. In fairness to the legislators it should be observed that Congress was continually under pressure from the taxpayers to reduce service appropriations—Navy and Army.

Throughout the 1920's the Navy was tortured by its own consistency of viewpoint. The contradictions inherent in representative governments constantly thwarted naval attempts to prepare for war in the Pacific. The instability in the nation's dealings with Japan was a natural result of sharing the work of foreign policy formulation with Congress. A firmer hand by Harding and Coolidge would possibly have prevented some of the difficulties that arose, but neither man was selected as a presidential candidate because he promised executive firmness. With the passage of years the General Board never changed its interpretation of American Far Eastern policy and could see no reason to change its premise that Japan was a serious menace to American interests in the Far East. The State Department, until Secretary of State Stimson took the helm, hewed fairly close to traditional policy lines. In Congress, however, the one outstanding commitment of the United States in eastern Asia was in the process of liquidation. By 1930 it was obvious to many that the Philippines would be set adrift in the not very distant future, and hence there was reluctance to create a strong Navy to defend them. This same view also promoted acceptance of the London Naval Treaty by the Senate.

With a stubbornness born of conviction the Navy resisted the Philippine independence movement with a rationalization that the islands were necessary for defense of trade in the Far East. But United States trade in the Far East was a mere 10 per cent of its world trade, and the heaviest percentage of that commerce was with the theoretical enemy, Japan. Yet. as the General Board recognized, a Navy capable of defending the Philippines or of thoroughly protecting the trade routes to the Far East would be in a position to defend the nation against Japanese aggression on either side of the Pacific.

From the Navy's point of view it was acting in a rational and logical manner. Officered by men trained in engineering and science, it tended to view foreign relations and naval diplomacy quantitatively. It counted ships and men, measured tonnages and weights of broadsides, and evolved mathematical ratios. The General Board kept abreast of technical developments abroad and constantly sought teries on foreign naval vessels were weighed carefully, and these new limits, the addition of catapults, or the installation of antiaircraft bat-improvements for its vessels. Changes in capital ship gun-elevation developments often resulted in a re-evaluation of existing ratios.

ERRATUM

From the Navy's point of view it was acting in a rational and logical manner. Officered by men trained in engineering and science, it tended to view foreign relations and naval diplomacy quantitatively. It counted ships and men, measured tonnages and weights of broadsides, and evolved mathematical ratios. The General Board kept abreast of technical developments abroad and constantly sought improvements for its vessels. Changes in capital ship gun-elevation limits, the addition of catapults, or the installation of antiaircraft batteries on foreign naval vessels were weighed carefully, and these new developments often resulted in a re-evaluation of existing ratios.

At the Naval War College more was done than refighting the Battle of Jutland on the war game board. Foreign policy seminars were a part of the curriculum, and most officers were required to write at least one analytical paper in this area. Generally those who studied foreign relations accepted as axiomatic that there should be a balance between commitments abroad and naval support for them. As eminently practical men and managers of a bureaucratic institution, these naval officers believed growth was necessary for health. They were reluctant to see a cutback in commitments; naval reductions might logically follow the withdrawals. While some people in the State Department and Congress could see merit in finally acceding to Filipino independence demands, the average naval officer felt that this was foolish. Years of support for a foreign policy based on unequal treaties and on immigration laws that forbade entrance to those from the barred zone could not help but reinforce an existing attitude that Filipinos were as backward as the Chinese, Japanese, or Malays.

In contrast to the Navy's "scientific" approach to foreign relations in the 1920's was the nation's emotionalism. Beginning with the eviction of the Democratic majority in the election of 1918, the country began its prolonged reaction to Wilsonism. The war was fought under the banner of the Fourteen Points, but in 1920 the electorate chose Warren G. Harding, the standard-bearer of the party that had rejected the fourteenth point—the League of Nations. In almost whimsical manner Americans sided with the Chinese when Japan put them under pressure, contributed handsomely to Japanese rehabilitation after the 1923 earthquake, then excluded Orientals from immigration to America, pressed European debtors to repay loans contracted in wartime, and raised tariff barriers to close the American markets to credit-hungry European traders. Though capricious, American actions during the 1920's are not beyond fathoming.

Spurred by a bullish market, blessed with an annually mounting gross national product, and having wrought miracles of industrial production during the eighteen months of war, the nation could afford to be optimistic. Though abstaining from League membership, America had fostered naval disarmament and had taken the lead in abolishing war "as an instrument of national policy." Seen against this background, the average American of the 1920's can probably be excused

191

if he refused to worry about war with Japan or to concern himself with the taxeating naval establishment. Since he often favored the underdog in competitive sports, the man in the street could be sympathetic with the troubled Chinese or the reparations-harassed German.

It is hard to imagine the average naval officer of the 1920's becoming overly troubled about the Japanese threat to America. The Navy never doubted that Japan could be defeated, even in the Far East, given time and a full mobilization of the national economy, but the professional officer considered it wasteful to wait for the approach of war before moving to a state of readiness. The General Board believed that Japan was a calculating nation which would probe to the limits of American sufferance. It knew that the Japanese understood force, appreciated a superior adversary, and would treat with contempt any move to block them with declarations rather than deeds. In the eyes of the board members a properly constituted fleet was the best deterrent to Japanese ambitions in the Far East.

For the Navy of the 1920's its most critical problem was convincing Congress of the need for a balanced fleet, and here it chose to dissemble. With Japan outraged by the 1924 immigration act, the Navy could not publicly use the island empire as its theoretical enemy. The British, however, fitted the role nicely. There was no possibility of war between Great Britain and the United States, and Americans had twisted the lion's tail for ages eternal. Hence American planners now used the British as a standard for comparisons, encouraged naval equality in all categories of vessels, and quickly called attention to any strengthening of the Royal Navy. To a degree this approach worked admirably, but from the big-Navy viewpoint it miscarried miserably. Prime Minister MacDonald and President Hoover recognized the existing community of interests between Britain and America and together agreed to work for naval limitation and reduction. The end product of their labors was the London Treaty of 1930. Of vastly greater significance for the next decade was the resultant alignment of Anglo-American interests and the diplomatic isolation of Japan.

In terms of the present, one other lesson can be drawn from this study. The inconsistencies between foreign policy formulation and support during the 1920's were caused by the heavy hand of Congress in foreign affairs. Stronger Presidential leadership and greater loyalty from the party in Congress could have resulted in a more consistent policy from conception to implementation. As it was, the Navy was a coordinate member of the executive branch of the Government, at the command of the President, and defending policies created by Congress and the Chief Executive. Lacking were the close reasoning and evaluation that exist when policy creation and fulfillment are vested in one person. If the Navy's premise concerning Japan's future conduct was correct, Congress needed information in the most candid terms, but candor did not exist; nor was it sought. An acceptance of the Navy's views would have blasted a balanced budget far beyond the reach of a Congress striving to achieve "normalcy."

Bibliography

PRIMARY MATERIALS

Private Papers—Manuscript

BORAH, WILLIAM E. Collection. Manuscripts Division, Library of Congress.

BRISTOL, [ADMIRAL] MARK L. Collection. Manuscripts Division, Library of Congress.

BRYAN, WILLIAM JENNINGS. Collection. Manuscripts Division, Library of Congress.

COOLIDGE, CALVIN. Collection. Manuscripts Division, Library of Congress.

COTTEN, LYMAN A. [CAPTAIN, USN]. Collection. Southern Historical Collection, University of North Carolina.

FORBES, W. CAMERON. Collection. Manuscripts Division, Library of Congress.

FULLAM, [REAR ADMIRAL] WILLIAM F. Collection. Naval Historical Foundation Collection, Manuscripts Division, Library of Congress.

GLEAVES, [REAR ADMIRAL] ALBERT. Collection. Naval Historical Foundation Collection, Manuscripts Division, Library of Congress.

HARRISON, LELAND. Collection. Manuscripts Division, Library of Congress.

HUGHES, CHARLES EVANS. Collection. Manuscripts Division, Library of Congress.

JOHNSON, NELSON TRUSLER. Collection. Manuscripts Division, Library of Congress.

JONES, [ADMIRAL] HILARY P. Collection. Naval Historical Foundation Collection, Manuscripts Division, Library of Congress.

LONG, [REAR ADMIRAL] ANDREW T. Collection. Southern Historical Collection, University of North Carolina.

MAHAN, [REAR ADMIRAL] ALFRED T. Collection. Manuscripts Division, Library of Congress.

McCOY, [MAJOR GENERAL] FRANK R. Collection. Manuscripts Division, Library of Congress.

NORRIS, GEORGE W. Collection. Manuscripts Division, Library of Congress.

ROOT, ELIHU. Collection. Manuscripts Division, Library of Congress.

STATON, ADOLPHUS [CAPTAIN, USN]. Collection. Southern Historical Collection, University of North Carolina.

TRAIN, [REAR ADMIRAL] HAROLD C. Papers. In possession of Admiral Train at Annapolis, Maryland.

WALSH, THOMAS J. Collection. Manuscripts Division, Library of Congress.

WELLES, [VICE ADMIRAL] ROGER. Collection. Naval Historical Foundation Collection, Manuscripts Division, Library of Congress.

WOOD, [GENERAL] LEONARD. Collection. Manuscripts Division, Library of Congress.

Private Papers—Printed

MORISON, ELTING E. (ed.). *The Letters of Theodore Roosevelt.* 8 vols. Cambridge, Mass.: Harvard University Press, 1951-1954.

Government Documents—Manuscript

DEPARTMENT OF STATE

The general serial files are arranged by subject matter as it concerns relations between the United States and other countries. Heaviest emphasis was placed on those files dealing with Japanese-American and British-American naval relations. All records used are kept at the Foreign Affairs Section of the National Archives; arrangements to use the post-1929 files must be made through the State Department. The records of the London Naval Conference of 1930 form a special collection of 83 file boxes, and are kept at the National Archives, Foreign Affairs Section.

The documentation of this study shows most of the State Department files that were searched. The principal files examined were:

500.A4b	Washington Naval Conference
500.A12	U. S. and League Disarmament matters
500.A15A1	Geneva Naval Conference 1927
500.A15A3	London Naval Conference 1930
711.94	U. S.-Japanese relations
711.945	1924 Immigration Act
811.30	U. S. naval matters
811.3394	U. S. ship visits to Japanese territory
841.30	British naval matters
841.34546d	Singapore naval base
894.00	Japanese political matters
894.20211	Japanese in the U. S.
894.20256d	Japanese in the East Indies
894.30	Japanese naval matters
894.51	Japanese finances
894.51So8	So. Manchurian Railroad

DEPARTMENT OF THE NAVY

The bulk of the Navy Department's files for the years before 1941 is kept at the Navy Department Section of the National Archives. Permission to use classified materials must be obtained through the Office of the Chief of Naval History. In this study the records of the General Board were examined and used. Permission to use the records of the General Board must be obtained from the Chief of Naval History. The principal files examined were:

General Correspondence of the Secretary of the Navy, 1921-1931.
Record Group 80.
Correspondence (Unclassified) of the Chief of Naval Operations.

Alphabetical File of the Assistant Secretary. Record Group 129.

Alphabetical File of the Assistant Secretary, 1921-1940. Record Group 130.

Minutes of the Secretary's Council, 1921-1926. General File 12753-14½.

Reports of the General Board of the Navy, 1915-1928.

DEPARTMENT OF THE ARMY (WAR DEPARTMENT)

Records of the War Department (Department of Army after 1947) are divided between the Old Army Records Section (before 1917) and New Army Records Section (1917 and after) at the National Archives. The principal source examined was Record Group 94, "Records of The Adjutant General." Access to classified records, regardless of their age, is difficult to obtain by the civilian or nongovernment-supported researcher.

DEPARTMENT OF THE INTERIOR

Records pertaining to the Philippine Islands are housed at the Interior Department Section of the National Archives. Like most government files they are arranged by subject matter. The principal files examined were:

File 364-467   Japanese Penetration of the Philippine Islands
File 6144   Japanese Matters, Miscellaneous.

BUREAU OF THE BUDGET

Records of the Budget Bureau for the years 1921 to 1941 are kept at the Treasury Department Section of the National Archives. These records were examined in order to ascertain, where possible, the significance of fiscal control in the determination of naval policy. Use of these files can give the researcher a very clear picture of the power of the Director of the Budget and the role he played in determining the size of the armed forces during the 1920's. The principal files examined were:

Navy Dept: Increase in Navy #1.
U. S. Navy 1923-1928.
Navy Dept: Vessels—Repairs.

Government Documents—Printed

UNITED STATES.

CONGRESS. HOUSE OF REPRESENTATIVES. Subcommittee of the Committee on Appropriations. *Hearings on Navy Department Appropriation Bill for 1923.* 67th Cong., 2d Sess., 1922.

————. Committee on Naval Affairs. *Hearings on Sundry Legislation Affecting the Naval Establishment, 1922-1923.* 67th Cong., 2d, 3d, 4th Sess., 1923.

————. Subcommittee of the Committee on Appropriations. *Hearings on Navy Department Appropriation Bill for 1924.* 67th Cong., 4th Sess., 1923.

_____. Subcommittee of the Committee on Appropriations. *Hearings on Navy Department Appropriation Bill for 1925.* 68th Cong., 1st Sess., 1924.

SENATE. Subcommittee of the Committee on Naval Affairs. *Hearings on Naval Omnibus Bill, S. 1808.* 68th Cong., 1st Sess., 1924.

_____. Committee on Naval Affairs. *Hearings on H. R. 8687, Alterations to certain naval vessels and construction of additional naval vessels.* 68th Cong., 1st Sess., 1924.

HOUSE OF REPRESENTATIVES. Subcommittee of the Committee on Appropriations. *Hearings on Navy Department Appropriation Bill for 1926.* 68th Cong., 2d Sess., 1924.

SENATE. Subcommittee of the Committee on Appropriations. *Hearings on Navy Department Appropriation Bill for 1926, H. R. 10724.* 68th Cong., 2d Sess., 1925.

HOUSE OF REPRESENTATIVES. Subcommittee of the Committee on Appropriations. *Hearings on Navy Department Appropriation Bill for 1927.* 69th Cong., 1st Sess., 1926.

SENATE. Subcommittee of the Committee on Appropriations. *Hearings on Navy Department Appropriation Bill for 1928, H. R. 15641.* 69th Cong., 2d Sess., 1927.

HOUSE OF REPRESENTATIVES. Subcommittee of the Committee on Appropriations. *Hearings on Navy Department Appropriation Bill for 1929.* 70th Cong., 1st Sess., 1928.

_____. Committee on Naval Affairs. *Hearings on H. R. 7359, A bill to provide for an increase of the Naval Establishment.* 70th Cong., 1st Sess., 1928.

SENATE. *Records of the Conference for the Limitation of Naval Armament. Doc. No. 55.* 70th Cong., 1st Sess., 1928.

HOUSE OF REPRESENTATIVES. Subcommittee of the Committee on Appropriations. *Hearings on Navy Department Appropriation Bill for 1930.* 70th Cong., 2d Sess., 1929.

SENATE. Subcommittee of the Committee on Appropriations. *Hearings on Navy Department Appropriation Bill for 1930, H. R. 16714.* 70th Cong., 2d Sess., 1929.

HOUSE OF REPRESENTATIVES. Committee on Naval Affairs. *Hearings on Sundry Legislation Affecting the Naval Establishment, 1928-1929.* 70th Cong., 2d Sess., 1929.

_____. Committee on Naval Affairs. *Hearings on Sundry Legislation Affecting the Naval Establishment, 1929-1930.* 71st Cong., 2d Sess., 1930.

SENATE. Committee on Foreign Relations. *Hearings on Treaty on the Limitation of Naval Armaments.* 71st Cong., 2d Sess., 1930.

————. Committee on Foreign Relations. *Limitation and Reduction of Naval Armament*. Report No. 1080, Part 2. 71st Cong., 2d Sess., 1930.

————. Committee on Naval Affairs. *Hearings on London Naval Treaty of 1930*. 71st Cong., 2d Sess., 1930.

HOUSE OF REPRESENTATIVES. Subcommittee of the Committee on Appropriations. *Hearings on Navy Department Appropriation Bill for 1931*. 71st Cong., 2d Sess., 1930.

————. Subcommittee of the Committee on Appropriations. *Hearings on Navy Department Appropriation Bill for 1932*. 71st Cong., 3d Sess., 1931.

————. Committee on Naval Affairs. *Hearings on Sundry Legislation Affecting the Naval Establishment, 1930-1931*. 71st Cong., 3d Sess., 1931.

————. Select Committee of Inquiry Into Operations of the United States Air Services. *Hearings*. 68th Congress, 1925.

Congressional Record. 68th Congress, 2d Session.

        71st Congress, 2d Session.

        71st Congress, Special Session.

        71st Congress, 3rd Session.

Statutes at Large. Volumes XXXXIII (68th Congress), XXXXVI (71st Congress).

DEPARTMENT OF COMMERCE. *Foreign Commerce and Navigation of The United States, 1921-1931*. 11 vols. Washington: Government Printing Office, 1922-1932.

NAVY DEPARTMENT. *Annual Reports of the Navy Department for the Fiscal Year 1922*. Washington: Government Printing Office, 1923.

————. *Annual Reports of the Navy Department for the Fiscal Year 1923*. Washington: Government Printing Office, 1924.

————. *Information Concerning the U. S. Navy and Other Navies*. Washington: Government Printing Office, 1925.

————. *Report of the General Board on Limitation of Armaments*. Washington: Government Printing Office, 1921.

————. *Ships' Data U. S. Naval Vessels: July 1, 1922*. Washington: Government Printing Office, 1922.

———— *Ships' Data U. S. Naval Vessels: July 1, 1931*. Washington: Government Printing Office, 1931.

DEPARTMENT OF STATE. *Memoranda for the American Delegates to the Conference on Limitation of Armament*. Washington: Government Printing Office, 1922.

————. *Papers Relating to the Foreign Relations of the United States, 1918-1930*. Washington: Government Printing Office, 1930-45.

————. *Papers Relating to the Foreign Relations of the United States: The Lansing Papers, 1914-1920.* 2 vols. Washington: Government Printing Office, 1940.

————. *Papers Relating to Pacific and Far Eastern Affairs Prepared for the Use of the American Delegation to the Conference on the Limitation of Armament, Washington, 1921-1922.* Washington: Government Printing Office, 1922.

————. "Proceedings of the London Naval Conference of 1930 and Supplementary Documents." *Conference Series, No. 6.* Washington: Government Printing Office, 1931.

INTER-DEPARTMENTAL COMMITTEE ON THE PHILIPPINES. *Report on Philippine-United States Trade Relations.* 2 vols. Washington: Government Printing Office, 1935.

PRESIDENT. *Message of the President of the United States to Congress, December 3, 1924.* Washington: Government Printing Office, 1924.

————. *Report of the Special Mission to the Philippines.* Manila: Bureau of Printing, 1921.

SUPREME COURT. Reports: 260 (1922).

GREAT BRITAIN.

Parliamentary Debates (Commons.) 1923.

Parliamentary Papers. "Singapore Naval Base." *Correspondence with the Self-Governing Dominions & India Regarding the Development of the Singapore Naval Base.* Cmd. 2083. March 25, 1924. London: H. M. Stationery Office, 1924.

Parliamentary Papers. "Papers Regarding the Limitation of Naval Armament." *Miscellaneous No. 6 (1928).* Cmd. 3211. London: H. M. Stationery Office, 1928.

WOODWARD, E. L. and ROHAN BUTLER (eds.). *Documents on British Foreign Policy, 1919-1939.* Second Series. 2 vols. London: H. M. Stationery Office, 1946.

JAPAN.

Foreign Office. *The Present Condition of China: With Reference to Circumstances Affecting International Relations and the Good Understanding between Nations upon Which Peace Depends: Document "A".* Printed, 1932.

LEAGUE OF NATIONS.

Records of the Conference for the Limitation of Naval Armament. Genève, 1927.

SECONDARY MATERIALS

Autobiography, Biography, Memoirs, and Journals

ARPEE, EDWARD. *From Frigates to Flat-Tops.* Chicago: Privately printed, 1953.

BACON, ADMIRAL SIR R. H. *The Life of John Rushworth Earl Jellicoe.* London: Cassell & Co., Ltd., 1936.

COONTZ, ROBERT E. *From the Mississippi to the Sea.* Philadelphia: Dorrance and Company, 1930.

DAWES, CHARLES G. *Journal as Ambassador to Great Britain.* New York: The Macmillan Company, 1939.

GARRATY, JOHN A. *Henry Cabot Lodge: A Biography.* New York: Alfred A. Knopf, Inc., 1953.

GREW, JOSEPH C. *Turbulent Era: A Diplomatic Record of Forty Years.* 2 vols. Boston: Houghton Mifflin Company, 1952.

HAGEDORN, HERMANN. *Leonard Wood: A Biography.* 2 vols. New York and London: Harper and Brothers, 1931.

ISHII, KIKUJIRO. *Diplomatic Commentaries.* Edited by William R. Langdon. Baltimore: The Johns Hopkins Press, 1936.

JESSUP, PHILIP C. *Elihu Root.* 2 vols. New York: Dodd, Mead & Company, 1938.

LEACH, PAUL R. *That Man Dawes.* Chicago: Reilly & Lee Company, 1930.

LOHBECK, DON. *Patrick J. Hurley.* Chicago: Henry Regnery Company, 1956.

MORISON, ELTING E. *Admiral Sims and the Modern American Navy.* Boston: Houghton Mifflin Company, 1942.

————. *Turmoil and Tradition: A Study of the Life and Times of Henry L. Stimson.* Boston: Houghton Mifflin Company, 1960.

PULESTON, CAPTAIN W. D. *Mahan.* New Haven: Yale University Press, 1939.

PUSEY, MERLO J. *Charles Evans Hughes.* 2 vols. New York: The Macmillan Company, 1951.

ROOSEVELT, NICHOLAS. *A Front Row Seat.* Norman: University of Oklahoma Press, 1953.

STIMSON, HENRY L. and McGEORGE BUNDY. *On Active Service in Peace and War.* New York: Harper and Brothers, 1947.

STIRLING, YATES. *Sea Duty.* New York: G. P. Putman's Sons, 1939.

TAYLOR, CHARLES C. *The Life of Admiral Mahan.* London: John Murray, 1920.

WILEY, HENRY A. *An Admiral From Texas.* Garden City: Doubleday, Doran & Company, 1934.

WILSON, EUGENE E. *Slipstream, The Autobiography of an Air Craftsman.* New York: McGraw-Hill Book Company, Inc., 1950.

Books, Monographs, and Treatises

ADAMS, BROOKS. *America's Economic Supremacy.* New York: The Macmillan Company, 1900.

_____. *The New Empire*. New York: The Macmillan Company, 1902.

BAILEY, THOMAS A. *The Man in the Street: The Impact of American Public Opinion on Foreign Policy*. New York: The Macmillan Company, 1948.

_____. *Theodore Roosevelt and the Japanese-American Crises*. Stanford: Stanford University Press, 1934.

BLAKESLEE, GEORGE H. *The Recent Foreign Policy of the United States: Problems in American Cooperation with Other Powers*. New York and Cincinnati: The Abingdon Press, 1925.

BORG, DOROTHY. *American Policy and the Chinese Revolution 1925-1928*. New York: American Institute of Pacific Relations and the Macmillan Company, 1947.

BUELL, RAYMOND L. *The Washington Conference*. New York: D. Appleton & Company, 1922.

BYWATER, HECTOR C. *The Great Pacific War: A History of the American-Japanese Campaign of 1931-1933*. London: Constable & Company, Ltd., 1925.

_____. *Navies and Nations: A Review of Naval Developments Since the Great War*. Boston and New York: Houghton Mifflin Company, 1927.

_____. *Sea Power in the Pacific: A Study of the American-Japanese Problems*. 2d ed. London: Constable & Company, Ltd., 1934.

CAMPBELL, CHARLES S., JR. *Special Business Interests and the Open Door Policy*. New Haven: Yale University Press, 1951.

CLINARD, OUTTEN J. *Japan's Influence on American Naval Power 1897-1917*. University of California Publications in History, No. 36. Berkeley and Los Angeles: University of California Press, 1947.

COHEN, JEROME B. *Japan's Economy in War and Reconstruction*. Minneapolis: University of Minnesota Press, 1949.

CONROY, HILARY. *The Japanese Frontier in Hawaii, 1868-1898*. Berkeley and Los Angeles: University of California Press, 1953.

CORBETT, SIR JULIAN S. *Some Principles of Maritime Strategy*. 2d ed. London: Longmans, Green & Company, 1919.

CRAIG, GORDON A. and FELIX GILBERT. *The Diplomats, 1919-1939*. Princeton: Princeton University Press, 1953.

DAVIS, GEORGE T. *A Navy Second to None: The Development of American Naval Policy*. New York: Harcourt, Brace & Company, Inc., 1940.

DECONDE, ALEXANDER (ed.). *Isolation and Security: Ideas and Interests in Twentieth-Century American Foreign Policy*. Durham, N. C.: Duke University Press, 1957.

DENNETT, TYLER. *Americans in Eastern Asia*. New York: The Macmillan Company, 1922.

_____. *Roosevelt and the Russo-Japanese War*. Garden City: Doubleday, Page & Company, 1925.

FEIS, HERBERT. *The Diplomacy of the Dollar, First Era 1919-1932*. Baltimore: The Johns Hopkins Press, 1950.

FERRELL, ROBERT H. *American Diplomacy in the Great Depression: Hoover-Stimson Foreign Policy, 1929-1933.* New Haven: Yale University Press, 1957.

FIELD, FREDERICK V. *American Participation in the China Consortiums.* Chicago: University of Chicago Press, 1931.

FIFIELD, RUSSELL H. *Woodrow Wilson and the Far East; the Diplomacy of the Shantung Question.* New York: Thomas Y. Crowell Company, 1952.

FISHEL, WESLEY R. *The End of Extraterritoriality in China.* Berkeley and Los Angeles: University of California Press, 1952.

FORBES, W. CAMERON. *The Philippine Islands.* 2 vols. New York and Boston: Houghton Mifflin Company, 1928.

FROST, HOLLOWAY H. *The Battle of Jutland.* Annapolis: U. S. Naval Institute, 1936.

GRASSMUCK, GEORGE A. *Sectional Biases in Congress on Foreign Policy.* The Johns Hopkins University Studies in Historical and Political Science, Series LXVIII, No. 3. Baltimore: The Johns Hopkins Press, 1951.

GRENFELL, CAPTAIN RUSSELL. *Main Fleet to Singapore.* London: Faber & Faber, Ltd., 1951.

GRISWOLD, A. WHITNEY. *The Far Eastern Policy of the United States.* New York: Harcourt, Brace & Company, 1938.

GRUNDER, GAREL A. and WILLIAM E. LIVEZEY. *The Philippines and the United States.* Norman: University of Oklahoma Press, 1951.

HACKWORTH, GREEN H. *Digest of International Law.* 8 vols. Washington: Government Printing Office, 1940-1944.

HICKS, JOHN D. *Republican Ascendancy, 1921-1933.* New York: Harper and Brothers, 1960.

ICHIHASHI, YAMATO. *Japanese in the United States.* Stanford: Stanford University Press, 1932.

————. *The Washington Conference and After.* Stanford: Stanford University Press, 1928.

ISLEY, JETER A. and PHILIP A. CROWL. *The U. S. Marines and Amphibious Warfare.* Princeton: Princeton University Press, 1951.

KIRK, GRAYSON L. *Philippine Independence.* New York: Farrar, Rinehart, Inc., 1936.

KNOX, CAPTAIN DUDLEY W. *The Eclipse of American Sea Power.* New York: The Army and Navy Journal, 1922.

LEE, DWIGHT E. and GEORGE E. McREYNOLDS. *Essays in History and International Relations in Honor of George Hubbard Blakeslee.* Worcester, Mass.: Commonwealth Press, 1949.

LI, T'IEN-YI. *Woodrow Wilson's China Policy, 1913-1917.* New York: University of Kansas City Press, 1952.

LIPPMANN, WALTER. *U. S. Foreign Policy: Shield of the Republic.* Boston: Little, Brown & Company, 1943.

MAGRUDER, THOMAS P. *United States Navy.* Philadelphia: Dorrance and Company, 1928.

MAHAN, CAPTAIN A. T. *The Influence of Sea Power Upon History 1660-1783.* 25th ed. Boston: Little, Brown & Company, 1918.

_____. *The Interest of America in International Conditions.* Boston: Little, Brown & Company, 1918.

_____. *The Interest of America in Sea Power, Present and Future.* Boston: Little, Brown & Company, 1898.

_____. *Naval Administration and Warfare.* Boston: Little, Brown & Company, 1908.

MAYO, KATHERINE. *The Isles of Fear.* New York: Harcourt, Brace & Company, Inc., 1925.

MILLARD, THOMAS F. *Conflict of Policies in Asia.* New York: The Century Company, 1924.

NORTON, HENRY KITTREDGE. *China and the Powers.* New York: The John Day Company, Inc., 1927.

O'CONNOR, RAYMOND G. *Perilous Equilibrium: The United States and the London Naval Conference of 1930.* Lawrence: University of Kansas Press, 1962.

O'GARA, GORDON C. *Theodore Roosevelt and the Rise of the Modern Navy.* Princeton: Princeton University Press, 1943.

OSGOOD, ROBERT E. *Ideals and Self-Interest in America's Foreign Relations: The Great Transformation of the Twentieth Century.* Chicago: University of Chicago Press, 1953.

PARKES, OSCAR (ed.). *Jane's Fighting Ships, 1934.* London: Sampson Low, Marston & Co., Ltd., 1934.

PARKES, OSCAR and FRANCIS E. McMURTRIE (eds.). *Jane's Fighting Ships, 1923.* London: Sampson Low, Marston & Co., Ltd., 1923.

PAUL, RODMAN W. *The Abrogation of the Gentlemen's Agreement.* Cambridge, Mass.: Phi Beta Kappa Society, 1936.

PEARSON, DREW and CONSTANTINE BROWN. *The American Diplomatic Game.* Garden City, New York: Doubleday, Doran & Company, 1935.

PERLO, VICTOR. *American Imperialism.* New York: International Publishers, 1952.

POMEROY, EARL S. *Pacific Outpost: American Strategy in Guam and Micronesia.* Stanford: Stanford University Press, 1951.

POTTER, E. B. and FLEET ADMIRAL CHESTER W. NIMITZ. *Sea Power: A Naval History.* Englewood Cliffs, New Jersey: Prentice-Hall, Inc., 1960.

PRATT, JULIUS W. *America's Colonial Experiment.* New York: Prentice-Hall, Inc., 1951.

_____. *Expansionists of 1898: The Acquisition of Hawaii and the Spanish Islands.* Baltimore: The Johns Hopkins Press, 1936.

RAPPAPORT, ARMIN. *The Navy League of the United States.* Detroit: Wayne State University Press, 1962.

REMER, C. F. *Foreign Investments in China*. New York: The Macmillan Company, 1933.

ROOSEVELT, NICHOLAS. *The Philippines: A Treasure and A Problem*. New York: Sears Publishing Company, 1927.

_____. *The Restless Pacific*. New York: Charles Scribner's Sons, 1928.

SIMONDS, FRANK H. *American Foreign Policy in the Post-War Years*. Baltimore: The Johns Hopkins Press, 1935.

SPROUT, HAROLD and MARGARET. *Toward a New Order of Sea Power: American Naval Policy and the World Scene*. Princeton: Princeton University Press, 1943.

TAKEUCHI, TATSUJI. *War and Diplomacy in the Japanese Empire*. Garden City, New York: Doubleday, Doran & Company, 1935.

TANSILL, CHARLES C. *Back Door to War: The Roosevelt Foreign Policy 1933-1941*. Chicago: Henry Regnery Company, 1952.

TATE, MERZE. *The Disarmament Illusion: The Movement for a Limitation of Armament to 1907*. New York: The Macmillan Company, 1942.

_____. *The United States and Armaments*. Cambridge, Mass.: Harvard University Press, 1948.

TOYNBEE, ARNOLD J. *Survey of International Affairs, 1927*. London: Oxford University Press and Humphrey Milford, 1929.

TREWARTHA, GLEN T. *Japan: A Physical, Cultural & Regional Geography*. Madison: University of Wisconsin Press, 1945.

TUPPER, ELEANOR and GEORGE McREYNOLDS. *Japan in American Public Opinion*. New York: The Macmillan Company, 1937.

TURNBULL, ARCHIBALD D. and CLIFFORD L. LORD. *History of United States Naval Aviation*. New Haven: Yale University Press, 1949.

UNITED STATES NAVAL INSTITUTE. *The Navy and Its Relation to the Nation*. Annapolis: The U. S. Naval Institute, 1930.

VINSON, JOHN CHALMERS. *The Parchment Peace: The United States Senate and the Washington Conference, 1921-1922*. Athens: The University of Georgia Press, 1955.

_____. *William E. Borah and the Outlawry of War*. Athens: The University of Georgia Press, 1957.

WALTERS, F. P. *A History of the League of Nations*. 2 vols. London: Oxford University Press, 1952.

WHEELER-BENNETT, JOHN W. *Disarmament and Security Since Locarno, 1925-1931*. London: George Allen & Unwin, Ltd., 1932.

WILLIAMS, BENJAMIN H. *The United States and Disarmament*. New York and London: Whittlesey House, 1931.

WILLOUGHBY, WESTEL W. *Foreign Rights and Interests in China*. 2 vols. Baltimore: The Johns Hopkins Press, 1927.

WRIGHT, PHILIP G. *Trade and Trade Barriers in the Pacific*. Stanford: Stanford University Press, 1935.

Articles

ALBION, ROBERT GREENHALGH. "The Naval Affairs Committees, 1816-1947," *United States Naval Institute Proceedings*, November, 1952.

ANDERSON, CAPTAIN WALTER S. "Limitation of Naval Armament," *United States Naval Institute Proceedings*, March, 1926.

BEARD, MIRIAM. "Our War-Advertising Campaign," *The Nation*, March 25, 1925.

BYWATER, HECTOR C. "Japan: A Sequel to the Washington Conference," *United States Naval Institute Proceedings*, May, 1923.

DENNETT, TYLER. "The Open Door Policy As Intervention," *The Annals of the American Academy of Political and Social Science*, 168 (July, 1933).

DUNCAN, FRANCIS. "Mahan—Historian With a Purpose," *United States Naval Institute Proceedings*, May, 1957.

EBERLE, ADMIRAL EDWARD W. "A Few Reflections On Our Navy and Some Of Its Needs," *United States Naval Institute Proceedings*, September, 1924.

FIFIELD, RUSSELL H. "Disposal of the Carolines, Marshalls, and Marianas at the Paris Peace Conference," *American Historical Review*, April, 1946.

GARDINER, WILLIAM HOWARD. "National Policy and Naval Power," *United States Naval Institute Proceedings*, February, 1926.

————. "The Philippines and Sea Power," *North American Review*, August, 1922.

GILL, COMMANDER C. C. "The New Far East Doctrine," *United States Naval Institute Proceedings*, September, 1922.

GLADDEN, C. T. "The Uses of Aircraft in Naval Warfare," *United States Naval Institute Proceedings*, February, 1929.

HOWARD, COMMANDER H. S. "Light Cruisers," *United States Naval Institute Proceedings*, September, 1926.

HUNTINGTON, SAMUEL P. "National Policy and the Transoceanic Navy," *United States Naval Institute Proceedings*, May, 1954.

JONES, ADMIRAL HILARY P. "A Just Man Armed Keepeth His House In Order," *United States Naval Institute Proceedings*, May, 1923.

KNAPP, REAR ADMIRAL H. S. "The Limitation of Armament at the Conference of Washington," *United States Naval Institute Proceedings*, May, 1923.

KNOX, CAPTAIN DUDLEY W. "The Navy and Public Indoctrination," *United States Naval Institute Proceedings*, June, 1929.

MASLAND, JOHN W. "Missionary Influence Upon American Far Eastern Policy," *Pacific Historical Review*, X (September, 1941).

McNAMEE, CAPTAIN LUKE. "Keep Our Navy Strong," *United States Naval Institute Proceedings*, May, 1923.

MORTON, LOUIS. "Military and Naval Preparations for the Defense of the Philippines During the War Scare of 1907," *Military Affairs*, Spring, 1949.

————."War Plan ORANGE: Evolution of a Strategy," *World Politics*, XI (January, 1959).

O'CONNOR, RAYMOND G. "The 'Yardstick' and Naval Disarmament in the 1920's," *The Mississippi Valley Historical Review,* XLV (December, 1958).

O'DWYER, SIR MICHAEL. "Self-Government in the Philippines and in British India," *The Living Age,* May 6, 1922.

OVERSTREET, CAPTAIN L. M. "Danger of Disarming America," *United States Naval Institute Proceedings,* September, 1924.

PARKINSON, C. NORTHCOTE. "The Pre-1942 Singapore Naval Base," *United States Naval Institute Proceedings,* September, 1956.

PRATT, REAR ADMIRAL W. V. "Some Considerations Affecting Naval Policy," *United States Naval Institute Proceedings,* November, 1922.

RAPPAPORT, ARMIN. "The Navy League of the United States," *South Atlantic Quarterly,* April, 1954.

RODGERS, REAR ADMIRAL W. L. "Military Preparedness Necessary to the Economic and Social Welfare of the United States," *United States Naval Institute Proceedings,* October, 1925.

ROOSEVELT, NICHOLAS. "Philippine Independence and Peace in the Pacific," *Foreign Affairs,* April, 1930.

————. "The Strategy of Singapore," *Foreign Affairs,* January, 1929.

RUSSELL, SIR HERBERT. "The Pacific Zone: British View of American Naval Policy," *United States Naval Institute Proceedings,* August, 1925.

SCHOFIELD, CAPTAIN FRANK H. "Incidents and Present Day Aspects of Naval Strategy," *United States Naval Institute Proceedings,* May, 1923.

TAUSSIG, CAPTAIN J. K. "A Balanced Fleet for the Navy," *United States Naval Institute Proceedings,* July, 1925.

VINSON, J. CHALMERS. "The Annulment of the Lansing-Ishii Agreement," *Pacific Historical Review,* XXVII (February, 1958).

WEBSTER, LT.(jg) WILLIAM. "The Cruiser," *United States Naval Institute Proceedings,* April, 1926.

WHEELER, GERALD E. "Isolated Japan: Anglo-American Diplomatic Cooperation, 1927-1936," *Pacific Historical Review,* XXX (May, 1961).

————. "Mitchell, Moffett and Air Power," *The Airpower Historian,* VIII (April, 1961).

————. "Republican Philippine Policy, 1921-1933," *Pacific Historical Review,* XXVIII (November, 1959).

————. "The United States Navy and the Japanese 'Enemy': 1919-1931," *Military Affairs,* XXI (Summer, 1957).

WRIGHT, LIEUTENANT H. J. "Discussion on 'The Cruiser'," *United States Naval Institute Proceedings,* June, 1926.

YARNELL, CAPTAIN H. E. "The Peace Time Service and Costs of the Navy," *United States Naval Institute Proceedings,* September, 1924.

207

Unpublished Dissertations and Manuscripts

CUSTER, [CAPTAIN] BEN SCOTT. "The Geneva Conference for the Limitation of Naval Armament—1927." Unpublished Ph.D. dissertation, Georgetown University, 1948.

FAGAN, GEORGE V. "Anglo-American Naval Relations, 1927-1937." Unpublished Ph.D. dissertation, University of Pennsylvania, 1954.

HELLER, ROGER K. "Factors Influencing Naval Construction in the United States, 1922-1929." Unpublished Master's thesis, University of California, 1952.

LINCOLN, ASHBROOK. "The United States Navy and Air Power, A History of Naval Aviation 1920-1934." Unpublished Ph.D. dissertation, University of California, 1946.

SNOWBARGER, WILLIS E. "The Development of Pearl Harbor." Unpublished Ph.D. dissertation, University of California, 1950.

Unpublished Naval War College Theses

CLUVERIUS, W. T. "Class of 1922 Thesis: Policy." Manuscript, Naval War College, 1921.

EARLE, CAPTAIN RALPH. "Class of 1923 Thesis: Policy in Its Relation to War." Manuscript, Naval War College, 1922.

HART, CAPTAIN T. C. "Class of 1923 Thesis: Policy in Its Relation to War: With Special Reference to U. S. Policy in the Pacific." Manuscript, Naval War College, 1922.

KEMPF, CAPTAIN CLARENCE S. "Class of 1923 Thesis: Policy—In Its Relation to War: With Special Reference to U. S. Policy in the Pacific." Manuscript, Naval War College, 1922.

NIMITZ, COMMANDER CHESTER W. "Class of 1923 Thesis: Policy, Its Relation to War." Manuscript, Naval War College, 1922.

CLASS OF 1927. "Class of 1927 Report of Committee on: A Logistic Study of the Pacific Area as a Theatre of Operations in an Orange-Blue War." Manuscript, Naval War College, 1927.

Periodicals

Army and Navy Register. Washington. January, 1921—December, 1931.
Army and Navy Journal. Washington. September, 1919.
The Literary Digest. New York. January, 1921—December, 1931.

Index

209

212